Suffixal rivalry in adjective formation

Dedication

To my mother

a symbol of affection and a spring of compassion

Suffixal rivalry in adjective formation

A cognitive-corpus analysis

Zeki Hamawand
University of Hamburg

LONDON OAKVILLE

Published by
UK: Equinox Publishing Ltd., Unit 6, The Village, 101 Amies St.,
London SW11 2JW
USA: DBBC, 28 Main Street, Oakville, CT 06779
www.equinoxpub.com

First published 2007

British Library Cataloguing-in-Publication Data
A catalogue record for this book is available from the British Library.

ISBN-10 1 84553 180 9 (hardback)
1 84553 181 7 (paperback)

ISBN-13 978 1 84553 180 5 (hardback)
978 1 84553 181 2 (paperback)

Library of Congress Cataloging-in-Publication Data
Hamawand, Zeki.
Suffixal rivalry in adjective formation : a cognitive-corpus analysis / Zeki Hamawand.
p. cm.
Includes bibliographical references and index.
ISBN-13: 978-1-84553-180-5 (hb)
ISBN-10: 1-84553-180-9 (hb)
ISBN-13: 978-1-84553-181-2 (pbk.)
ISBN-10: 1-84553-181-7 (pbk.)
1. English language--Adjective. 2. English language--Word formation. 3. English language--Suffixes and prefixes. I. Title.
PE1241.H326 2006
425--dc22
2006019029

Typeset by Catchline, Milton Keynes (www.catchline.com)
Printed and bound in Great Britain and the USA

Contents

List of Figures

List of Tables

Preface

Aims

This book deals with the semantics of adjective formation through suffixation in English, namely the process of attaching an affix to the end of a root. Its scope of analysis is confined to the formation of adjective pairs that share a single root but end in different suffixes. Theoretically, the book adopts Cognitive Semantics and attempts to substantiate some of its principles. One principle is that a linguistic item is polysemous by nature. On this basis, the aim is to show that an adjectival suffix forms a *category* consisting of multiple senses, which gather around a centre. Another principle is that the meaning of a linguistic item is described relative to the *domain* of knowledge to which it belongs. In this respect, the aim is to group the adjectival suffixes into sets, where they stand for one concept but differ in the specifics. A further principle is that the use of a linguistic item is governed by the particular *construal* imposed on its content. In this regard, the aim is to show that no two adjectives are synonymous even if they share the same root. They differ, as evidenced by corpus data, in terms of the alternative ways the speaker construes their common root. Empirically, the book adopts Corpus Linguistics which, through the provision of a concordancer, helps the linguist to identify the distinctive collocates of the members of an adjective pair and, consequently, reveal the differences in meaning between them.

Features

The book aims to integrate cognitive and corpus models in the processes of adjective formation. The new finding it arrives at is that meaning differences between adjective pairs are attributable to rival suffixes. To achieve its mission, the book is written in an approachable style and embellished with a few illustrations. One unique feature of the book is that it combines two aspects of language: derivation and usage. Concerning derivation, the book serves to familiarise speakers with the mechanisms of adjective formation. The book covers around 32 adjectival suffixes. To solve riddles of derivation, the book groups the suffixes in different domains with a view to uncovering their specifics, an issue that is applied for the first time to the analysis of adjectival suffixation. Concerning usage, the book serves to familiarise speakers with the ways in which adjective pairs differ. The book covers around 300 adjective pairs, the majority of which are mentioned as head words. To solve problems of usage, the book focuses on the association patterns of the adjectives, an issue that is applied for the first time to the analysis of adjectival derivation. One is lexical association, which concerns words used in association with each other. The other is grammatical association, which concerns words used in specific environments. The book uses actual data offered in the British National Corpus, and in rare cases surveys Web pages on the Internet which are retrieved by the search engine Google.

Readership

Over the years, I have found myself, as an EFL teacher and a linguist, disagreeing with the way dictionaries and usage manuals treat suffixes and words. Dictionaries give suffixes separate entries, which lack information on their specifics and so consider the adjective pairs they form as synonymous in meaning. Usage manuals give differences in a very small number of cases, but do not relate them to the suffixes and so disregard the significance of their functions in words. To fill such gaps, I felt the need to write the present book. The book is directed towards native and non-native speakers of English. Primarily, the book targets researchers working within Cognitive Linguistics by offering a full-length study of suffixal rivalry in English. Secondarily, the book targets researchers who have a basic knowledge of linguistics but want to know more about its developments. In addition, the book will be a useful source for readers who have no background in linguistics but want to make use of its contribution to language analysis. It suits students of English who want to improve their language skills, both spoken and written. It informs teachers more fully about such thorny areas in language as suffixation and rivalry. It guides textbook writers about what to cover and how. It aids lexicographers to improve their entries by making the reader aware of meaning differences. It helps translators to improve their work by making correct choices. As such, the book will appeal to a large audience.

Organisation

The book falls into six chapters. Chapter 1 presents an overview of adjectival suffixation in English and sets the framework for subsequent chapters. Chapter 2 reviews the role of categorisation in the semantic description of adjectival suffixes. Relative to the word class of the root and the structure of the suffix, it classifies the suffixes into three categories: de-verbal bound, de-nominal bound and de-nominal free. Chapter 3 addresses the role of domains in the semantic description of de-verbal suffixes. Relative to their meanings, it groups the suffixes into two domains: *voice* and *aspect*. To spell out the rivalry between the suffixes, it investigates a considerable number of adjective pairs and explores the roles of the construals of *participant choice* and *profiling* in their differentiation. Chapter 4 considers the role of domains in the semantic description of de-nominal suffixes. Relative to their meanings, it groups the suffixes into seven domains: *evaluation*, *possession*, *relation*, *resemblance*, *motion*, *trouble* and *disposition*. To expound the rivalry between the suffixes, it probes a large number of adjective pairs and explores the role of the construal of *perspective* in their differentiation. Chapter 5 deals with the interaction between suffixes belonging to different domains. To explicate the rivalry between the suffixes, it sifts through a substantial number of adjective pairs. Chapter 6 recapitulates the findings of the analysis, presented as key points and reported in tabular form.

Acknowledgements

Writing a book is a task that is both exhausting and exhilarating. It is exhausting because its preparation requires enormous energy. It is exhilarating because its completion produces satisfying results. In this onerous experience, many people have been supportive. Firstly, I owe a special debt of gratitude to Wendy Anderson, of the University of Glasgow, for her acute observations, perceptive insights and sagacious comments in the course of reading the draft, all of which helped to get the manuscript into its present form. Secondly, I would like to acknowledge the contribution of fellow linguists who answered my queries in a friendly manner and with an inspiring spirit: Guenter Radden, Juliane House, Klaus-Uwe Panther, Thomas Berg, Paul Chilton, and Terry Shortall. Thirdly, I would like to place on record my thanks to Tristan Palmer and Janet Joyce at Equinox for working hard to bring the project to fruition. Fourthly, I am grateful to my friends who provided moral support in the preparation process: Iris Koepen, Susannah Ewing, Evgenia Sokolinskaja, Christian Vogel, Guillaume Fréchette, Gerd Samland and Christopher Baum. Needless to say, none of the people mentioned so far is responsible for the book's imperfections. Finally, the book could not have been completed without the constant encouragement, ceaseless support and permanent love of my mother. To her, I owe my warmest acknowledgement.

1 Adjectival suffixation

This chapter introduces the descriptive framework that is necessary for a discussion of the semantics of adjective formation in English. On its agenda, there are four main items. Section 1 defines the notion of suffixation and specifies the intricacies involved in its description. Section 2 reviews the linguistic approaches. It shows how they treat the issues of form-meaning relationship, morphological rivalry and lexical alternation, touches upon some existing research and offers an assessment of the treatments posited. At the end, a new approach is outlined, covering its underpinnings, assumptions, goals and procedures. Section 3 presents the methods of analysis within which my treatment of adjectival suffixation is conducted. It falls into two subsections. The first tackles the theoretical method represented by Cognitive Linguistics, elaborating on the principles related to adjectival suffixation and the mechanisms responsible for morpheme combination. The second handles the empirical method represented by Corpus Linguistics, describing the corpus consulted and the techniques employed in the analysis.

1.1 Introduction

Morphology is the study of the internal structure of words. It is rife with instances of subtlety, one of which pertains to derivation. Traditionally defined, *derivation* is the process of forming a new word by adding an affix to a root[1]. In some cases, the root undergoes a phonetic change as in *defensive* from *defend*. In other cases, the root preserves its phonetic shape as in *careful* from *care*. Along with compounding, derivation is one of the two principal means of forming new words in language. Derivation includes three modes. The first mode of derivation is *prefixation*, which consists in the attachment of a prefix to a root, as in *indirect*. The second mode of derivation is *infixation*, which consists in inserting an infix into a root, as in *speedometer*. The third mode of derivation is *suffixation*, which consists in the attachment of a suffix to a root, as in *lovable*. In each example, the affix functions as a bound morpheme, whereas the root functions as a free morpheme. In each mode, the affix used to build a derivation is called a *derivational morpheme*. Of the three modes of derivation, the present study is concerned with suffixation.

Suffixation covers various processes of word formation such as the derivation of verbs, nouns and adjectives. Verbs can be derived from nouns as in *symbolise* from *symbol*, and from adjectives as in *simplify* from *simple*. Sometimes, only one verb is derived from a root as in *legalise* from *legal*. Sometimes, two or more verbs are derived from a root as in *plasticise/plastify* from *plastic*. Nouns can be derived from verbs as in *development* from *develop*, and from adjectives as in *darkness* from *dark*. Sometimes, only one noun is derived from a root as in *operation* from *operate*. Sometimes, two or more nouns are derived from a root as in *admission/admittance* from *admit*. Adjectives can be derived from nouns as in *dirty* from *dirt*, and from verbs as in *breakable* from *break*. Sometimes, only one adjective is derived from a root as in *accidental* from *accident*. Sometimes, two or more adjectives are derived from a root as in *awesome/awful* from *awe*. Of the three types of suffixation, the present study is confined to the adjectival one, specifically to cases where pairs of adjectives relate to the same root but end in different suffixes.

The prevalence of such pairs of adjectives highlights three phenomena and subsequently raises a few questions. One phenomenon pertains to form-meaning relationship. With regard to this, two questions are posed. The first is: do suffixes have a single meaning or numerous meanings? The second is: if numerous, how are the meanings related? The other phenomenon relates to *rivalry*, which refers to the existence of two, or more, suffixes which attach to the same root and profile distinct aspects of its meaning. With respect to this, two questions are posed. The first is: can suffixes sometimes perform the same function? The second is: if yes, how can one distinguish between them? The third phenomenon relates to alternation. With reference to this, two questions are posed. The first is: is an adjective pair formed by the rival suffixes synonymous? The second is: if not, is the meaning difference in the adjective pair relatable to the rival suffixes? The task of the present study will be to address such questions. Before performing the task, it is worth showing how such issues are treated by different linguistic approaches.

1.2 Linguistic approaches

There is a continuing controversy surrounding the issues of form-meaning relationship, morphological rivalry and lexical alternation. In modern linguistics, two broad approaches address such issues. Each approach has its own stance on the form-meaning co-occurrence, the treatment of rival elements and the distinction between alternatives. Each approach makes quite an impact on the way language is described. To identify the position of each approach, I take three steps. In the first step, I classify the literature into key linguistic approaches according to the different ways of tackling such issues. In the second step, I give a general sketch of each approach and then mention the different affiliates that lie under its rubric. In the third step, I describe the general hypothesis of each affiliate about language and then its treatment of morphology. In assessing the linguistic approaches, my intention is not to criticise them but to see how relevant they are to the present work. For a general discussion of the form-meaning issue in linguistics, the reader is referred to Croft (1995, 1998) and Newmeyer (2000).

1.2.1 Form-centred approaches

Form-centred approaches focus centrally on linguistic form, so they are referred to as *formalist*. They include both Structural and Generative Linguistics. Structuralism is an approach to linguistic description that characterises the formal properties of sentences independently of their functions. Generativism is an approach to linguistic description that characterises all and only the well-formed sentences of a language. For these approaches, the form of language embodies a system which should be studied in isolation, both from its users and its cognitive context. Language is described separately from cognitive faculties and abstracted away from actual use, and so its principles of combination make no reference to system-external factors. The central task of a formal linguist is therefore to describe the formal relationships among linguistic elements independently of the meanings they hold. This is due to the theoretical position that divides language into distinct modules, and so its explanation should be entirely internal.

For form-centred approaches, morphology is treated as segmentation into separate components seen as building blocks. These components and the means to assemble them are conceived of as being independent of the language user. This model is depicted by the simple algebra in A+B=C, in which A and B are the building blocks of the composite structure C. Morphology is seen only as a matter of objective composition independently of the language user. The foundation of this way of thinking is *objectivist*. According to the premise of *objectivism*, words can be looked upon as objects. As objects, they are made up of building blocks represented by roots and affixes. The parts stand in various relationships to one another depending on their building-block structure and their formal properties. As Lakoff & Johnson (1980:204) comment, 'Linguistic expressions are objects that have properties in and of themselves and stand in fixed relationships to one another independently of any person who speaks them or understands them'.

In a building-block view, morphology operates independently of general cognitive principles, and the components of a composite expression are objects being stacked together in some appropriate fashion. The gist of this view of morphology has been advocated by some linguists. Halle (1973:3) describes morphology as including a list of morphemes as well as rules of word formation. Speakers should know the words of their language, the number of morphemes such words contain, and the ways they are combined. Jensen (1990:21) stipulates that a word must be exhaustively divided into morphemes. Accordingly, a composite word is seen as being made up of components and the aim is to find these building blocks and the rules that combine them. In other words, a composite word is seen as a whole constructed out of smaller components, called building blocks. Analysing a composite word amounts to listing its components and stating how they are combined.

1.2.1.1 Structuralism

Saussure (1916) drew a contrast between *langue* (language) and *parole* (speaking). Langue is a system of signs, whereas parole is the use of the signs in speech. A linguistic system is the association of a signifier (sound or morpheme) and a signified (meaning). For example, the signifier *–ed* associates with the signified *past tense*. Two fundamental relationships among signs define the linguistic system: syntagmatic (co-occurrence) and paradigmatic (substitution). The sign *–ed*, for example, is in a syntagmatic relationship with verbs to which it is suffixed, e.g. *stop, seem* and *wait*, and it is in a paradigmatic relationship with other suffixes such as the present tense *–s*, the past participle *–en* and the present participle *–ing*. Thus, a verb plus a suffix constitute a syntagmatic frame in that they co-occur with each other as a regular pattern. The constituents of the pattern, namely the verb and the suffix, represent substitution classes. Syntagmatic and paradigmatic relations among signs constitute the structure of language, and it is this structure, and not its meaning, that is the proper field of morphological analysis.

The relationship between a linguistic form and its meaning is arbitrary, i.e. unprincipled. Practitioners of this approach hold that there is no predictable relationship between a phonological form and its meaning. There is no a priori relationship, for example, between the word *tree* and the physical reality to which it refers. The speaker experiences the reference as something established. Under this formulation, a suffix is adduced to be a meaningless element, which is summoned simply to derive a new word. The presence of rival suffixes is a matter of coincidence, and the existence of the resulting alternatives is an instance of synonymy. The rules of morphology build up a word piece by piece, adding something at each step until its structure is complete. Stageberg (1965:94) writes: 'The words with which derivational suffixes combine is an arbitrary matter. To make a noun from the verb *adore*, we must add *–ment*, and no other suffix will do, whereas the verb *fail* combines only with *–ure* to make a noun *failure*'. This is so because the structural rationale considers language a self-contained system of relations, where every element is defined by the way it relates to the others.

1.2.1.2 Generativism

Chomsky (1957) proposes a distinction between *competence* and *performance*. Competence refers to a native speaker's knowledge of his or her language, whereas performance refers to the use of that knowledge in speech. Performance is very close to Saussure's parole, but competence includes both the linguistic system and the native speaker's knowledge of it. At the centre of this approach is the description of the regular patterns of language, relegating the irregular ones to the lexicon. The regular patterns serve as rules that are capable of generating well-formed sentences. This is so because grammarians have been concerned with the idea of a universal grammar. Such a grammar should be elegant in describing aspects that apply to all languages. In Aronoff's (1976) view, morphology should concentrate on regular and productive rules of word formation and leave lexical exceptions to lexicology. Words are built by means of morphological operations, which consist in setting up underlying structures from which divergent morphological forms are derived by rules. It is these operations that should be the proper sphere of linguistic analysis.

Within Generativism, there are two practices in morphology. Adherents of the first practice believe that words are formed by transformational rules. There is no relationship between a linguistic form and the meaning it denotes. Lees (1960) derives composite words from deep structures by means of obligatory transformations. A word pair is treated as having one deep structure. The surface differences are the result of transformations. A suffix turns up in the final position of a word and plays no role in its semantic make-up. Rival suffixes are treated as alternatives; their presence is a matter of idiosyncrasy. Since transformations do not change meaning, the resulting derivatives are synonymous. Spencer (2001:227) writes: 'Thus, the derivational morphology which creates the adjectives changes the syntactic category of the word but does not add any element of meaning and thus, strictly speaking, is a kind of cranberry suffix'. This is so because the generative rationale is preoccupied with rules that characterise formal elements of language. Semantics is too messy; therefore the focus should be laid solely on syntax.

Adherents of the second practice believe that words are formed by lexical rules. There is a relationship between the form and the use of a linguistic item. Selkirk (1982) analyses the form of a word as consisting of a set of morphemes arranged in sequence by a system of rules. A word pair is generated by syntactic rules. The presence of rival suffixes is governed by different sorts of restrictions, mainly syntactic or phonological in nature. There is no mention of alternation between word pairs; it is left untouched. Lieber (2004) thinks that words are generated by means of lexical rules. She suggests including semantics in the formation of words. She treats affixes as lexical items on a par with stems. She attributes broad semantic content to affixes, which serve to create new lexemes and extend the lexicon. Each affix contributes a distinct meaning to the complex word. Affixes differ from simple free forms in that they are subcategorised for attachment to items of specific categories. Lieber's view is insightful, but unfortunately she doesn't provide any interpretation as to the use of rival suffixes or rival pairs of words.

The assumptions of the form-centred approaches are inadequate for my purposes. First, the structural approach aims to describe the existing patterns found in language, while the generative approach, as Chomsky (1965) claims, aims to provide rules for the established patterns and help the speaker to generate all the new ones. Neither approach achieves its aims. While many such patterns can be described, a large number of exceptions remain unaccounted for. Consequently, they stop short of supplying a complete listing of all the patterns. Second, the approaches sharply separate knowledge of language from the use of language. For them, language faculty is divorced from cognitive influence. Consequently, they exclude the role of the speaker in shaping language. Third, the approaches have concentrated on structural and phonological issues concerning word formation to the neglect of semantic issues. As Lieber (2004:2) mentions, there is no comprehensive treatment of the semantics of word formation in Generative Morphology. The theory is built primarily on the basis of a study of inflectional phenomena at the expense of derivation.

1.2.2 Meaning-centred approaches

Meaning-centred approaches focus centrally on linguistic meaning, so they are referred to as *functionalist*. They include both Functional and Cognitive Linguistics. Functionalism is a theory that studies the discourse functions of syntactic forms. Cognitivism is a theory that studies the mental processes responsible for syntactic forms. According to these approaches, the function of conveying meaning has so affected grammatical form that it is senseless to compartmentalise it. Language serves many functions, among which the communication of information is paramount. The structure of language reflects what people use language for. There is a conceptual interface between syntax and semantics. The central task of a functional linguist is therefore to describe how the formal properties of grammar are motivated by the communicative functions that language carries out. This is due to the theoretical assumption that draws no boundaries between language components, and so its explanation is considerably external.

For meaning-centred approaches, morphology is treated as a reservoir of linguistic units structured in the mental lexicon as networks. More specifically, morphology is seen as the study of the relationship between sounds and meaning in composite words. This way of thinking is characterised as *subjectivist.* According to the postulate of *subjectivism*, words stand for meaning. Humans employ speech sounds to symbolise meaning. Morphology thus consists of a complex web of parallel phonological and semantic connections. Although the component status of a composite word is an important aspect of morphology, there is more to its morphological structure than the building-block model implies. The segmentation of a word into separate components is merely one dimension, valid or useful up to a point, but their status is not that of building blocks. Rather, they are secondary to the word as a whole, and can only be singled out on the basis of relations to other items in the web which makes up morphology.

In a network-relation view, morphology is seen as a collection of meaningful units involving links between form and meaning. It is not a set of rules for the language user to follow. Rather, it is a network in which the language user associates the units with each other in conformity with cognitive principles. A morphological analysis is then the study of how a language user handles a composite word by studying the relationships between its components. The thrust of this view of morphology has been supported by some linguists. Langacker (1987:452–457) contends that a word should primarily be seen as a coherent structure in its own right, and its segmentation into components is only secondary. The components are not the building blocks out of which it is assembled, but function instead to motivate selected facets of it. Bybee (1985) considers morphology as a set of lexical connections within the mental lexicon. When a word is used, its morphological elements are sequentially activated through relationships.

1.2.2.1 Functionalism

Nichols (1984:97) explains that functional grammar analyses the entire communicative situation: the purpose of the speech event, its participants and its discourse context. It is the communicative situation which motivates, constrains, explains or otherwise determines grammatical structure. This approach, as Foley & Van Valin (1984) claim, extends the study of langue/competence to cover the communicative functions of linguistic forms. It seeks to describe language in terms of types of speech activities in which language is used as well as types of constructions which are used in speech activities. It does not try to predict the occurrence of particular constructions in actual speech events. It takes the pragmatic view that language is mainly an instrument of communication and a medium of social interaction rather than an abstract system. The primary concern is to attach importance to the uses to which language is put. Language is not a question of following rules but of possessing a repertoire of strategies for building discourses.

The link between the form and meaning of an expression is isomorphic. Followers of this approach stress that syntactic structure is to a significant degree a response to discourse pressure. For Bolinger (1977:19), the natural condition of language is to preserve one form to one meaning and one meaning to one form. Such a principle has mostly been applied to the internal structure of sentences rather than to words. However, there are a few studies where morphology has been alluded to. In Givón (1993:60), derivation is governed by semantic rules, in part by the history of the vocabulary and in part by idiosyncratic word-specific considerations. The potential context in which a suffix appears is a response to the communicative constraint on its distribution. A suffix is used to change the semantic class of the word to which it is added. This suggests that there is a connection between the context and the type of suffix used. This is so because functionalism is, as Prince (1991:79) contends, about the discourse functions of syntactic forms.

1.2.2.2 Cognitivism

Lakoff (1987:228) argues that the primary purpose of language is to frame thoughts and convey them in communication. If thought were independent of language and language were a way of expressing thought, then one would expect that many aspects of natural language would be dependent in some way on the thoughts expressed. Language knowledge and language use appear to interact. The grammar of a language provides its speakers with alternative options of expressing the same conceptual content. The speaker's choice of a particular option in discourse is determined in part by the way he or she construes the content. A grammatical structure reflects a conceptual structure; hence it is determined by a set of cognitive principles. Namely, the occurrence of formal elements tends to be inextricably tied to particular conceptual effects. An adequate treatment of any language involves, to a profound degree, the role of the speaker in determining the patterning of the grammatical elements.

The link between form and meaning in complex words is not arbitrary but motivated. Proponents of this approach, notably Langacker (1987:82), emphasise that a construction involves pairing between conceptual and phonological structures. In morphology, expressions correlate directly with the aspects of meaning expressed. In Bybee's (1985:6–7) analysis, a morphophonemic rivalry should be described in terms of features present on the surface, which include not only phonological but also semantic information. The working hypothesis is that each distinct sense of a word is associated with a distinction in form, and that the form of a word is shaped in part by a conceptual motivation. Under this formulation, a suffix is associated with a variety of meanings. The rival suffixes are quite distinct from each other. The derivatives formed represent different conceptualisations of content. This is due to the theoretical position that all language elements have semantic values which motivate their linguistic behaviour.

In theory, the assumptions of the functional approach are adequate because the approach downplays the role of constituent structure, focuses on the functions of language and perceives linguistic forms as closely corresponding to characteristics of the entities to which they refer. In practice, however, the assumptions are inadequate for two reasons. For one, the approach has paid morphology very little attention. The approach, as Watters (1985:85) explains, is concerned with the internal structure of sentences rather than words. For another, the approach maintains a monosemic view of meaning. For Bolinger (1977:19), it is inappropriate to chop the meaning of a word into distinct senses. To solve the problem, the present study chooses the cognitive approach because it provides the principles on the basis of which language analysis can be convincingly conducted. One principle shows that a linguistic item encodes distinct but related sets of senses, which are structured around one central sense. Another principle shows that the meaning of a linguistic item can be defined by contrasting it with the other items in the same domain. A further principle shows that the use of a linguistic item is the result of the way its content is viewed. These principles will be discussed in depth in Section 3.

1.2.3 Research samples

On English morphology, there is a substantial amount of literature concerning many of its areas. A large number of works such as Hockett (1954), Adams (1973), Matthews (1974), Aronoff (1976), Dressler (1985), Bauer (1988), Jensen (1990), Spencer (1991), Katamba (1993), Beard (1995), Haspelmath (2002), Booij (2005) and Aronoff & Fudeman (2005) serve as introductions to the basic notions used in morphology. A considerable number of studies such as Aronoff (1980), Cutler (1980), Fabb (1988), Baayan & Lieber (1991), Plag (1999) and Bauer (2001) deal with the productivity of English affixes conducting corpus-based analyses. Within word-formation, some handbooks such as Marchand (1969), Urdang (1982), Bauer (1983), Szymanek (1998), Adams (2001), Plag (2003) and Lieber (2005) shed light on aspects of derivation and offer detailed surveys of English affixes. A few sources such as

Beard & Szymanek (1988), Carstairs-McCarthy (1992), and Stekauer (2000) survey the history of research done so far in morphology. Because the topics of lexicalisation, productivity and semantic drift are extensively covered in the literature, they will be outside the scope of my project.

The main focus of my project is on the semantics of morphological rivalry, i.e. investigating near-synonymous pairs of adjectives that are derived by rival pairs of suffixes with a view to elucidating their differences. In this area, the literature can be characterised as rather scarce. The majority of the works mentioned above fail to mention its existence. The remaining minority, as we will see, confirm its existence but never try to tackle it in a systematic way. In most cases, the sorts of restrictions they propose on affixation are non-semantic in nature, where the combinability of morphemes is based on their phonological behaviour, and not on their meanings. This is so because their major contributions were made to the above-mentioned general issues in morphology. To identify the restrictions that have been proposed, I will give the literature a brief review. In what follows, I will divide the works into trends relative to the type of restriction placed on the choice of rival suffixes. In a separate section, I will present my new approach that is capable of accounting for the semantics of rivalry in adjectives.

1.2.3.1 Formal trends

One group of scholars argues for the role of the base form in the choice. In the sphere of nominal suffixation, two rival suffixes that have received attention by some studies on morphology are *–ness* and *–ity*. Anshen & Aronoff (1984) argue that the choice of a rival suffix hinges on the morphological form of the base. For example, the suffix *–ity* is said to be more productive with bases ending in *–ible*, while the suffix *–ness* is more productive with bases ending in *–ive*. As for stress, Aronoff (1976:40) argues that *–ness* follows a word boundary and *–ity* a morpheme boundary. Cutler (1980) argues that the choice of a rival suffix is regulated by its effect on the morphological transparency of the base. For example, *–ity* changes the stress pattern of the base as in *sénsible/sensibílity*, while *–ness* preserves it as in *sénsible/sénsibleness*. In addition, *–ity* may cause velar softening as in *toxic/toxicity*, and trisyllabic laxing as in *grave/gravity*. The difference in stress behaviour may cause some Latinate bases to prefer *–ness* to *–ity*. From what they say, the implication is that the rival suffixes are synonymous in meaning.

Another group of scholars argues for the role of the suffix phonology in the choice. In examining verbal suffixation, Plag (1999:227–234) argues that the choice between the rival suffixes *–ize, –ify* and *–ate* is governed by the phonological property of each suffix. Plag considers the suffixes as allomorphs of a single morpheme. They are phonologically different but semantically synonymous. In his opinion, true rivalry does not exist. For example, *–ize* and *–ify* express the same range of meanings, and so are equivalent. The meanings of *–ate* are a subset of those of *–ize* and *–ify*. These suffixes are complementarily distributed with regard to two restrictions. According to syllable pattern, the suffix *–ise* attaches to disyllabic stems as in *technicise*, whereas the suffix *–ify* attaches to monosyllabic stems as in *technify*. According to stress pattern, formations in *–ise* are stressed on the pre-penultimate syllable as in *flúoridise*, while formations in *–ate* are stressed on the penultimate syllable as in *fluorídate*. As is clear, the difference between rival suffixes is imputed to phonology, and by inference they are alike in meaning.

Let us now assess the works. These works are incompatible with my account of suffixation because in my account the co-occurrence restrictions are simply motivated by meaning. As can be seen, the sorts of restrictions they have suggested are either morphological or phonological in nature. Also, the descriptions they have conducted are based largely on individual suffixes. Excluding semantics from morphological investigation can be ascribed to two reasons. One reason is that it is onerous to establish the concepts in which the morphological rivals are embedded. The other reason is that it is thorny to define the specific meanings of the morphological rivals. Accordingly, these works are entirely unsuitable to tackling the issue of suffixal semantics in word formation. They do not provide the means to discuss the questions raised at the outset of the study. Given such a situation, the existence of these works should not prevent one from looking for other constraints on derivational suffixation as well.

1.2.3.2 Semantic trends

One group of researchers opts for the meaning of the suffix. In contrast to the previous views, Riddle (1985:435–461) claims that the primary factor that determines the choice between the suffixes *–ness* and *–ity*, with respect to a large portion of the lexicon, is semantics. While the suffix *–ness* tends to denote an embodied attribute, the suffix *–ity* tends to denote an abstract or concrete entity. To clarify the distinction, she gives some examples. In *The brutalness/brutality of Jill's remarks shocked us*, either word is possible but the resulting sentences have different senses. The form ending in *–ness* focuses on the brutal nature of the remarks themselves, while the form ending in *–ity* focuses on their utterance as being brutal. To support her claim, she provides some evidence. Colour words, which describe inherent traits, only take *–ness* as in *redness*. Ethnic names, which describe inherent traits, almost always take *–ness* as in *Slavicness*. Finally, count nouns, which denote abstract or concrete entities, mostly take *–ity* as in *oddities*, although the bases of some count nouns can take *–ness* to denote an attribute. The conclusion drawn is that the rival suffixes are distinguishable; each has meaning of its own.

Another group of researchers opts for the meaning of the base. According to Aronoff & Cho (2001:167–173), the choice of a rival suffix is predictable from the meaning of the host predicate. They explore the distinction between stage- and individual-level bases whereby the selection of a given suffix is determined by the semantics of the base. A stage-level base expresses a temporary property. Such bases select the suffix *–ship*. For example, *friendship* denotes a property that holds at a given time. In contrast, an individual-level base expresses a stable property. Such bases select the suffix *–hood*. For example, *sisterhood* denotes a property that holds all the time. Some bases, however, have both properties, and so accept both suffixes. The word *father* serves as a base for both *–ship* and *–hood*. Yet, the derived nouns do not have the same meaning. *Fathership* means 'the state or condition of being the oldest member of a community', a property that is transient in nature. By contrast, *fatherhood* means 'the state or condition of being a father', a property that is permanent in nature. From the description above, one infers that the suffixes play no role of any sort in the distinction between the derivatives.

Let us now assess the works. Although each of the works has some attractive characteristics, neither of them is suitable to tackle the issue of morphological semantics, or answer the questions about the construction of complex words. For one, the type of meaning analysis they have proposed is insufficient for exploring the semantics of rivalry, and so incapable of solving the riddles surrounding the uses of the existing confusable pairs. For another, their descriptions are limited mainly to individual nominal suffixes, and so do not provide a general view of the subject. More importantly, it is not clear how robust their analyses are. Riddle's generalisation is sound, but its reliance on invented data reduces its appeal. Some members of the pairs she exemplifies, e.g. *senileness* and *suaveness*, cannot be found in the British National Corpus. Aronoff & Cho's generalisation seems at best to be a tendency, not a general rule. It is not hard to find counterexamples. Words like *cousinship, sonship* or *twinship*, all listed in Lieber (2005), seem to be based on individual-level nouns, yet they take *–ship* rather than *–hood*.

Finally, some usage manuals like Partridge (1961), Greenbaum & Whitcut (1988) and Fowler (1996), among others, refer to the existence of such pairs and in some cases handle a few of them. They treat such pairs as confusable words, meaning that the words belong to the same part of speech but differ in one segment, and so have different meanings. Although some of the ideas suggested are worth considering, the comments on the use of such rival pairs are based on individual cases. As a result, they fail to do any service to the exploration of the matter. It is true that they instruct language users to judge the difference between the rival words on the basis of meaning, but none of them considers the choice to be the function of a difference in meaning between the rival suffixes, as the present study assumes. They do not give the rival suffixes any explicit meaning, and so ignore their functions altogether. Given the ineffective solutions to the problem of suffixal rivalry, there is then a need for a new research that is based on empirical data and capable of talking about the semantics of word formation in a systematic way.

1.2.4 New approach

The point in my study is to develop an approach that sheds light on the semantic aspects of word formation in English, an approach that has the right properties for characterising the meanings of complex words. The scope of the study is limited to the description of adjective derivation in English, capturing specifically the nuances expressed by rival pairs of suffixes. Cognitively defined, *derivation* is the process by means of which a dependent substructure (morpheme) is integrated, due to phonological and semantic correspondences, with an autonomous substructure (root) to form a composite structure (new word). The general theme of the discussion is to show that meaning is directly relevant to the phenomenon of rivalry in morphology because of the light it sheds on two issues. First, it justifies the existence of a set of pairs formed on one root. Second, it demonstrates a clear-cut differentiation in the usages of the derived forms. The specific theme of the discussion is to show that although adjective pairs share a single root, they certainly differ in meaning. The suffix variants seem to be interchangeable, but the meanings of the adjectives they form never overlap. The suffixes have meanings of their own, and so shift the meanings of the host roots in different directions.

1.2.4.1 Underpinnings

In view of the cognitive thesis adopted here, the semantic interpretation of an expression is a function of two important underpinnings. One underpinning resides in *conceptual content*, which is the meaning carried by an expression. In this respect, the composite structure of a derived adjective is made up of two component substructures: that of the root and that of the suffix. The two component substructures are argued to have conceptual content. The root has a multiple facet of content. The suffix has its own content which it adds to that of the root. Of the two component substructures, the suffix is the most important one because it is responsible for the character of the derived adjective. Precisely, the suffix serves to highlight a particular facet within the root's content. An adjective consisting of a root plus a suffix has, thus, a new meaning. The combination of the contents of the two component substructures is governed by the semantic compatibility between them, which in turn determines the distribution of the derivative.

Another underpinning resides in *construal*, which is the particular image the speaker selects to structure the content of an expression. It is the image that the speaker imposes on the conceptual content of a root relative to the communicative needs of the discourse. Because the root has a multiple facet of content, the speaker has the option to construe it alternatively. Making use of the lexical resources provided by language, the speaker can map his or her construals into different morphological realisations. Each morphological realisation describes the same content but does so in a peculiar way. That is, the speaker construes the content of a situation differently, and so chooses a different adjective to represent each construal. In each construal, the speaker opts for a different suffix, as a different suffix is associated with a different nuance of meaning. The construal chosen by the speaker thus determines the morphological form of the derivative. To illustrate what is meant by all this, we shall examine some practical examples.

Before I go on to the examples, it is necessary to elaborate on the descriptive steps taken to unveil the semantic distinctions between the rival pairs. Obviously, the aim is to elucidate differences in meanings between near-synonymous pairs of adjectives or more specifically pairs of adjectival suffixes. In the first step, I check the meanings of the rival suffixes by studying their occurrences in numerous adjectives in the corpus. In the second step, I diagnose the subtle nuances of the rival suffixes by contrasting their occurrences in example adjectives which host both of them. In the third step, I cite pairs of sentences, which are concise but clear in reflecting the meanings diagnosed. In the fourth step, I analyse the pairs of sentences in precise details. In the fifth and final step, I provide evidence to support the analysis, which comes in the form of different sorts of discriminating collocations. To corroborate the analysis, I give further pairs of sentences to see if analogous differences in meaning turn up when contrasting them.

In the examples under (1), the rival suffixes *–ive* and *–ory* are categorised as de-verbal because they form adjectives on verbal roots. Both suffixes mean 'performing or tending to perform the action referred to in the verbal root', but there is a line of demarcation between them. As the concordances in the corpus testify, the suffix *–ive* describes an action that is initiated by an agent and affects the self, whereas the suffix *–ory* describes an action that is initiated by an agent and affects others. Such specific meanings come out when the suffixes derive a pair from the same root. In the derivation, they single out different facets of the conceptual content of the root which is the outcome of alternative construals. To comprehend the distinction, consider the adjective pair below:

(1) regulative vs. regulatory
 a. The regulative faculty guides one's practices in a certain direction.
 b. The regulatory agency is established to promote public awareness.

The two adjectives in (1) are derived from the verbal root *regulate*, which means 'to control something according to a principle or a law'. Despite the similarity in derivation, the two adjectives differ in terms of construal. In (1a), the adjective *regulative* means 'tending to regulate'. A regulative faculty is a faculty which tends to regulate something according to a principle. Differently phrased, the action of regulating is initiated by an agent or things characteristic of him or her such as ability or belief and directed towards the self, viz. one's own faculty regulates one's own practices. This meaning is borne out by certain collocations of the adjective which are nouns implying one's behaviour based on morals such as *convention, custom, ethic, principle, tradition*; one's duty and the skill needed to do it such as *ability, faculty, function, property, role*, etc.

In (1b), the adjective *regulatory* means 'tending to regulate'. A regulatory agency is an agency which tends to regulate something according to a law. Differently phrased, the action of regulating is initiated by a group of people or things characteristic of it such as rules or orders and directed towards others, viz. the agency regulates the public's awareness. This meaning is borne out by certain collocations of the adjective which are nouns referring to a group of people with official responsibility such as *agency, board, body, council, organisation*; the system they use for operating things such as *policy, procedure, programme, regime, scheme*; the means, namely money, they impose on particular services such as *charges, costs, fees, rates, tariffs*, etc.

Let us summarise what has been said so far. The suffixes *–ive* and *–ory* are added to verbs to form adjectives. Both ascribe to the head noun following the adjective the property of performing the action expressed in the root, but each profiles a different aspect of it. The suffix *–ive* profiles an action that is initiated by an agent and imposed on the self, i.e. the agent and the patient are the same. As evidence, none of the nouns that collocates with the adjective *regulative* is compatible with the adjective *regulatory*. For example, it would not be possible to say *a regulatory faculty* because one's faculty cannot be controlled by an outside source. The *–ory*, on the other hand, profiles an action that is initiated by an agent and imposed on others, i.e. the agent and the patient are different. As evidence, none of the nouns that collocates with the adjective *regulatory* co-occurs with the adjective *regulative*. For example, it would not be possible to say *a regulative agency* because an agency exists to control others, not the self.

In the examples under (2), the rival suffixes *–al* and *–ary* are categorised as de-nominal because they derive adjectives from nominal roots. Both suffixes mean 'relating closely to the thing named by the nominal root', but they have unequal use. As the concordance listings in the corpus manifest, the suffix *–al* describes something as fundamental or original, whereas the suffix *–ary* describes something as chief or important. The difference in meaning arises when the suffixes form a pair on the same root. In the formation, they pick out discrete facets of the conceptual content of the root which is the result of alternative construals. To realise the distinction, consider the adjective pair below:

(2) primal vs. primary
a. They describe the primal instinct of the human for survival.
b. Their primary concern is to preserve and protect human life.

The two adjectives in (2) are derived from the nominal root *prime*, which means 'something that is first in time or in a sequence'. In spite of the similarity in derivation, the two adjectives vary with regard to construal. In (2a), the adjective *primal* means 'relating closely to prime'. A primal instinct is an instinct that is first in time. Precisely expressed, the adjective implies that the instinct is fundamental, viz. the instinct for survival is basic. This meaning is compatible with certain collocates following the adjective which are nouns implying natural tendencies that guide human behaviour such as *desire, impulse, inclination, instinct, urge*; unpleasant emotions caused by upsetting experiences such as *cry, fear, panic, scream, trauma*, etc.

In (2b), the adjective *primary* means 'relating closely to prime'. A primary concern is a concern that is first in a sequence. Precisely expressed, the adjective implies that the concern is chief, viz. the concern about human life is main. This meaning is compatible with certain collocates following the adjective which are nouns implying goals such as *aim, concern, objective, purpose, target*; procedures used in attaining them such as *design, means, method, mode, pattern*; aspects of socio-cultural organisation such as *curriculum, degree, discipline, stage, subject*, etc.

The following is a summary of the discussion. The suffixes *–al* and *–ary* are added to nouns to form adjectives. Both ascribe to the head noun following the adjective the quality of the thing expressed in the root, but each takes a different perspective on it. The suffix *–al* ascribes to the noun the quality of being fundamental or original. As evidence, none of the nouns that collocates with the adjective *primal* is compatible with the adjective *primary*. For example, it would be odd to say *a primary instinct* because an instinct cannot be main but basic. The suffix *–ary*, on the other hand, ascribes to the noun the quality of being chief or important. As evidence, none of the nouns that collocates with the adjective *primary* is compatible with the adjective *primal*. For example, it would be infelicitous to say *a primal concern* because a concern cannot be basic but main.

In the examples under (3), the rival suffixes *–ible* and *–ful* belong to the categories de-verbal and de-nominal, respectively. The suffix *–ible* means 'capable of undergoing the action referred to in the verbal root', while the suffix *–ful* means 'full of the thing denoted by the nominal root'. Both suffixes can make a pair out of a single root, but they select discrete facets of its conceptual content. As the lists of collocates in the corpus demonstrate, the suffix *–ible* describes an action that involves physical power, whereas the suffix *–ful* describes a thing that abounds in mental power. To understand the distinction, consider the adjective pair below:

(3) forcible vs. forceful
a. Police used forcible measures to remove the protesters.
b. She made some forceful arguments against the project.

In (3a), the adjective *forcible* is derived from the verb *force* and means 'capable of being forced'. A forcible measure is a measure that is capable of being forced. Clearly restated, the action of forcing includes physical power, viz. the measure used is coercively exercised. It is aggressive, hostile and violent. This meaning is bolstered by the usage patterns of the adjective which tends to collocate with nouns referring to processes such as *conquest, expulsion, repatriation, seizure, suppression*; ways to carry them out such as *means, measures, ploys, steps, tactics*, etc.

In (3b), the adjective *forceful* encompasses the noun *force* and means 'full of force'. A forceful argument is an argument that is full of force. Clearly restated, the thing produced swarms with mental power, viz. the argument made is strongly expressed. It is confident, emphatic and persuasive. This meaning is bolstered by the usage patterns of the adjective which tends to collocate with nouns referring to people such as *dean, member, president, spokesman, team*; their oral productions such as *argument, disclaimer, speech, statement, view*, etc.

By way of summary, let us repeat the basic points. The suffixes *–ible* and *–ful* are added to roots that function as verbs and nouns to form adjectives. Each suffix adds to the head noun following the adjective a certain property or quality which is expressed by the root. The suffix *–ible* is used in concrete contexts, indicates physical property and signifies disapproval. As evidence, none of the nouns that collocates with the adjective *forcible* is compatible with the adjective *forceful*. For example, it would be incongruous to say *a forceful measure* because a measure can only have a physical influence. The suffix *–ful*, on the other hand, is used in abstract contexts, indicates mental quality and signifies approval. As evidence, none of the nouns that collocates with the adjective *forceful* is compatible with the adjective *forcible*. For example, it would be infelicitous to say *a forcible argument* because an argument can only have a mental influence.

From the foregoing analyses of the examples, one can draw a number of conclusions. One conclusion is that the rival suffixes are virtually distinguishable and the meanings of the words which host them are entirely different. Another conclusion is that the juxtaposition of a suffix with another is the best way to specify their meanings. The consideration of the collocations that the adjectives take reveals the meanings of the adjectives and the specifics of the suffixes. A further conclusion is that the choice of a specific suffix in preference to another is dictated by meaning. This is represented by the particular construal the speaker imposes on the content of a root. The presence of a suffix, therefore, adds one additional layer of meaning to the semantic make-up of a word. The crux of the argument is that a given content can be conceived in different ways, and that the different conceptualisations are morphologically encoded by different suffixes. Each adjective conveys a meaning that would not be possible without the specific suffix.

1.2.4.2 Assumptions

To proceed to a fruitful discussion of adjective formation, the analysis needs to be based on solid arguments. In the present study, three central arguments based on cognitive assumptions underlie the analysis.

The first assumption is that all elements of language, lexical or grammatical, are attributed semantic values which motivate their syntactic behaviour. The linguistic form of an element is motivated by its semantic organisation, thus form and meaning are inseparable. On the basis of this assumption, I argue that an adjectival suffix has a distinctive meaning, and therefore has a special role to play in the language. A suffix does not only serve the function of changing a word's speech part, but also gives it a certain type of semantic information. A suffix forms a category which involves prototypical as well as peripheral senses. For instance, the prototypical sense of the suffix *–ant* is 'liable to do the action specified by the verbal root'. This sense originates when the suffix is attached to transitive verbs, as in *reliant*. From this, another sense develops, which is 'apt to do the action specified by the verbal root'. This sense originates when the suffix is attached to intransitive verbs, as in *deviant*. Peripherally, the suffix means 'being in the condition specified by the verbal root'. This sense originates when the root ends in *–ate*, as in *communicant*.

The second assumption is that the meaning of a lexical item is described relative to the cognitive domain to which it belongs, not in terms of an invariable set of necessary and sufficient features. A *domain* is a context of background knowledge with regard to which linguistic items are characterised. In view of this assumption, I argue that adjectival suffixes form sets, where they are related in such a way that in some respects they are similar to each other, while in others they are different from each other. The reason is that a suffix does not exist in isolation in the mind of the speaker, but forms together with other suffixes a structured set. For instance, to understand the meanings of *–ive* or *–ory* the speaker has to think of the subdomain of *agentivity* within the domain of *voice*. Both suffixes mean 'performing or tending to perform the action referred to in the verbal root', but with the former the speaker initiates the action, whereas with the latter the hearer initiates it. *A derisive remark* is a remark that expresses the attitude of the speaker, whereas *a derisory remark* is a remark that expresses the attitude of the hearer.

The third assumption is that no two expressions are synonymous even if they look similar. Similar-looking expressions are not transformationally related but conceptually motivated. Two expressions may share the same conceptual content, but differ in terms of the construal imposed on that content. Each expression is a vehicle of a certain semantic structure, and so the alternatives available to the speaker should not be treated on an equal footing. In the light of this assumption, I argue that adjectives pairs, which the suffixes help to form, are by no means synonymous. Each adjective has its own individuality that requires recognition. Their interchange is conditional, depending upon the type of construal the speaker employs to structure their common content. For instance, both *triumphal* and *triumphant* derive from *triumph*, but they are far apart in use. In describing events, the speaker uses *triumphal*, with the suffix *–al* meaning 'relating to triumph', as in *a triumphal march*. In describing people, the speaker uses *triumphant*, with the suffix *–ant* meaning 'apt to triumph', as in *a triumphant marcher*[2].

1.2.4.3 Goals

The general goal in the present study is to develop a semantic framework that is capable of describing adjectival suffixation in English. The study attempts to achieve this goal by exploring the semantic effects that contribute to adjective formation processes. Given the arguments formulated previously, the study sets a number of specific goals and seeks to attain them. The goals are:

1. Confirming that the multiple senses of a suffix can be understood in terms of a category which it forms. To achieve this goal, the study draws a categorial characterisation for each suffix. The category of a suffix subsumes all of its senses, both prototypical and peripheral. The present

analysis adopts the *prototype* approach, which assumes that not all senses of a category are equal. Some senses are typical, while others are atypical. Using the *prototype* approach, the study posits for each suffix a prototypical sense, from which the peripheral senses are derived. The category of a suffix cannot be defined in terms of attributes applicable to all its senses. Rather, it is marked by vague boundaries between the peripheral zones that gather around a centre. That is, it may have marginal instantiations that do not conform rigidly to the central sense. In the *prototype* approach, the meaning of an existing lexical item is not fixed. Through the creativity of the language user, it can be extended into new realms of experience, thus resulting in new senses.

2. Demonstrating that the meaning of a suffix can be identified through comparison with the meanings of other suffixes in the same domain. A *domain* is an integrated conceptualisation into which our mental experiences are registered. To reach this goal, the study furnishes complete descriptions of the cognitive domains which the suffixes presuppose as a basis for their characterisation. The present analysis adopts the *domain* approach, which assumes that lexical structures are characterised relative to the cognitive domains in which they are embedded. Each domain consists of a number of members, but their membership is based on perceived similarity rather than identity. The members converge at some general points but diverge at some minute details. Employing the *domain* approach, the study groups the suffixes into semantic sets relative to the common features they display. In the *domain* approach, the meaning of an expression is describable in terms of a configuration, and not in terms of a bundle of semantic primitives.

3. Elucidating that the difference between seemingly similar adjectives can be explained by the different ways of conceiving their common content. To attain this goal, the study compiles a list of adjective pairs that share the same content. These adjective pairs are neither synonymous nor free variants, and so should not be turned about in their uses. The distinction between them is quite subtle but significant. The distinction is not based on the operation of formal rules; it is exclusively a property of *construal*, which gives the speaker the flexibility to construe the same conceptual content in alternate ways. The present analysis adopts the *construal* approach, which assumes that the specific form of an expression reflects the particular way in which the speaker chooses to describe its scene. Utilising the *construal* approach, the study seeks to relate some of its dimensions to the area of adjectival suffixation. In the construal approach, the form

of an expression is characterised by the particular image it presents of the scene it describes.

1.2.4.4 Procedures

To achieve the goals, the study adopts a number of procedures. In order of importance, the procedures are:

1. *Retrieving data.* Before starting the work with the corpus, I compiled a list of thirty-two suffixes by relying on major dictionaries and reference books. Relative to the part of speech of the combining root, I then classified the suffixes into three categories. De-verbal bound suffixes comprise *–able*, *–ant*, *–ed*, *–en*, *–ible*, *–ing*, *–ive* and *–ory*. As the list shows, the suffixes *–ed*, *–en* and *–ing* are included because they meet the requirements of derivation in that they change category, add meaning and occur in adjectival position. De-nominal bound suffixes include *–al*, *–ary*, *–ful*, *–ic*, *–ical*, *–ish*, *–ly*, –ous, *–some* and *–y*. De-nominal free suffixes include *–based*, *–bound*, *–conscious*, *–free*, *–less*, *–like*, *–minded*, *–prone*, *–related*, *–ridden*, *–stricken*, *–style*, *–type* and *–ward*. Then, I used the Wordsmith Tools concordancer to retrieve all the contextual occurrences of the suffixes as they form adjectives. The occurrences allow the researcher to reveal the multiple senses of the suffixes, and provide their schematic definitions based on their linguistic behaviour.

2. *Establishing pairs*. Given lack of technical devices, I conducted, relying on the occurrences of the suffixes in normal contexts, a manual search of adjective pairs. I did that by putting the lists of adjectives containing the suffixes side by side with a view to picking out the pairs. Prototypically, an adjective pair shares a root of the same word class and displays a contrast in the suffixes only, as in *derisive* and *derisory* which share the verb *deride*. In some marginal cases, the pair displays a contrast in the word class of the root, as in *forcible* which relates to the verb *force* and *forceful* which relates to the noun *force*. The use of a pair has double import. Theoretically, it achieves emphasis by placing focus on a particular segment within a word, and provides evidence that the segments compared have different meanings. Empirically, it helps, by relying on a corpus, to determine the contextual preferences of the pair members, and stress the role of the rival suffixes in signalling the meaning differences that exist between them.

3. *Providing examples.* After collecting the adjective pairs, I provided examples of sentences to demonstrate their uses. I took the majority of

the examples from the corpus. To make the examples easy to understand but rigorous in effect, I condensed them. In a few cases, I took examples from major dictionaries and/or usage manuals when these were found to be clearer in explaining semantic distinctions. Through these examples, it becomes relatively easy to see how the arguments posited work in real life, how related adjectives are used in different ways, and how they are appropriate in different contexts. To back up the arguments, I gave more than one example for each argument. Though *repetitive* and *repetitious* seem interchangeable, their implications are different. *A repetitive theme* occurs again and again without implying boredom, whereas *a repetitious joke* occurs again and again implying boredom[3]. These examples and the like provide sufficient data for the researcher to arrive at meaningful generalisations.

4. *Analysing meaning*. In distinguishing pairs of adjectives and identifying their individual behaviour, I made use of the two corpus techniques of *collocation* and *colligation*. *Collocation* deals with the occurrence of two words next to each other in a text. It serves to allocate a semantic value to the search word. For example, the collocations of *sensual* describe something as appealing to the body as in *They were moved by the sensual movements of the dancer*, whereas the collocations of *sensuous* describe something as appealing to the mind as in *They appreciated the sensuous music of the concert*[4]. *Colligation* deals with the positioning of a word in a sentence and/or its complements. It serves to allocate a syntactic value to the search word. For example, the concordances of *woollen* restrict its use to an attributive position as in *the woollen pullover*. By contrast, the concordances of *woolly* permit it both in an attributive position as in *the woolly pullover* as well as in a predicative position as in *the pullover is woolly*[5].

1.3 Methods of analysis

To address the issue of suffixal rivalry, the present study integrates two kinds of methods in the analysis. One is theoretical; the other is empirical. It is assumed that the two methods can work together and provide a cogent description of the way language is used. The theoretical method, represented by Cognitive Linguistics, makes the necessary assumptions. It is chosen because it explains linguistic structure with reference to cognitive processing and concentrates on the link between linguistic and non-linguistic worlds. The empirical method, represented by Corpus Linguistics, provides the useful tools to verify the assumptions. It is chosen because it fulfils the conditions of objectivity, reliability and validity, which are the pillars of scientific research. The data used are actual, the evidence presented is incontrovertible and the results attained are solid. Significantly, it is the linguist who conducts the analysis and unearths the semantic distinctions.

1.3.1 Theoretical method

In broad terms, the theoretical framework within which the analysis of adjectival suffixation is conducted is Cognitive Linguistics (CL). Being a relatively young but promising theory of language, CL exemplifies a new way of doing science. Foremost among its assumptions is the belief that language forms an integral part of human cognition and linguistic structures reflect patterns of mental activity. CL aims, therefore, to base grammatical description on our understanding of the mental operations in the human brain and on the intimate relationship between the worlds of thought and language. CL seeks to characterise how the human mind understands the world and encodes that understanding in language. Linguistic structures are motivated by conceptual knowledge, which is grounded in experience. CL's ideal objective is, therefore, to offer an insightful analysis that is embedded in human cognitive abilities, an analysis that goes beyond the description of linguistic phenomena. For overviews of the scope of CL, see Rudzka-Ostyn (1988), Dirven & Verspoor (1998), Ungerer & Schmid (1996), Lee (2001), and Croft & Cruse (2004).

One specific theory of language within CL is Cognitive Grammar (CG). The standard text of CG is found in Langacker (1987, 1988a, 1991a, 1991b, 1994, 1997a, 1999). At the forefront of its general characteristics is the claim that language is inherently symbolic in nature and linguistic expressions stand for conceptualisations. Any linguistic expression can be described in terms of three kinds of structure: a phonological structure, which refers to its form, a semantic structure which refers to its meaning, and a symbolic structure which refers to the link between the two. CG bases knowledge of language on actual usage. Speakers create novel expressions on the basis of frequently occurring expressions stored in the mind. Grammatical structure does not conceal any underlying organisation. Rather, it is entirely overt and represents a means for symbolising semantic content. CG rejects the division of language into components. Lexicon, morphology and syntax form a continuum, and so cannot be divided into separate modules. Semantics and pragmatics are inseparable, and so interact in the meaning of an expression. For an exposition of CG, see Taylor (2002) and Dirven & Radden (in press).

1.3.1.1 Principles

In specific terms, the theoretical framework within which the analysis of adjectival suffixation is carried out is Cognitive Semantics (CS), which is exemplified by linguists such as Fillmore (1977, 1982), Talmy (1983, 1985), Fauconnier (1985, 1997), Lakoff (1987, 1990) and Langacker (1988b, 1997b), among others. CS is a theory that identifies meaning with conceptualisation and describes a linguistic expression as encoding a particular way of conceptualising a given situation. Meaning is not a property of an expression but a product of the interaction between the expression and the human knowledge. CS therefore takes into account the role of the human being in providing the basic meanings coded in language. CS presupposes a conceptualist account of semantics that recognises the capacity of the human being to construe a given situation in alternate ways. All linguistic elements are reasonably attributed some kind of semantic import. CS operates with an encyclopaedic view of meaning, not recognising a clear boundary between linguistic and non-linguistic worlds. Everything that is known about an entity is allowed to contribute to its meaning.

In CS, linguistic structure is a direct reflection of cognition in the sense that a particular linguistic expression is associated with a particular way of perceiving a given situation. This view of meaning makes CS different from earlier theories of meaning, where linguistic expressions are described by a formal rule system that is largely independent of meaning. The meaning of an expression includes not only an objective description of its content, but also how it is construed. Many expressions that are objectively the same are nonetheless semantically distinct. The viability of CS rests on several fundamental principles. Such principles are not specific to language, but part of our general system of cognition. They are, at the same time, considered the mental capacities on which the creation of linguistic units rests. Below are some of the cognitive principles that relate to the phenomenon of suffixation. In most cases, the description of these notions will be brief, but they will be discussed in greater detail in the relevant chapters.

1.3.1.1.1 Category

At the conceptual level, a *category* is a concept of thought. It subsumes a meaningful set of experiences which gather around an exemplary representative. At the linguistic level, a *category* consists of a meaningful set of items, lexical or grammatical, which can be described with respect to an ideal archetype. The process of grouping together conceptual experiences or linguistic expressions into a category is referred to as *categorisation*. Most linguistic expressions are polysemous, comprising a wide range of senses. These senses form a network which is structured around a central sense, referred to as the *prototype*. A prototype then is the primary sense which is felt to be the best member of a category. It is the most representative instance of a category, which serves as a reference point for the other instances. It is the instance that first comes to the mind of a language user when he or she thinks of the category. The other senses, referred to as the *periphery*, are linked to each other by means of extension from the *prototype.*

The other instances conflict in some way with the specifications of the prototype, but they are assimilated to the category on the basis of some similarity. These instances differ in contrasting ways, yet they are rounded up because of sharing some features. To make this clear, let us take an example. Internally, a lexical category like *chair* exhibits a network of prototype-extension relations among its members. It includes a prototype represented by *a kitchen chair*, and peripheral members represented by *rocking chair*, *swivel chair*, *armchair*, *wheelchair*, *highchair*, etc. These members share common semantic features, but they differ in minute details. Externally, the category *chair* forms part of a large system of category known as *taxonomy*, a conceptual hierarchy that includes three levels established by kind-of relations. At the superordinate level, *chair* is a member of the category *furniture*. At the basic level, it exists with other kinds such as *bed, table, cupboard*, etc. At the subordinate level, it subsumes its own instantiations.

The prototype-periphery relation applies equally to all components of language. Over the years, a number of linguists have applied it to grammar. On prepositions, see Brugman (1988), Dewell (1994), Vandeloise (1994), Sandra & Rice (1995), Kreitzer (1997) and Tyler & Evans (2001). On non-finite complementisers, see Hamawand (2003a). In this work, I apply it to morphology. In Chapter 2, I assume that a suffix forms a category of its own, with its multiple senses organised around a prototype. For instance, prototypically the suffix *–some* means 'having the thing denoted by the nominal root', as in *toilsome*. One extension involves the meaning 'causing or inspiring the thing denoted by the nominal root', as in *fearsome*. Another extension involves the meaning 'willing to do the thing denoted by the nominal root', as in *quarrelsome*. Peripherally, it means 'retaining the thing denoted by the nominal root', as in *mettlesome*. When we describe the suffixes, we find that sometimes they perform the same kind of function or create the same kind of word. On this basis, the suffixes can be grouped into sets, referred to as *domains*. It is within these domains that the suffixes can act as rivals, where they stand for one concept but differ in the specifics. This cognitive tenet will be elaborated on in the next section.

1.3.1.1.2 Domain

In CS, the meaning of a linguistic expression is equated with the concept it expresses. A *concept* is a mental image of something. It is the element of a proposition in the same way that a word is the element of a sentence. Concepts do not occur as isolated units in the mind, but can only be comprehended in a context of background knowledge referred to as a *domain*. Conceptually, a *domain* is a body of knowledge within our conceptual system that contains and organises ideas. It is a mental representation with respect to which concepts are characterised. Linguistically, a *domain* is a configuration which provides the basis for characterising items. Any chunk of knowledge can function as a domain regardless of its complexity or abstractness. Knowledge is encyclopaedic; it is organised into cognitive domains and grounded in our experience of the world. A *domain* refers to the area of experience covered by a set of conditions in a particular field. This term, which is proposed by Langacker (1987), is similar to Fillmore's (1977) theory of Frame Semantics and Lakoff's (1987) notion of an *Idealised Cognitive Model*.

At this point, it is useful to make a distinction between the *base* against which an entity is profiled and the *domain* against which concepts take shape. The *base* of an expression is the conceptual content that is immediately invoked by the expression. A linguistic expression cannot be conceptualised without reference to the base. A *domain* is the more generalised background knowledge against which an expression or its property is conceptualised. An example will clarify the distinction. The concept of a *thumb* constitutes the base against which *thumb-nail* is profiled. The concept *human* is the domain against which a cluster of body-part concepts are characterised. A domain itself may be a complex of domains; any concept can in turn function as a domain for another concept. To see how this works, let us consider some examples. The concept of *space* serves as the domain against which the meaning of the concept *circle* gets characterised. The concept *circle*, in turn, can function as a domain for characterising the concept *arc*. This shows that the semantic value of a concept is specified in terms of a domain.

The evocation of domains is important for the description of both lexical and grammatical items. In Hamawand (2002), I applied the notion of *domain* to the area of verbal complementation. In this work, I extend its significance to the area of morphology. In Chapters 3 and 4, I assume that suffixes form domains, areas of background knowledge within which their meanings are characterised. In the domains, the suffixes stand as rivals sharing common features but differing in specifics. To take an example, I will show that the domain of *voice* consists of two subdomains. One subdomain pertains to *agentivity* and is evoked by the suffixes *–ive*, *–ory* and *–ing*. Another subdomain pertains to *patientivity* and is evoked by the suffixes *–able*, *–ible* and *–ed*. Each suffix, as we will see in Chapter 3, is associated with a particular aspect of meaning that plays a part in the composition of the subdomain. This means that to understand a given suffix, one has to consider the other suffixes in the subset. When and how to use a suffix is a matter decided by the speaker. The choice of the speaker comes under the rubric of *construal*. Two suffixes that stand as rivals construe a situation in different ways. The elaboration of this cognitive tenet will be the task of the following section.

1.3.1.1.3 Construal

The cognitive domain an expression evokes is necessary to its meaning, but it is not sufficient. The meaning of an expression cannot be derived from the sole observation of characteristics intrinsic to the entity described. CS embraces a subjectivist view of meaning in that the meaning of an expression involves the way the speaker chooses to think about it and represent it as well as the properties inherent to the scene conceptualised. Language is the product of our interaction with the world around us. Language structure is an immediate reflection of thought, of the way the mind works. The way we build discourses and develop linguistic categories can be derived from the way we experience our environment and use that experience to communicate with others. The meaning of an expression is, therefore, characterised in terms of the particular construal imposed on its conceptual content. Langacker (1997a:4–5) writes: 'A semantic structure includes both conceptual content and a particular way of construing that content'. Two expressions may have the same conceptual content, yet differ semantically by virtue of the construals they represent.

An important facet of meaning, then, is the speaker's ability to construe a situation in more than one way. The speaker's attitude in shaping his or her utterances is incorporated in the notion of *construal*. Langacker (1987:487–488) defines it as 'the relationship between a speaker (or hearer) and a situation that he conceptualises and portrays'. At the conceptual level, *construal* is a mental operation that allows the speaker to conceive a given situation in alternate ways. At the linguistic level, *construal* involves mapping the alternate conceptualisations onto structural realisations. Language provides the speaker with plentiful symbolic structures to draw on in expressing ideas. These symbolic structures are the linguistic manifestations of the speaker's conceptualisations. Langacker (1991b:ix) points out: 'There are many different ways to construe a given body of content, and each construal represents a distinct meaning; this is my intent in saying that an expression imposes a particular image on the content it evokes'.

Building on a *conceptualist* theory of meaning, the selection of an adjective is therefore a matter of two parameters. First, the semantic value of a construction is based on the type of construal imposed on the scene by a given conceptualiser. A lexical construction is a meaningful symbolic unit. The construction as a whole has its own semantic import, which is characterised in terms of the particular construal it presents of the scene it describes. Second, the semantic value of a construction is based on the semantic match-up between all the component parts of the construction. The consideration of the construction itself as a meaningful template imposes constraints of semantic compatibility between its own meaning and that of every one of its internal elements. For example, attributes of *child* can be construed differently and symbolised by different suffixes. It can be construed positively, and so symbolised by the suffix *–like* as in *childlike*. It can be construed negatively, and so symbolised by the suffix *–ish* as in *childish*.

The premise that linguistic structure derives from conceptual structure has been explored in some detail in other areas of language by linguists such as Haiman (1985), Johnson (1987), Wierzbicka (1988), Dixon (1991), Deane (1992), Casad (1995), Heine (1997), and Hamawand (2002, 2003a, 2003b, 2005), among others. *Construal* consists of several dimensions. Of all, the present study applies only two dimensions to adjectival suffixation.

The first dimension of *construal* is *prominence*. In CS, a conceptualisation can be described as consisting of various facets. These facets differ in terms of the different levels of *prominence* they receive. Prominence is the quality of eminence given, often in different degrees, to the facets of a conception relative to their importance. The very wording that one chooses to encode a situation rests on the manner in which the different facets of a conception are construed. Linguistically, the degree of prominence accorded to the different substructures of an expression is crucial to its value. It characterises the internal organisation of the expression by highlighting different aspects of it. The substructures are, accordingly, placed in different positions within the expression. Two expressions may have the same conceptual content, but they differ by virtue of the prominence their substructures receive. This is so because in CS the meaning of an expression cannot be based on conceptual content alone, but also on the alternate ways that content can be construed. *Prominence* can be applied to numerous linguistic phenomena and subsumes various types.

The first type of *prominence* pertains to the *choice of participant* in a relationship. One participant, termed the *trajector*, is analysed as the primary figure and associated with the function subject. The other, called the *landmark*, is analysed as the secondary figure and associated with the function object. (Langacker,1988b:75–84) The subject-object function of an entity arises as a result of different conceptualisations. This is so because in CS there is a difference between the semantic role of an entity and its syntactic function. For instance, in an active sentence like *He opened the door*, the subject status is conferred on the trajector, whereas in a passive sentence like *The door was opened* it is conferred on the landmark. Relating this notion to the present topic, I will show that the realisation of the form of a derived adjective undergoes the same analysis. In Chapter 3, I will show that the trajector-landmark status can also be signalled by suffixes. In *The drug is preventive*, the focus is on a trajector having the property of performing the prevention, and so the adjective ends in *–ive*. In *The disease is preventable*, the focus is on a patient having the property of undergoing the prevention, and so the adjective ends in *–able*.

The second type of *prominence* pertains to *profiling*. Within its base, every expression singles out a substructure, referred to as *profile*, which functions as its focal point. The *profile* is the component that is elevated to a special level of prominence and functional significance. The imposition of a profile on a base is crucial to the semantic value of the expression because the expression inherits its character from it. In order to illustrate this, consider Langacker's (1988b:60) examples: *the lamp above the table* and *the table below the lamp*. These expressions contrast semantically, but not by virtue of any difference in their conceptual content. The semantic contrasts are attributable primarily to the imposition of alternate profiles on the base. In the first *lamp* is profiled, while in the second *table* is profiled. Relating this notion to the present topic, I will show that the particular realisation of the form of a derived adjective represents the speaker's choice to express what is most prominent depending on its communicative needs. In Chapter 3, I will show that profiling different components of a root can be signalled by different suffixes. In *She exercises a repressing influence on him*, the durative nature of repression is profiled, and so the adjective ends in *–ing*. In *They rebel against the repressive system*, the holistic nature of repression is profiled, and so the adjective ends in *–ive*.

The second dimension of *construal* is *perspective*. In CS, a particular situation can be construed in different ways. The different ways of linguistically encoding a situation constitute different conceptualisations. One factor involved in alternative construals has to do with *perspective*, referring to the view the speaker takes on a situation. Consider, for example, the contrast between *The roof slopes gently downwards* and *The roof slopes gently upwards*. The two sentences describe exactly the same scene, that of a roof sloping at a certain angle, but they hardly express the same meaning. The difference is that in the first the roof is mentally viewed from above, while in the second it is mentally viewed from below. Each sentence casts a particular perspective on the scene in question, and so produces a distinct interpretation. (Langacker,1988b:84–90) Relating this notion to the present topic, I will show that the particular realisation of the form of a derived adjective represents the speaker's perspective of a situation. In Chapter 4, I will show that different perspectives taken on a root can be signalled by different suffixes. In *After days of manful defence, they surrendered*, the speaker describes the quality, e.g. courage, that the defence is construed as having or showing, and so the adjective ends in *–ful*. In *It is manly to confess one's mistakes*, the speaker describes the manner, e.g. bravely, in which the confession is construed as being carried out, and so the adjective ends in *–ly*.

1.3.1.2 Mechanisms

In CS, morphological analysis is not a question of breaking up a composite word into its building-block components. It is a matter of the conceptual integration of the semantic structures of its components. Conceptual integration proceeds in parallel with the integration of phonological structures. Langacker (1987:277–327) addresses the issue of conceptual integration in terms of the establishment of *valence relations. Valence* is the mechanism whereby two linguistic units combine to form a composite unit. The term *valence* is taken from chemistry, where it refers to the combining properties of atoms. Langacker (1988c:102) writes: 'A valence relation between two predications is possible just in case these predications overlap, in the sense that some substructure within one corresponds to a substructure within the other and is construed as identical to it'. This means that the integration of component subparts in a grammatical construction depends on the perceived sharing of some features between them. The presence vs. absence of these features often has striking consequences for the semantic value and the grammatical behaviour of the construction.

A grammatical construction refers to an entire ensemble which includes the *component substructures*, their mode of integration and the resulting *composite structure*. A *component substructure* is a substructure that is integrated with one or more other substructures to form a *composite structure*. A *composite structure* is a structure formed by unifying two or more identical substructures. An expression like *complaining* represents a grammatical construction, which integrates the component substructures *complain* and *–ing* to form the composite structure *complaining*. Such integration, both phonological and semantic, between the two substructures is established by means of certain mechanisms. Relating the notion of valence to the present topic, I will describe adjectival derivation on the basis of the internal structures of the participating elements and examine the nature of their integration. Consequently, a central concern of CS is to pin down the mechanisms on the basis of which a valence relation can be established.

1.3.1.2.1 Correspondence

The first valence mechanism responsible for combining two substructures into a composite structure pertains to *correspondence*. By this, it is meant that two substructures can be integrated to form a coherent composite structure only if they have certain elements in common at both semantic and phonological poles. A composite structure is formed by unifying identical substructures and merging their specifications. Typically, one substructure corresponds to, and serves to elaborate, a schematic substructure within the other. Let us apply this mechanism to our topic by taking an example. The composite structure *complaining* is composed of the two component substructures *complain* and *–ing*. The integration of the two substructures is affected by correspondences established between them. Phonologically, the participial morpheme *–ing* makes schematic reference to a stem, which *complain* elaborates to yield *complaining*. Semantically, the *–ing* profiles an ongoing process which corresponds to the process profiled by *complain*. By unifying the two corresponding processes, one obtains the composite structure *complaining*. As an adjective, *complaining* profiles a property although internally it has the structure of a verb.

1.3.1.2.2 Dependence

The second valence mechanism responsible for combining two substructures into a composite structure pertains to *autonomy* and *dependence*. This means the extent to which one substructure can be conceptualised independently of its syntagmatically linked partner. The question is whether a unit can be conceptualised in and of itself, without the need to make reference to structures beyond the unit itself. Of the two component substructures that make a composite structure, one qualifies as *autonomous* (A), the other as *dependent* (D). The asymmetry between A and D substructures resides in the fact that A exists on its own without need of D to complete its meaning, whereas D is dependent on A to complete its meaning to the extent that A constitutes a salient substructure within D. In other words, the D substructure has a hole and its A partner fills that hole. The hole in the D substructure is called an *elaboration site*, or more briefly *e-site*. The A substructure elaborates the e-site, which is a salient sub-part within the semantic structure of the D substructure.

Let us apply this mechanism to the example above. An adjective containing two component parts also shows an A/D asymmetry: D representing the suffix substructure, whereas A the root substructure. In *complaining*, the root *complain* represents the A substructure. Phonologically, it can stand by itself as a fully autonomous form. Semantically, it can stand as a fully acceptable unit. It is possible to conceptualise it without making any necessary reference to anything outside the concept itself. By contrast, the suffix *–ing* represents the D substructure. Phonologically, it cannot occur as an autonomous form. Semantically, it cannot stand by itself as a fully acceptable unit. It has to attach itself to a host of an appropriate kind. The integration of the suffix with the root is, as mentioned earlier, determined by the phonological and semantic correspondences that exist between them. Thus, the root *complain* elaborates a salient sub-part within the semantic structure of the suffix *–ing* and adds conceptual substance to it.

1.3.1.2.3 Determinacy

The third valence mechanism responsible for combining two substructures into a composite structure relates to *profile determinacy*. By this, it is meant that one of the component substructures lends its profile to the entire composite structure. A composite structure usually inherits its profiling from one of the component substructures, which is called the *profile determinant*. Traditionally, the profile determinant is known as the *head*, meaning an element in a construction which is central because it is primarily responsible for the character of the construction, and because the other elements are in syntactic and semantic relationship to it. On applying this mechanism to the example above, we find that in the adjective *complaining* the suffix *–ing* is the key substructure in that it lends its profile to the entire composite structure. The root *complain* is describable as one whose profile is overridden by that of the suffix. Although the composite structure *complaining* has the internal structure of a verb, it designates a property and this is determined by the suffix *–ing*.

Two component substructures are integrated with the head: either a *complement* or a *modifier*. (Langacker, 1994:592–593) A *complement* is an autonomous substructure that elaborates a schematic entity in the semantic structure of the dependent head. It adds intrinsic conceptual substance to the profile determinant. Within the participial construction *complaining*, the substructure *–ing* is the profile determinant, whereas the substructure *complain* is its complement. A *modifier*, by contrast, is a dependent substructure that has a schematic entity in its semantic structure which is elaborated by the profile determinant. It adds non-intrinsic specifications to the profile determinant. In the expression *complaining neighbour*, for instance, the noun *neighbour* elaborates the trajector and functions as a profile determinant, whereas *complaining* qualifies the trajector and functions as a dependent modifier, hence it is extrinsic to the meaning of *neighbour*. The composite expression profiles an atemporal relation and not a thing.

1.3.1.2.4 Constituency

The fourth valence mechanism responsible for combining two substructures into a composite structure relates to *constituency*. This refers to the order in which component substructures are successively integrated to yield composite structures. Cognitive processing involves multiple levels of organisation, such that elements at one level combine to form a composite structure that functions as a unitary entity at the next higher level and so on. A *constituent* is a composite structure formed by integrating two or more components. Though related to the traditional notion of *constituent structure*, constituency is not to be identified with an autonomous level of syntactic organisation. Rather, constituency has to do with the assembling of meaningful symbolic units into structures of progressively increasing semantic and phonological complexity. Let us return to the example to illustrate this mechanism. In *complaining neighbour*, at the first or lower level of constituency, the root *complain* is integrated with the suffix *–ing* to form the adjective *complaining*. At the second or higher level, *complaining* combines with *neighbour* deriving thus the composite structure of the overall expression.

In the syntagmatic combination, one substructure forces a change in the specification of another substructure with which it combines. In addition to meaning, the change involves some kind of morphological and/or phonological marking. This is referred to as *coercion* and defined by Taylor (2002:287) as: 'the phenomenon whereby a unit, when it combines with another unit, exerts an influence on its neighbour, causing it to change its specification'. In morphology, the internal structure of a word may also be obscured by coercion effects. Suffixes affect not only the semantic character of the word but determine at least some of the phonological properties of the composite word. Suffixes in English can be divided into two broad categories: those that coerce the root to which they combine and those that do not. Example of the former is the adjective-forming suffix *–ive*, which changes the phonological shape of the root word, as in *permissive* from *permit*. Example of the latter is the adjective-forming suffix *–ly*, where the phonological shape of the root word remains unchanged, as in *lovely* from *love*.

1.3.1.2.5 Interpretability

The final valence mechanism concerns the interpretation of a composite structure. The question is: how can one account for the meaning of a complex expression? The answer resides in terms of compositionality which exists in two types: strict and partial. Under strict compositionality, which is a key principle in Formal Semantics, the meaning of a complex expression is fully determined by the meanings of its components and the manner in which they are combined.

For example, the meaning of *mendable* in *a mendable fault* is a combination of the meanings of the root and the suffix: a fault that can be mended. Although this type works for a number of expressions, it fails in others like idioms and compounds. The reason is that the meaning of any expression is not fixed, but tends to vary according to contextual use. Under partial compositionality, which is a fundamental principle of CS, the meaning of a complex expression is determined by both the semantic contribution of its components and the pragmatic knowledge behind what is actually symbolised. For example, the meaning of *questionable* in *a questionable theory* is not only a function of the meanings of the root and the suffix: a theory that can be questioned, but rather a theory that is dubious. Presumably, every theory can be questioned.

As clarified by Taylor (2002:116), strict compositionality fails for two reasons. First, 'the conventionalised resources of a language are abstractions over usage events. Their semantic content encapsulates common features of their many uses, filtering out the specifics of individual events. Even when a ready-made expression is applied to a situation, the specifics need to be filled in again'. Second, when component substructures come together, they need to adjust to each other in certain details. This requires shifting in their values relative to the intended conceptualisation. This process is referred to by Langacker (1991:543) as *accommodation*: 'the adjustment a component structure undergoes when integrated with another to form a composite structure'. For example, the meaning of the word *child* has both positive and negative qualities. In *childish*, the root *child* accommodates itself to the meaning of the suffix *–ish* to denote immaturity. In CS, it is claimed that linguistic units do not normally have fixed meaning which they contribute to the composite expression in which they occur. Just as the articulation of a phonetic segment adjusts to the articulation of an adjacent segment, so a contributing semantic unit typically varies according to the units with which it combines.

1.3.2 Empirical method

The empirical framework within which the analysis of adjectival suffixation is conducted is Corpus Linguistics, as exemplified by linguists such as Sinclair (1991), Stubbs (2001), McEnery & Wilson (2001), Tognini-Bonelli (2001) and Meyer (2002), among others. Corpus Linguistics is simply the study of authentic examples of a language which are presented in a *corpus*. A *corpus* is a collection of linguistic data, either recorded utterances or written texts, from a language, which serves as an empirical basis for linguistic description. Corpus Linguistics provides a methodology to describe language, which involves a given set of computational procedures to retrieve data from a corpus, sort them and process them for analysis. Corpus Linguistics can be seen as an empirical approach because the starting point is actual data. Since the data are based on language as it really is, the arguments formulated can be verified, the examples analysed can be objective, the evidence presented can be indisputable, and the findings arrived at can be valid.

The question then is: why the need for a corpus? In any language, most linguistic items, words or morphemes, are polysemous. Dictionaries, however, differ in presenting them. Some dictionaries give only one main entry, with the meanings unrelated one to another. Other dictionaries give more than one entry, with the definitions varying from one to another. With this variability in presentation, it is difficult for a language user to guess the common uses of such items. Likewise, many linguistic items look alike. Dictionaries often characterise them as synonymous in meaning. This is misleading because such items are used in different ways. To resolve such problems, we need a corpus. The importance of a corpus is twofold. Theoretically, it helps investigators to make accurate observations about the real linguistic behaviour of people. It can thus provide investigators with highly reliable facts about a language, free of personal judgements or prescriptive attitudes. Practically, it provides important tools for language description. It provides the natural contexts in which words are used, and so allows the investigators to work out the differences.

Concerning polysemy, for example, a corpus makes it possible to identify the multiple meanings of a linguistic item by looking at its occurrences in normal contexts. Concerning synonymy, a corpus helps to show that supposedly synonymous items are not at all equivalent in meaning when their actual patterns of use are analysed. There are systematic differences in the use of these seemingly similar items. A number of works using corpora have shown how closely related words can be differentiated. These include Collins (1991), Kennedy (1991), Zernik (1991), Francis (1992), and Biber, Conrad & Reppen (1998), among others. These works have demonstrated the important role played by corpus data in studying the frequency or productivity of different components of a language. They have shown that a corpus is used as a means of verifying hypotheses about a language on the basis of examples derived from real discourse. Moreover, the possibility of verifying results leads to the accountability of the investigator.

1.3.2.1 Precepts

Corpus Linguistics considers language a social phenomenon and an applied science with practical implications. It hinges on some fundamental precepts. One precept is that linguistics should describe actual instances which are realised in texts. Another precept is that linguistics should study meaning which is inspected in context. Meaning and form are interdependent. A text is regarded as an integral part of the context, and so the main vehicle for the creation of meaning. The main task of a corpus linguist is to analyse performance rather than competence. Given such precepts, the empiricist view taken by Corpus Linguistics runs counter to Chomsky's rationalist view, where the focus is on sentences composed by the researcher and advanced as credible data, and where priority is given to syntax at the expense of semantics. For Chomsky, the task of a linguist is to model language competence rather than performance. Rather than try to account for language observationally, the linguist should try to account for it introspectively.

Below are detailed explanations of two precepts of Corpus Linguistics that apply to the phenomenon of suffixation.

1.3.2.1.1 Authenticity

The corpus offers authentic, not intuitive, data. Because the data are factual, not invented, the results the corpus linguist arrives at are indubitable. The data come in the form of whole texts, not isolated sentences or text fragments. By *text*, it is meant a spoken or written instance of language which has occurred naturally, without intervention on the part of the linguist. This precept squares with the cognitive principle that knowledge of language emerges from language use, including both regular and irregular patterns. However, it contrasts with the generative practice which prefers abstract data. In order to illustrate a linguistic point, the generative linguist relies on data, usually of his or her own or of an informant and passes judgement on the basis of intuition. This is against the scientific norm in two ways. First, it reveals only narrow aspects of the human competence. Second, the invention of the data precedes the development of the theory, which should be the other way round. In Corpus Linguistics, the linguist relies on attested data, which allow him or her to make useful generalisations about the overall tendencies of usage.

As the major source of data, I have chosen the *British National Corpus* (BNC). This is a 100-million-word corpus of modern British English of the late twentieth century. It includes different styles and varieties, and comprises 90% written texts and 10% spoken texts. It contains different registers: academic prose, fiction and scientific language. So, the characterisation of linguistic items cannot be misleading. The data surveyed include a finite set of linguistic utterances that are based on actual data and represent current usage. The use of different texts is advantageous. The examples studied represent a high diversity of speakers and situational contexts. Therefore, they serve to minimise the impact of idiolects or dialects on the research results. In rare cases where the corpus fails to provide information on a given item, I solicit help from Internet pages. For this, I examine the total number of hits returned by the search engine

Google. The aim is to show that feedback of different kinds can give a boost to the analysis.

1.3.2.1.2 Semanticity

Since the main function of language is to mean, one task of the corpus linguist then is to explain how it means. Meaning is conveyed in spoken or written discourse. Written discourse is represented in texts. The meaning of a text can only be derived from the context in which it occurs. In studying any text, the corpus linguist tries to extract its meaning and relate it to the form it assumes. This precept accords with the cognitive principle which stipulates that every entity has identity, and that there is no meaning without form in language. However, it contrasts with the generative tendency which views meaning independently of its form, or gives priority to form at the expense of meaning. Although some generative linguists consider meaning in their description, their accounts are not adequate. In Corpus Linguistics, any text can be viewed under two aspects: meaning and form. Meaning and form are different aspects of a text, which cannot be separated. By evidence, when the speaker wants to describe a future action, s/he uses the *to*-infinitive after the main verb, as in *I regret to say so*. When the speaker wants to describe a past action, s/he uses the *–ing* gerund after the main verb, as in *I regret saying so*.

In Corpus Linguistics, two types of meaning analysis exist: qualitative and quantitative. The difference between the two is that the former assigns no frequencies to the linguistic phenomena identified in the data, whereas the latter looks at the frequency of such phenomena using statistical measures. In fact, the former is a precursor for the latter because linguistic phenomena must first be identified before they are classified or counted. Of the two types, the present study applies the qualitative analysis to the data. The reason behind the choice, as McEnery & Wilson (2001:76) stress, is that a qualitative analysis is both rich in detail and precise in perspective. In a qualitative analysis, the data are meant to describe aspects of usage in the language and provide real-life examples of particular phenomena. In a qualitative analysis, both rare and frequent phenomena receive equal attention. This is so because its aim is to provide a detailed description, not quantification, of the data. Accordingly, it enables delicate distinctions to be drawn since it is not necessary to fit the data into a finite number of classifications.

1.3.2.2 Techniques

To retrieve the occurrences of linguistic items, the study uses a powerful tool called a *concordancer*. In this work, WordSmith Tools has been used. A *concordancer* is a software programme that searches and displays the occurrences of a chosen word with its surrounding context. To achieve the task of disambiguation, each word selected will be accompanied by a maximum of 70 characters to the left and to the right. The displays of occurrences, referred to as *Key Word in Context* (KWIC), help to identify the main senses of a word and produce definitions for each of the senses identified. Recall that one advantage of a corpus is that it can be used to show a large number of contexts in which a word occurs. From these contexts, the researcher can reveal the semantic and syntactic patterning of a word. In the present study, the aim is not to consider the frequency of any of the suffixes nor of their host words. Rather, the aim is to consider the range of different but related meanings which adjectival suffixes have and the roles they play in distinguishing between words. On the issue of affixal frequency, see Ljung (1974), among others.

To discriminate between senses of adjective pairs, the study builds on two effective techniques provided by Corpus Linguistics. One is called *collocation*. It shows how a word is systematically associated with particular words. The other is called *colligation*. It shows how a word is systematically associated with particular grammatical features. The techniques help remove the confusion surrounding the use of rival items, and make generalisations about their usage patterns. The techniques imply that in Corpus Linguistics there is no demarcation between lexical and grammatical associations.

1.3.2.2.1 Collocation

Collocation refers to the recurrent co-occurrence of words. It helps to identify collocates that come, for the purposes of the present study, to the right of the keyword. All lines of concordances available will be examined for the sake of identifying the discriminating collocates associated with an adjective. These collocates will then be classified into semantic fields, for which around five examples will be given as evidence. It is to be noted that the focus will be placed only on those discriminating collocates that form patterns of use and help to distinguish adjective pairs that have gone unnoticed in many, if not all, previous analyses. From such collocates, it becomes fairly clear what the meaning of an adjective is. For example, a thorough examination of the concordances in the corpus shows that the collocates of the adjective *observable* pertain to inanimate entities as in *There is no observable evidence in support of his claim*, whereas the collocates of its counterpart *observant* pertain to animate entities as in *Cook is the most observant man.*

1.3.2.2.2 Colligation

Colligation refers to the grammatical patterning in which words are embedded. It helps to show the pattern of use of the search word. This covers the positioning of the adjective, its complements and the constructions in which it occurs. For example, a close look at the collocations in the corpus shows that the adjective *preventive*, as opposed to *preventable*, occurs always in an attributive position as in *They incorporated preventive measures in the treatment.* When used in a predicative position, the adjective *suggestive*, as opposed to *suggestible*, is followed by the preposition *of* as in *His inaction is suggestive of his lack of interest.* The adjective *advisable*, as opposed to *advisory*, almost always occur in an *it+be+adj+to* construction as in *It is advisable to practise each exercise individually.* Throughout the study, I will provide information concerning the adjectives that undergo syntactic restrictions. The absence of such information means that the adjectives occur freely in both positions.

2 Categorisation of adjectival suffixes

This chapter explores the role of categorisation in the semantic description of adjectival suffixes. It attempts to substantiate two principles of CS. One principle is that all language items, lexical or grammatical, have semantic values which motivate their linguistic behaviour. Applying this principle to morphology, I argue that a suffix has semantic import and adds to the meaning of the root which hosts it. Another principle is that linguistic items are polysemous by nature. Applying this principle to morphology, I argue that a suffix has a wide range of senses which gather around a central one. To that end, the chapter is organised as follows. Section 1 reviews the status of categorisation in language in the main theories of thought. Section 2 introduces the *prototype* approach by touching upon its mechanisms and enumerating its advantages. Section 3 applies the *prototype* approach to the characterisation of adjectival suffixes by grouping them into categories relative to the word class of the root and the structure of the suffix, namely into de-verbal bound, de-nominal bound and de-nominal free suffixes.

2.1 Introduction

In describing the world, a speaker needs to form concepts. Concepts come in the form of single entities such as *orange*, or a whole set of entities such as *fruit*. In the latter case, the speaker automatically slices the entity into relevant units such as *apples, bananas, oranges, pears*, etc. These concepts which structure the speaker's thoughts form a *category*, and the process of putting them into a category is called *categorisation*. To communicate the concepts, the speaker needs to use items. Category then is a class of linguistic items having properties in common, whereas categorisation is the process of organising them into a category. Category sheds light on how specific concepts relate to each other in the speaker's mind, and so makes an important contribution to the analysis of lexical items. Categorisation has received attention in both classical and cognitive theories of language, but with differences in view. The different views of the two theories follow from their underlying assumptions. For a detailed coverage of the opposition between the two theories, see Lakoff (1987:xi-xvii), Taylor (1989:21–37) and Geeraerts (1988:652–657).

In the classical view, meaning is literal. Human cognitive capacities play no role in shaping the nature of categories. Meaning is primarily about propositions that can objectively be either true or false. This view is inspired by the theory of *objectivism*, which stipulates that symbols used in language get their meaning via correspondence with things in the external world. Meaning is objective in the sense that it is not influenced by the physical or emotional feelings of a language user. In the cognitive view, meaning is imaginative: mental imagery play a role in shaping the nature of categories. Meaning is derived from the different ways a language user construes a situation and the structures chosen to encode them. This view holds on to the theory of *subjectivism*, or alternatively *experientialism*, which stipulates that symbols used in language get their meaning via correspondence with conceptualisations of the world. Meaning is experiential in the sense that it grows out of real-world scenarios and user-specific background data.

In the classical view, a single meaning approach, *monosemy*, is advocated. In view of this approach, different senses of a lexical item pair up with different forms. This means the different senses are separated from each other and assigned to the lexicon. The lexicon is, as Jackendoff (1997:4) describes, a repository consisting of a finite list of discrete word senses that happen to share the same phonological form. This view is also asserted by Chomsky (1995:235): 'I understand the lexicon in a rather traditional sense: as a list of 'exceptions', whatever does not follow from general principles'. In the cognitive view, a multi-meaning approach, polysemy, is advocated. In the light of this approach, different senses of a lexical item are subsumed under one form. The lexicon represents a network of form-meaning associations, in which each lexical item is associated with a set of distinct but related senses. Langacker (1991a:43–50) believes that the description of any lexical item should include both its regular and irregular properties, which are determined by their productivity, specificity and symbolic complexity.

In the classical view, meaning is disembodied. A category is constructed independently of the human doing the categorising and defined in terms of conditions, which are necessary and sufficient for membership in the category. According to this view, membership in a category is an all-or-nothing matter, such that an entity is included in a category if it meets such conditions, whereas an entity is excluded if it lacks any of them. All members of a category should have equal status. In the cognitive view, meaning is embodied. A category is constructed on the basis of the human encountering a physical or social world and defined in terms of experiences gained or conceptions of reality. According to this view, membership in a category is a gradient phenomenon, such that some members of a category carry more weight as better examples than others. Membership in a category is based on degrees of similarity to its best example. What characterises the various members is a family resemblance relationship in which they, as Geeraerts (1989) notes, share general properties but exhibit incidental nuances.

2.2 The prototype approach to suffixation

To provide a semantic characterisation of adjectival suffixes in English, the present study favours the *prototype* approach[6]. The approach is based on the works of Rosch (1975,1977,1978), and discussed extensively in Lakoff (1987) and Taylor (1989). Before going into the details, one note merits attention. In addition to elaborating on the internal organisation of the suffixes, the descriptions given here will serve as a base for the subsequent chapters. The descriptions show that there are senses where suffixes converge and diverge. That is, when two or more suffixes perform the same or a separate function. On the basis of the converging senses, the suffixes are grouped into (sub)sets, which are referred to as *(sub)domains*. It is within these (sub)domains that suffixes can stand against each other as rivals. Two suffixes may stand for one concept but differ in the specifics. The assortment of the suffixes into (sub)domains and the detection of their peculiarities will be the subject matter of Chapters 3 and 4.

2.2.1 Essence of the approach

The *prototype* approach holds that a linguistic item is polysemous and its numerous senses constitute a category. Precisely, a linguistic item forms a network in which the peripheral senses extend out from a prototype. As Langacker (1987:371) defines the terms, a *prototype* is a typical member which has all of the properties of a category, whereas *peripheral* senses are the atypical members which have only some of those properties. To determine the prototype of a category, I follow the criteria proposed by Evans (2003) and Tyler & Evans (2001). First, it is the sense which is the earliest and the first learned in the process of language acquisition. Second, it is the sense whose meaning components are most frequent in other senses. Third, it is the sense which gives rise to additional senses through extensions. A sense is counted as peripheral if it meets three criteria. First, it is the sense which has an additional meaning that is not apparent in the other senses. Second, it is the sense which is not derived from context or inferred from another sense. Third, it is the sense which has structural properties and displays collocational restrictions.

According to Langacker (1991a:266–272), the peripheral senses represent either separate senses or separate sense types of the item in question. The semantic extensions of the item may involve some twists or bends. Some extensions may be directly derivable from the prototypical sense. Others are traceable to a sense that is derived from the prototype. However, the senses are related to each other like the members of a family, where they share the general properties of the category but differ in specific details. That is the extended senses differ from the prototypical sense by having special specifications but resemble it by elaborating the same category. To clarify the point, let us look at an example. *A sparrow* can be regarded as the prototype of the *bird* category because it possesses all the typical features of birdness such as having a beak, wings and feathers, or being able to fly. By contrast, *duck, falcon, ostrich*, or *penguin* can be regarded only as the periphery because they possess only some of those features.

The *prototype* approach seems to be pervasive in all linguistic areas including morphology. Following Langacker's (1991a:16) claim that 'grammatical morphemes, categories and constructions all take the form of symbolic units', I argue that a suffix is a polysemous symbolic unit whose senses are conceptually related. Precisely, I maintain that the description of a given suffix requires the specification of its prototypical sense as well as its peripheral senses. Let us explain this through an example. Prototypically, the suffix *–ive* is added to a transitive root and means 'performing or tending to perform the action referred to in the verbal root'. *A defensive player* is a player who defends his goal. From this prototypical sense, two peripheral senses emerge. In *a talkative organiser*, the suffix is added to an intransitive root and means 'apt to do the action signified by the verbal root'. In *an excessive exercise*, the suffix is added to a nominal root and means 'marked by the property of the thing named by the nominal root'.

The meaning of a derived adjective, I argue, can be either strictly or partially compositional. In strict compositionality, which is rare, the meaning of a derived adjective is a function of the meanings of its component morphemes. The meaning of the combined form is the interaction between the root and the suffix. For example, the meaning of *wearable* in *a wearable dress* is a combination of the meanings of the root and the suffix: a dress that can be worn. In partial compositionality, which is often, the meaning of a derived adjective is a function of both the meanings of its component morphemes and the pragmatic interpretation of the combination as a whole. This is so because the meaning of any expression is not fixed, but tends to vary according to contextual uses. For example, the meaning of *watchable* in *a watchable movie* is not only a function of the meanings of the root and the suffix: a movie that can be watched, but rather a movie that is worth seeing. Presumably, every movie can be watched.

To describe adjective-forming suffixes, I take three steps. First, I identify the central sense of each suffix, from which all the other senses are derived. To determine the central sense of a suffix, I build on the first criterion. It is the first learned in the process of language acquisition. I checked that by asking some native speakers. Second, I point out the peripheral senses of each suffix in order of conceptual distance from the prototype, showing thus the suffix's much wider application. It becomes apparent that the endpoints of these extensions are unpredictable, but very well motivated. Third, I provide ample exemplification for the central and peripheral senses to support the description. In each example, the derived adjective functions as a template in which the root is the determinatum, while the suffix is the profile determinant. The aim behind all this is to confirm the claim that language is an evolving usage-based system. Its items need to be studied in terms of cognitive, rather than formal, principles.

2.2.2 Advantages of the approach

In CS, a language may be characterised as an inventory of linguistic units. The inventory is so structured that the units are interrelated in complex ways. The characterisation of any unit makes reference to two things. The first is the horizontal relationship which pertains to the disposition of a unit to combine with another unit. This is the case when the suffix *–ive* combines with the verbal root *defend* to form the adjective *defensive*. The second is the vertical relationship which pertains to the category of a unit to its instances. This is the case when the suffix *–ive* combines with roots of different nature to form adjectives as in *talkative* and *excessive*. A category is a unit which is specified in lesser detail, whereas an instance is a unit which is specified in greater detail. Because of that, the instances cannot be covered in a single definition. They are held together by devices such as a family resemblance. The adoption of a prototype-periphery model of categorisation to the description of suffixes has some practical advantages.

One advantage is that it embodies the notion of gradation in the characterisation of a lexical item. The parameters along which the senses of a lexical item vary are scalar or gradual, rather than binary, plus-or-minus qualities. The differences along such parameters are relative rather than absolute. This view shows that there is no place for absolute predictability. Rather, the use of a given suffix is influenced by context. To demonstrate this case, let us take an example. In dictionary descriptions, the derivative force of the suffix *–able* is restricted to the formation of adjectives from verbal roots with a passive meaning as in *eatable goods*, meaning 'goods that can be eaten'. In the present description, the derivative force of the suffix is extended to cover an active meaning as in *perishable stuff*, meaning 'stuff that can perish', or both meanings as in *changeable*, meaning 'can be changed or able to change'. This illustrates how categorisation facilitates the construal of a scenario in various ways, which differ relative to certain degrees.

Another advantage is that it includes the conforming as well as the non-conforming senses in the characterisation of a lexical item. Thus, it permits the study of more phenomena, where previously only those exhibiting absolute commonality were deemed amenable to empirical investigation. In doing so, it helps to delineate all the specific senses of a suffix, showing the points where they converge and the points where they diverge. To clarify the point, let us take an example. In forming adjectives, the suffix *–ish* is used mainly to show disapproval. It picks out an undesirable quality of the thing specified by the nominal root as in *freakish behaviour*, meaning 'behaviour that is strange'. In the present description, the suffix is used additionally, though rarely, to stand for a desirable quality of the thing specified by the nominal root as in *a stylish dress*, meaning 'a dress that is fashionable'. This indicates how categorisation allows for generality by embracing those uses that have hitherto been treated as exceptions to the rules.

A further advantage is that it embraces the role of the human in structuring the world and allows for the mental capacities to shape language. As Lakoff (1987:5–10) states, categories should be defined in terms of the peculiarities of human understanding or human capacity of conceptualisation, and not in terms of the shared properties of their members. If categories are defined only by properties that all members share, then no members should be better examples than others. To see how this works, let us look at an example. In dictionary descriptions, the suffix *–less* is simply employed to construe the absence of something undesirable as in *a noiseless flight*, meaning 'a flight that is without noise'. In the present description, the suffix is used also to construe the absence of something desirable as in *a powerless person*, meaning 'a person who is without power'. This demonstrates how categorisation helps to describe new phenomena on the basis of existing patterns without the need to create new words.

2.3 Categories of adjectival suffixes

Adjectival suffixes can be categorised according to two levels. At the external level, a group of adjectival suffixes can be categorised together because they meet certain criteria. In this respect, I propose two formal criteria to categorise adjectival suffixes. The first is the word class of the root, which can be either a verb or a noun. The second is the structure of the suffix, which can be either bound or free. The external categorisation allows one to see, among other things, how suffixes of different kinds form a group or how they are placed under one umbrella. For our purposes, adjectival suffixes form three external categories: de-verbal, de-nominal bound, and de-nominal free suffixes. At the internal level, any adjectival suffix forms a network made up of a range of senses exhibiting minimal differences. In this regard, I propose the *prototype* theory to categorise an adjectival suffix. The internal categorisation serves to reveal the various senses of a given suffix and show their relationships with one another.

In what follows, I group the adjectival suffixes into three major categories based on the two criteria: word class of the root and structure of the suffix. Then, I formulate a sketch of each of the adjectival suffixes. To do so, the sketch includes three steps. In the first step, I compile a list of adjectives containing each suffix, for which I rely on data provided by the BNC. The lists of adjectives compiled are not exhaustive, but they are numerous enough to reflect the suffix they represent. In the second step, I define each suffix, for which I rely on the analyses of the provided lists of instances. Meanwhile, I make use of insights offered in some major books on morphology like Marchand (1969), Urdang (1982), and *Collins COBUILD Word Formation* (1993). In the third step, I provide examples for each of the meanings diagnosed, for which I rely on major Online English dictionaries such as *Oxford English Dictionary*, *Cambridge Advanced Learner's Dictionary*, *Merriam-Webster Dictionary*, and a few others cited in the references.

2.3.1 De-verbal bound suffixes[7]

A de-verbal suffix is a word-final element that is commonly added to a verb to form an adjective. It is a bound morpheme because it never occurs by itself, but is attached to some other morpheme. It acts as a profile determinant of a derivation and has twofold import in its derivation. As a categorial marker, it changes a lexical item from one class into another. Here, it transforms a verb into an adjective. As a meaning marker, it contributes to the semantics of the derivative of which it is part. It causes a shift of a kind in the semantic structure of the root, and so adds a special meaning to the derived formation. In CS, the form of an expression is motivated by its cognitive organisation, which is reflected by both its conceptual content and the construal imposed by the speaker on it. In the case of a de-verbal adjective, the construal employed to structure its content is realised morphologically by the type of the suffix chosen. The suffix bears content; its use is not governed by a set of defining features, but rather by mental representations.

What is involved in the semantic description of a de-verbal suffix is an idealised model of *transitivity*. The model is scalar in dimension in that the root subsumes some components. The prototype is the transitive component, where the root evokes an action requiring both an agent and a patient. In *digestible food*, the verbal root *digest* is transitive. It features a process involving a patient, who is focused, and an agent, who is defocused. The combination means 'food that is capable of being digested'. One step removed from the prototype is the intransitive component, where the root evokes a process in which the subject is the actor and acts upon the self. Such a case is referred to as *middle voice*. In *a collapsible chair*, the verbal root *collapse* is intransitive. The combination means 'a chair that is capable of collapsing'. Furthest from the prototype is a formation where the root evokes a quality. In *a sensible person*, the nominal root *sense* denotes a quality. The combination means 'a person who shows an awareness of a situation'.

Below are the de-verbal bound suffixes used to derive adjectives together with their synchronic descriptions.

2.3.1.1 –able

The suffix *–able* is taken over from Old French. In its prototypical sense, the suffix *–able* is attached to verbs denoting action to form adjectives[8]. The meaning of the suffix varies relative to the nature of the combining root, which can be paraphrased as:

a. 'capable of undergoing the action referred to in the verbal root'. This meaning emerges when the suffix is attached to transitive verbs. The adjectives so formed have a passive interpretation in that the action performed on the patient requires an external agent. The patient is represented by an object with emphasis laid on the process that it undergoes. For example, *a washable shirt* is a shirt that is capable of being washed, *a movable screen* is a screen that is capable of being moved, and *a returnable bottle* is a bottle that is capable of being returned. Other coinages are *avoidable, breakable, countable, endurable, recognisable*, etc.

   The passive interpretation of the suffix does not always work. In some formations, it is the substance trait of the inanimate entity that is focused. As Lee (2001:54–55) notices, *drinkable water* does not mean water that is able to be drunk, but water that is safe to be drunk. Hydrochloric acid is also able to be drunk, but it is not drinkable. *A readable book* does not mean the book is able to be read, but a book that is enjoyable. Presumably, all books can be read. Other coinages are *breathable, crossable, eatable, payable, watchable*, etc. In other formations, it is the character trait of the animate entity that is focused.

For example, *an adorable child* does not necessarily mean a child who can be adored, but a child who is extremely charming. *Deplorable behaviour* does not necessarily mean behaviour that can be deplored, but behaviour that is bad. Other coinages are *agreeable, comparable, enjoyable, likeable, loveable,* etc.

b. 'capable of doing the action referred to in the verbal root'. This meaning emerges when the suffix is attached to intransitive verbs. In such formations, the adjectives realise a middle voice relationship between an entity and a process. The adjectives profile an entity that is responsible for performing the action, without an external influence. The entity is personified as having the agent-like properties of being self-moving or self-changing. For example, *perishable food* is food that is capable of perishing, *decayable victuals* are food and drink that are capable of decaying, and *a shrinkable sweater* is a sweater that is capable of shrinking. In all the examples, the roots evoke a process in which the nouns change themselves depending on their own properties and under certain circumstances.

c. 'capable of doing or undergoing the action referred to in the verbal root'. This meaning emerges when the suffix is attached to verbs that are both transitive and intransitive. In such formations, the adjectives have a dual interpretation: active and passive. For example, *adaptable* means either 'capable of adapting' or 'capable of being adapted', *changeable* means either 'capable of changing' or 'capable of being changed', and *variable* means either 'capable of varying' or 'capable of being varied'.

In its peripheral sense, the suffix *–able* is attached to nouns denoting quality to form adjectives. In this use, the suffix displays some degrees of variability in meaning according to the nature of the combining root, which can be paraphrased as:

a. 'worthy of or deserving the quality referred to in the nominal root'. This meaning arises when the suffix is attached to nouns applying to inanimate entities. In such formations, the adjectives have a passive interpretation with the entity being affected by an external agent. For example, *a habitable area* is an area that is worth living in, *a palatable meal* is a meal that is worth eating, and *a marketable product* is a product that is worth marketing. Other coinages are *creditable, impracticable, memorable, practicable, saleable*, etc.

b. 'having or showing the quality referred to in the nominal root'. This meaning arises when the suffix is attached to nouns applying to animate entities. In such formations, the adjectives have an active interpretation with the entity acting as an agent. For example, *a knowledgeable debater* is a debater who has a lot of knowledge, *a reasonable speaker* is a speaker who shows sound judgement, and *a peaceable campaigner* is a campaigner who shows calmness. Other coinages are *charitable, personable*, etc.

A graphical representation of the multiple senses of the de-verbal bound suffix *–able* is offered in Figure 1:

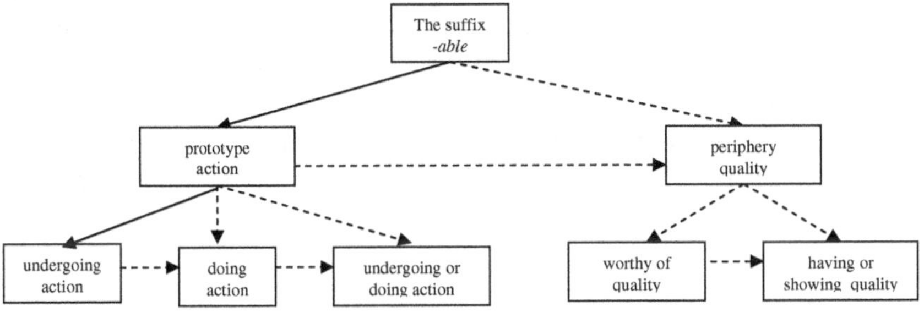

Figure 1: The semantic network of the de-verbal bound suffix *–able*

The solid arrow represents the prototypical sense, whereas the dashed arrows represent the semantic extensions.

2.3.1.2 –ant

Prototypically, the suffix *–ant* is attached to verbs denoting action to form adjectives. Relative to the nature of the combining root, the suffix shows some slight deviances in meaning. These meanings are:

a. 'liable to do the action signified by the verbal root'. This meaning emerges when the suffix is attached to transitive verbs. The adjectives so formed denote an action which involves both an agent and a patient. For example, *a defiant protester* is a protester who is liable to defy authority, *a resistant politician* is a politician who is liable to resist change, and *an observant guard* is a guard who is liable to observe things. Other adjectives with this meaning are *acceptant, attendant, continuant, ignorant, reliant*, etc.

b. 'apt to do the action signified by the verbal root'. This meaning emerges when the suffix is attached to intransitive verbs. The adjectives so formed denote an action which involves no patient. For example, *a compliant child* is a child who is apt to comply, and *an errant husband* is a husband who is apt to err, and *a hesitant leader* is a leader who is apt to hesitate. Other adjectives with this meaning are *deviant, emigrant, repentant, resultant, triumphant*, etc.

Peripherally, the suffix *–ant* is still attached to verbal roots, but in these derivations the roots specify a condition. In this use, the suffix means 'being in the condition signified by the verbal root'. This meaning emerges when the suffix is attached to verbal roots, ending mostly in *–ate*, which are both transitive and intransitive. For example, *a dominant issue* is an issue that is more important than anything of the same type, *a radiant bride* is a bride who is obviously happy or beautiful, and *a vibrant performer* is a performer who is energetic, exciting and full of enthusiasm. Some roots are only transitive: *a vacant room* is a room that is not filled or is available to be used. Other roots are only intransitive: *a stagnant pool* is a pool that does not flow and smells unpleasant.

2.3.1.3 –ed

The suffix *–ed* combines with the base forms of regular weak verbs to form simple past and past participles. In this use, the suffix is inflectional in character. It locates the event or state described by the base form at some point prior to the moment of speaking or writing. In *She walked away*, the suffix *–ed* refers to the past time of the action of walking, i.e. it ended before the time of speaking. However, there are contexts in which the suffix is derivational in character. In this use, the words so formed are adjectival by function and can occur in adjectival positions. In *a pleased expression*, the *–ed* derives the word *pleased*, which is an adjective and occurs before the noun it modifies. It means 'happy or satisfied'.

Prototypically, the suffix *–ed* is appended to verbs denoting action. In such combinations, the suffix triggers the following specialised connotations:

a. 'affected by the action referred to in the verbal root'. This meaning evolves when the suffix is appended to transitive verbs to form past participles. In this case, the adjectives so formed have a passive meaning and denote an action that involves a patient. For example, *an excited crowd* is a crowd which is excited, *an astonished spectator* is a spectator who is astonished, and *a frightened child* is a child who is frightened. Other adjectives which fall under this heading are *bored, confused, delighted, interested, worried*, etc.

b. 'having been in the state signified by the verbal root'. This meaning evolves when the suffix is appended to intransitive verbs to form past participles. In this case, the adjectives so formed have an active interpretation and denote an action that involves only an agent. For example, *a retired officer* is an officer who has retired, *an escaped prisoner* is a prisoner who has escaped, and *a qualified teacher* is a teacher who has received qualifications. Other adjectives which fall under this heading are *accumulated, dated, faded, wilted*, etc.

Peripherally, the suffix *–ed* is appended to nouns denoting feature. In such combinations, the suffix triggers the following specialised connotations:

a. 'demonstrating the feature signified by the nominal root'. This meaning develops when the suffix is appended to concrete nouns. So, the feature is explicit. For example, *a bearded man* is a man with a beard, *a spotted dress* is a dress with spots, and *a patterned wallpaper* is a wallpaper with a pattern. Other adjectives which fall under this heading are *flowered, hooded, pointed, striped, turbaned*, etc.

b. 'implying the feature signified by the nominal root'. This meaning, approving or disapproving, develops when the suffix is appended to abstract nouns. So, the feature is implicit. For example, *a cultured woman* is a woman who has a good education, *a fabled film director* is a director who is very famous, and *a jaundiced view* is a view that judges everything as bad. Other adjectives which fall under this heading are *bigoted, crooked, gifted, lettered, principled*, etc.

2.3.1.4 –en

Unlike the suffix *–ed* which combines with regular weak verbs, the suffix *–en* is added to irregular strong verbs to form past participles. In this use, the suffix is inflectional in character. It indicates the completion of a past action. In *She has written a book*, the suffix *–en* marks the end point of the action of writing. However, in some contexts the suffix *–en* is derivational in character. In this use, the words so formed are adjectival by function and can occur in adjectival positions. In *a fallen tree*, the *–en* derives the word *fallen*, which functions as an adjective and occurs before the noun it modifies. It means 'a tree that lies on the ground'.

Prototypically, the suffix *–en* is appended to verbs denoting action. In such extensions, the suffix means 'being in the state designated by the verbal root'. This meaning comes out when the suffix is added to verbs to form past participles. For example, *a forbidden subject* is a subject that is not allowed to be discussed, *a broken promise* is a promise that is not kept, and *a beaten path* is a path that has been made by people walking the same way.

Peripherally, the suffix *–en* is appended to nouns denoting things. In such extensions, the suffix indicates such meanings as:

a. 'resembling the thing designated by the nominal root in make'. This meaning comes out when the suffix is added to nouns denoting substance. For example, *a wooden fence* is a fence that is made of wood, *a golden necklace* is a necklace that is made of gold, and *a woollen scarf* is a scarf that is made of wool. Adjectives behaving similarly are *earthen, oaken, silken, waxen*, etc.

b. 'situated in the region expressed by the nominal root'. This meaning comes out when the suffix is added to nouns denoting location. In this use, the suffix takes the form *–ern*. For example, *an eastern suburb* is a suburb that is situated in the east, *a western border* is a border that is situated in the west, *a northern coast* is a coast that is situated in the north, and *southern England* is a region that is situated in the south.

2.3.1.5 –ible

The suffix *–ible* goes back to Latin. In its prototypical sense, the suffix *–ible* is attached to verbs denoting action to form adjectives. Based on the nature of the combining root, the meaning of the suffix can be rephrased as:

a. 'capable of undergoing the action referred to in the verbal root'. This meaning emerges when the suffix is attached to transitive verbs. In this nuance, the suffix denotes passivity. This meaning corresponds, therefore, to a passive construction in which the action performed involves an external agent. For example, *a discernible difference* is a difference that is capable of being recognised, *a comprehensible film* is a film that is capable of being understood, and *a reversible raincoat* is a raincoat that is capable of being reversed. A sample of similar adjectives includes *admissible, convertible, deductible, expressible, reducible*, etc.

b. 'capable of doing the action referred to in the verbal root'. This meaning emerges when the suffix is attached to intransitive verbs. In this nuance, the adjective has a middle voice interpretation in that the object acts on itself. The object is personified as having the agent-like properties of being self-moving or self-changing. For example, *a collapsible chair* is a chair that is capable of folding, *a contractible metal* is a metal that is capable of drawing together so as to become diminished in size, and *a combustible substance* is a substance that is capable of burning easily.

c. 'capable of doing or undergoing the action referred to in the verbal root'. This meaning emerges when the suffix is attached to verbs that are both transitive and intransitive. In this nuance, the adjective has a dual interpretation: active and passive. For example, *flexible* means 'capable of adapting to new requirements' or 'capable of being flexed', *responsible* means 'capable of controlling' or 'capable of being controlled', and *submersible* means 'capable of functioning while submerged' or 'capable of being submerged'.

In its peripheral sense, the suffix *–ible* is attached to nouns denoting quality. Due to the nature of the combining root, the suffix shows some variability in meaning, which can be rephrased as:

a. 'involving the quality referred to in the nominal root'. This meaning emerges when the suffix is attached to nouns applying to inanimate entities. In such formations, the adjective has a passive interpretation with the entity acting as a recipient of the action. For example, *forcible entry* is entry that involves the use of physical power, *a horrible accident* is an accident that involves fright and shock, and *a terrible crash* is a crash that involves fear and damage.

b. 'having or showing the quality referred to the nominal root'. This meaning emerges when the suffix is attached to nouns applying to animate entities. In such formations, the adjective has an active interpretation with the entity acting as a performer of the action. For example, *a sensible person* is a person who shows an awareness of a situation, and *an insensible person* is a person who lacks awareness of a situation. In some uses, the adjectives may also refer to inanimate entities. For example, *a sensible answer* is an answer that is based on practical ideas or understanding.

2.3.1.6 –ing

The suffix *–ing* combines with the base forms of verbs to form present participles. In this use, the suffix is inflectional in character. It denotes duration of the activity contained in the base form. In *She is dancing*, the suffix *–ing* refers to the activity of dancing which is going on at the moment of speaking. However, there are contexts in which present participles formed by the suffix *–ing* are used as adjectives. The words so formed are adjectival by function and can occur in adjectival positions. In this use, the suffix is derivational in character. In *a disturbing scene*, the *–ing* derives the word *disturbing*, which is an adjective and occurs before the noun it modifies. It means 'worried or upset'.

Prototypically, the suffix *–ing* is appended to verbs denoting action. In such combinations, the suffix evokes some specialised connotations:

a. 'causing the action referred to in the verbal root'. This meaning emerges when the suffix is appended to transitive verbs. In this function, the adjective has an active meaning in that it requires an agent and a patient. For example, *an interesting programme* is a programme that makes one feel interested, *an amusing story* is a story that makes one feel amused, and *a disgusting room* is a room that makes one feel disgusted. Adjectives of similar behaviour are *amazing, depressing, embarrassing, entertaining, surprising*, etc.

b. 'keep on the activity signified by the verbal root'. This meaning emerges when the suffix is appended to intransitive verbs. In this function, the adjective has an active meaning in that it requires only an agent. For example, *a recurring crisis* is a crisis which keeps on occurring, *dwindling circulation* is circulation that keeps on becoming less in number or smaller, and *a prevailing law* is a law that keeps on existing. Adjectives of similar behaviour are *ailing, decreasing, diminishing, increasing, reigning*, etc.

2.3.1.7 –ive

The prototypical use of the suffix *–ive* can be detected when it is appended to verbs denoting action to form adjectives. According to the nature of the combining root, the meaning of the suffix can be restated as:

a. 'performing or tending to perform the action referred to in the verbal root'. This meaning comes about when the suffix is attached to transitive verbs. The adjectives so formed indicate that the action involves a patient. In most cases, the roots end in *–d, –s* or *–t*. For example, *a creative designer* is a designer who tends to create new ideas, *productive land* is land that tends to produce something, and *a destructive weapon* is a weapon that tends to destroy things. A list of other adjectives includes *coercive, evasive, offensive, persuasive, repulsive,* etc.

b. 'apt to do the action signified by the verbal root'. This meaning comes into existence when the suffix is attached to intransitive verbs. The adjectives so formed indicate that the action involves no patient. The action is metaphorically performed by the object itself. For example, *a responsive engine* is an engine that is apt to make a reaction, *reactive manner* is manner that is apt to react to situations, and *a speculative article* is an article that is apt to guess. A list of other adjectives includes *intrusive, participative, regressive, talkative*, etc.

c. 'performing or apt to perform the action referred to in the verbal root'. This interpretation holds when the suffix is appended to verbs that are both transitive and intransitive. For example, *protective clothing* is clothing that gives protection, *conclusive evidence* is evidence that ends uncertainty, and *an operative agreement* is an agreement that is apt to work. A list of other adjectives includes *attentive, impressive, obtrusive, reflective, selective*, etc.

The peripheral use of the suffix *–ive* can be detected when it is attached to nouns denoting quality. In such formations, the suffix suggests a slight meaning deviation. The meaning is 'marked by the quality named by the nominal root'. This meaning comes into existence when the suffix is appended to nouns applying to inanimate entities. For example, *an abusive practice* is a practice that is marked by wrong use or improper action, *a combative mood* is a mood that is marked by eagerness to fight or contend, and *a massive iceberg* is an iceberg that is marked by large size. A list of other adjectives includes *defective, expensive, impulsive, reflexive, secretive,* etc.

2.3.1.8 –ory

Prototypically, the suffix *–ory* is appended to verbs denoting action to form adjectives. Relative to the nature of the conjoined root, the meaning of the suffix can be reworded as:

a. 'performing or tending to perform the action referred to in the verbal root'. This meaning happens when the suffix is attached to transitive verbs. The adjectives so formed indicate that the action has an impact on a patient. In many cases, the verbal roots end in *–ate*. For example, *an accusatory look* is a look that tends to disapprove something, *a deprecatory remark* is a remark that tends to criticise something, and *an intimidatory interview* is an interview that frightens people. More adjectives are *compensatory, congratulatory, derogatory, explicatory, obligatory*, etc.

b. 'apt to do the action referred to in the verbal root'. This meaning happens when the suffix is attached to intransitive verbs. For example, *a retaliatory measure* is a measure that is apt to retaliate, *a hallucinatory side-effect* is an effect that is apt to hallucinate, *a migratory bird* is a bird that is apt to migrate.

c. 'performing or apt to perform the action referred to in the verbal root'. This meaning happens when the suffix is attached to verbs that are both transitive and intransitive. For example, *an advisory board* is a board that gives advice, *an explanatory note* is a note that describes how something works, and *preparatory work* is work that is done to get ready for something. More adjectives are *amendatory, celebratory, conciliatory, contradictory, contributory*, etc.

Peripherally, the suffix *–ory* is attached to nouns denoting quality. In this use, the suffix departs from the central meaning to evoke some meaning deflections:

a. 'associated with the quality described by the nominal root'. This meaning happens when the nouns refer to specialised contexts. In most cases, the roots end in *–ion*. For example, *a respiratory disease* is a disease that is associated with the respiratory system, *sensory organs* are organs that are associated with the physical senses, and *statutory obligations* are obligations that are associated with a formally-approved law. More adjectives are *auditory, expository, interlocutory, migratory, transitory*, etc.

b. 'containing the quality described by the nominal root'. This meaning happens when the nouns refer to general contexts. In most cases, the roots end in *–ion*. For example, *a declamatory style* is a style that contains a loud voice or a forceful language, *a consolatory remark* is a remark that contains comfort and sympathy, and *an exclamatory phrase* is a phrase that contains exclamation.

2.3.2 De-nominal bound suffixes[9]

A de-nominal suffix is a word-final element that is usually added to a noun to form an adjective. It is a bound morpheme because it cannot stand on its own, but is combined with some other morpheme. It acts as a profile determinant in the derivation process and is significant in two ways. As a word class indicator, it changes the class of the lexical item to which it is appended. Here, it transposes a noun into an adjective. As a meaning indicator, it contributes to the semantic make-up of the lexical item to which it is linked. It adds meaning to the derived outcome, and serves to reflect the speaker's conceptualisation of a situation. In CS, the form of a composite word is motivated by its cognitive organisation, which is determined by both its conceptual content and the construal imposed by the speaker on that content. In the case of a de-verbal adjective, the construal employed to describe its content is realised morphologically by the type of the suffix chosen. The use of the suffix is therefore governed by meaning, and is not a formal feature.

The meaning of a de-nominal suffix, I argue, is established in the idealised model of *animacy*. This model is scalar in dimension in that the root with which the suffix is combined can be of two categories: inanimate and animate. Let us take an example on the suffix *–y*. In a prototypical sense, *–y* describes an inanimate entity. First is a formation which focuses on amount. In *a dusty sofa*, the combination means 'a sofa that is full of dust'. Further is a formation which focuses on appearance. In *a marshy coastline*, the combination means 'a coastline that has the appearance of a marsh'. Furthest is a formation which focuses on resemblance. In *silky fur*, the combination means 'fur that resembles silk'. In a peripheral sense, *–y* describes an animate entity. First is a formation in which a quality is in focus. In *a lucky escape*, the combination means 'an escape that has luck'. Second is a formation in which an action is in focus. In *a fidgety child*, the combination means 'a child that is inclined to fidget'.

Below are the de-nominal bound suffixes used to derive adjectives together with their synchronic descriptions.

2.3.2.1 –al

In its prototypical sense, the suffix *–al* is attached to nouns denoting inanimate entities to form adjectives. Its meaning varies relative to the nature of the joining root, which includes the following cases of semantic specialisation:

a. 'relating closely to the thing named by the nominal root'. This meaning comes to attention when the suffix is added to roots referring to inanimate entities. The suffix specifies the type of entity the noun modified is related to. For example, *an environmental issue* is an issue that is related to the environment, *a medicinal product* is a product that is related to medicine, and *a postal delivery* is a delivery that is linked to a mail service. A sample of other adjectives includes *cultural, global, occidental, oriental, tropical*, etc.

b. 'showing the location of the thing named by the nominal root'. This meaning comes to attention when the suffix is added to roots referring to names of places. The suffix modifies the noun as being situated in or near the thing named by the root. For example, *a coastal town* is a town that is located near the coast, *marginal land* is land that is located on the edge of a cultivated area, *a central hole* is a hole that is located in, at or near the centre of something, and *a frontal door* is a door that is located at the front.

c. 'showing the proportion of the thing named by the nominal root'. This meaning comes to attention when the suffix is added to roots referring to dimensionality. The suffix modifies the noun as having the number, size or degree of the thing named by the root. For example, *an occasional vacation* is a vacation that occurs at infrequent intervals, *a colossal statue* is a statue that is of gigantic size, and *a proportional punishment* is a punishment that corresponds with the degree of seriousness of a crime. A sample of other adjectives include *minimal, maximal, monumental*, etc.

In its peripheral sense, the suffix *–al* is attached to nouns denoting animate entities, or their deeds, to form adjectives. In such formations, the suffix means 'showing the character of the thing named by the nominal root'. This meaning comes to attention when the suffix is added to roots applying to humans. For example, *a brutal dictator* is a dictator who shows his people cruelty and inhuman feelings, *a maternal nurse*, from Latin *mater*, is a nurse who shows her patients the compassionate feelings of a mother, and *a cynical view* is a view that believes people are only interested in themselves and are not sincere. A sample of other adjectives includes *matriarchal, paternal, patriarchal, pivotal*, etc.

2.3.2.2 –ary

The suffix *–ary* is added to nouns to yield adjectives. In its prototypical sense, the suffix *–ary* is attached to nouns denoting inanimate entities to form adjectives. Its meaning changes according to the nature of the joining root. The suffix has the following slightly different denotations:

a. 'relating closely to the thing named by the nominal root'. This meaning comes to the surface when the suffix is applied to roots referring to inanimate entities. The suffix shows the type of entity the noun modified is related to. For example, *a budgetary policy* is a policy that relates to the budget, *dietary fibre* is fibre that relates to diet, and *a disciplinary measure* is a measure that relates to discipline. A handful of other adjectives includes *customary, documentary, elementary, sedimentary, summary*, etc.

b. 'serving to do the thing named by the nominal root'. This meaning comes to the surface when the suffix is applied to roots having inanimate characteristics. For example, *a complementary list* is a list that serves to complete another, *a complimentary review* is a review that serves to express admiration for someone or something, and *an exemplary punishment* is a punishment that serves to warn others. A handful of other adjectives includes *diversionary, fragmentary, inflationary, precautionary, supplementary*, etc.

Peripherally, the suffix *–ary* is attached to nouns denoting animate entities to form adjectives. In such formations, the suffix means 'embodying the characteristics of the entity referred to by the nominal root'. This meaning comes to the surface when the suffix is applied to roots having animate characteristics. For example, *a legendary broadcaster* is a broadcaster who embodies a legend in being famous and admired, *an honorary member* is a member who embodies honour in recognition of achievement or service without the usual obligations, and *a visionary leader* is a leader who embodies vision by having the powers of imagination or foresight.

2.3.2.3 –ful

The suffix *–ful* attaches to nouns to produce adjectives. Prototypically, it is attached to nouns applying to inanimates to form adjectives. Its meaning varies relative to the nature of the joining root. The suffix gives rise to some combinations having the following shades of meaning.

a. 'full of the thing denoted by the nominal root'. More precisely, the meaning might be glossed as 'abundant', meaning there is an unusually large supply of the thing stated in the joining root. This meaning arises when the suffix is added to roots which denote non-emotion. For example, *an eventful period* is a period that is full of important or interesting events, *a colourful picture* is a picture that is full of colours, and *purposeful work* is work that is full of aims. A collection of other adjectives includes *brimful, fruitful, playful, tuneful, useful*, etc. Some adjectives denote emotion. For example, *a disdainful expression* is an expression that is full of disdain, *a frightful mess* is a mess that is full of fright, and *a wonderful view* is a view that is full of wonder. A collection of other adjectives includes *gleeful, resentful, scornful, sorrowful, woeful,* etc.

b. 'giving rise to the quality denoted by the nominal root'. This meaning succeeds when the suffix is added to roots denoting negative emotion. For example, *a painful memory* is a memory that gives rise to pain, *a shameful act* is an act that gives rise to shame, and *a harmful scandal* is a scandal that gives rise to harm. A collection of other adjectives includes *disgraceful, hurtful, mournful, rueful, stressful*, etc.

c. 'displaying the quality denoted by the nominal root'. This meaning follows when the suffix is added to roots referring to skills. For example, *a graceful movement* is a movement that displays smoothness, *a tasteful arrangement* is an arrangement that displays good style, and *a tactful manner* is a manner that displays tact. A collection of other adjectives includes *bashful, fanciful, masterful, neglectful, successful*, etc.

Peripherally, the suffix *–ful* is attached to roots applying to animates to form adjectives. It takes the following meanings:

a. 'full of the quality denoted by the nominal root'. This meaning arises when the suffix is added to nouns denoting emotion. For example, and *a merciful ruler* is a ruler who is full of mercy, *a remorseful husband* is a husband who is full of remorse, and *a spiteful child* is a child who is full of spite. A collection of other adjectives includes *delightful, fearful, hateful, lustful, ruthful,* etc.

b. 'featuring the quality denoted by the nominal root'. This meaning arises when the suffix is added to nouns denoting cognition. For example, *a hopeful woman* is a woman who believes that something she wants will happen, *an insightful politician* is a politician who shows a clear understanding of a situation, and *a thoughtful person* is a person who shows signs of careful thought. A collection of other adjectives includes *artful, careful, faithful, heedful, mindful*, etc.

c. 'likely to do the action denoted by the verbal root'. This meaning ensues when the adjective is formed with verbs denoting animate entities. For example, *a forgetful child* is a child who is likely to forget, *a boastful woman* is a woman who is likely to praise herself and what she has done, *a fretful person* is a person who is likely to worry or be unhappy about something, and *a wakeful guard* is a guard who is likely to be awake and aware.

A graphical representation of the multiple senses of the de-nominal bound suffix *–ful* is offered in Figure 2:

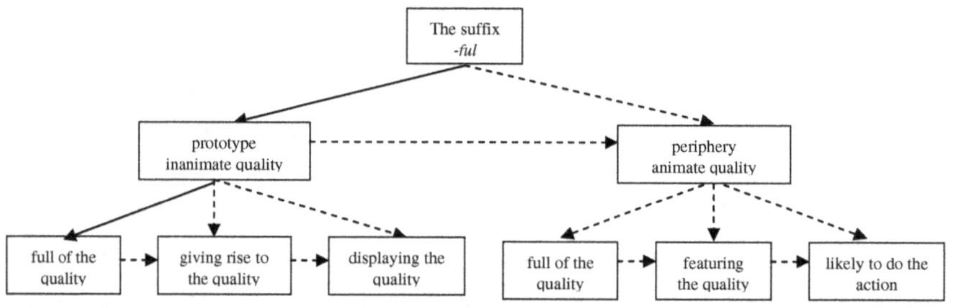

Figure 2: The semantic network of the de-nominal bound suffix *–ful*

The solid arrow represents the prototypical sense, whereas the dashed arrows represent the semantic extensions.

2.3.2.4 –ic

The suffix *–ic* is annexed to noun roots to form adjectives. In its central sense, the suffix *–ic* is attached to nouns denoting inanimate entities to form adjectives. Based on the nature of the joining root, the suffix conveys the following senses:

a. 'pertaining to the thing named by the nominal root'. This meaning proceeds when the suffix is attached to roots referring to common nouns of technological products, scientific subjects and medical terms. Such adjectives do not have a counterpart ending in *–ical*. For example, *a telegraphic apparatus* is an apparatus that pertains to telegraph, *atomic energy* is energy that pertains to atoms, and *photographic equipment* is equipment that pertains to photography. Similar adjectives are *alcoholic, allergic, cubic, mythic, phonemic*, etc.

b. 'pertaining to the place or the language named by the nominal root'. This meaning proceeds when the suffix is attached to roots referring to a small number of proper nouns, chiefly names of countries or languages. For example, *an Icelandic saga* is a saga that pertains to Iceland, *Teutonic mythology* is mythology that pertains to the Teutons, *Celtic music* is music that pertains to the Celts, and an *Arabic newspaper* is a newspaper that pertains to the Arabs or their language.

c. 'having the element named by the nominal root to a high degree'. This meaning proceeds when the suffix is attached to roots denoting chemistry. In such formations, the suffix *–ic* means that the chemical element borne by the nominal root has a valence higher than that denoted by the suffix *–ous*. For example, in *chloric/chlorous acid* the adjective ending in *–ic* contains a higher proportion of acid than the adjective ending in *–ous*. In *cupric/cuprous oxide*, the adjective ending in *–ic* contains oxide with a valence of two, whereas the adjective ending in *–ous* contains oxide with a valence of one. In *nitric/nitrous acid*, the termination *–ic* indicates a greater quantity of acid, while the termination *–ous* indicates a lesser quantity of acid.

d. 'pertaining to the typical feature of the thing named by the nominal root'. This meaning results when the suffix is attached to roots referring to fields of knowledge or art. In this nuance, both *–ic* and *–ical* are in competition. For example, *a philosophic stance* is a stance that is calm or unflinching in the face of trouble, *a poetic sunset* is a sunset that is very beautiful or expressive, *a prophetic statement* is a statement that is true and predictive, and *a tragic mistake* is a mistake that is regrettably serious or unpleasant. For the meanings of the adjectives in *–ical* and a list of adjectives ending in both suffixes, see the next section and Chapter 4.

Peripherally, the suffix *–ic* is attached to nouns denoting animate entities to form adjectives. The suffix conveys the following senses:

a. 'applying the typical feature of the thing named by the nominal root'. This is especially the case when the suffix combines with roots which refer to people or their deeds. Sometimes, the roots end in *–ist*. For example, *an optimistic person* is a person who has the belief that good things will happen in the future, *an idealistic planner* is a planner who believes that things can be better, and *an artistic writer* is a writer who applies, creates and enjoys art. Similar adjectives are *antagonistic, capitalistic, journalistic, linguistic, nationalistic*, etc. Sometimes, the roots end differently. For example, *a pedantic person* is a person who gives too much attention to formal rules or small details, *a patriotic citizen* is a citizen who shows love for and pride in his or her country, and *a heroic act* is an act that is brave or great.

b. 'pertaining to the person named by the nominal root'. This is especially the case when the suffix combines with roots which refer to personal names. For example, *Byronic style* is style that pertains to the English poet Byron, *Miltonic prose* is prose that pertains to the English poet Milton, and *Socratic wisdom* is wisdom that pertains to the philosopher Socrates.

2.3.2.5 –ical

The ending *–ical* looks like a combination of *–ic* and *–al*, but it is best regarded as a single suffix rather than a sequence of two. The central meaning of the suffix is 'pertaining to the thing named by the nominal root'. This meaning proceeds when the suffix is attached to roots denoting inanimate entities. For example, *a cyclical pattern* is a pattern that pertains to a cycle, *a geographical location* is a location that pertains to geography, and *a symmetrical shape* is a shape that pertains to symmetry.

However, quite a number of adjectives appear in two forms: *–ic* and *–ical*. Both forms mean 'pertaining to the thing named by the nominal root', but there is a difference in semantic range, although in some cases the distinction seems difficult to maintain or even recognise. In the present analysis, the suffix *–ic* is reserved to emphasise the core feature of the noun expressed in the root. By contrast, the suffix *–ical* is reserved to merely stress the relationship between the noun and the field of knowledge or subject of study expressed in the root. This analysis squares with Marchand's (1969:242) viewpoint, according to which the suffix *–ic* describes a relationship that is direct or close, whereas the suffix *–ical* describes a relationship that is indirect or remote. Adjectives formed with *–ical* have thus a wider or more transferred semantic range than corresponding adjectives in *–ic*.

Let us make this clear by means of some examples. *A philosophical essay* is an essay that pertains to philosophy, *a poetical work* is a work that pertains to poetry, *a prophetical study* is a study that pertains to prophets, and *tragical fate* is fate that pertains to tragedy. For the meanings of the adjectives in *–ic*, see the previous section and Chapter 4. Similar adjectives ending in both *–ic* and *–ical* include *classic/al, economic/al, geometric/al, graphic/al, historic/al, ironic/al, numeric/al, politic/al, problematic/al, rhythmic/al, symmetric/al*, etc. Before ending the section, a remark about the adjective *economic* is in order. According to Crystal (2002) and Oxford English Dictionary, *economic* nowadays tends to be used in the sense of 'money-saving', which has traditionally been associated with *economical*. This claim seems to be borne out by the data, as in *We had to close our London office with the rent so high it just was not economic.*

2.3.2.6 –ish

The suffix *–ish* is tacked on to nouns to form adjectives. In its prototypical sense, the suffix *–ish* is attached to nouns denoting inanimate entities to form adjectives. Dependent on the nature of the joining root, it has a variety of related senses:

a. 'having the character of the thing specified by the nominal root'. This meaning follows when the suffix is added to roots describing undesirable qualities. For example, *a raffish appearance* is an appearance that is vulgar or crude, *freakish weather* is weather that is unexpected, and *a hellish experience* is an experience that is unpleasant. A sample list of other adjectives with negative implications includes *amateurish, brackish, devilish, puckish, sluggish*, etc. In some very rare cases, the roots describe desirable qualities. This meaning follows when the suffix is added to roots denoting fashion or style. For example, *a modish outfit* is an outfit that is fashionable, *stylish dress* is dress that is high in design, and *a roguish skirt* is a skirt that is in fashion at a particular time.

b. 'given to or preoccupied with the thing specified by the nominal root'. This meaning follows when the suffix is added to roots denoting hobbies or activities. For example, *a bookish speech* is a speech which is preoccupied with literary style or pedantic tone, *a faddish theme* is a theme which is given to popularity but for a short time, and *an impish grin* is a grin which is given to annoyance or trouble. The adjectives could also be used to modify animates, as in *bookish reader*, *faddish eater* or *impish child.*

c. 'coming from or belonging to the thing specified by the nominal root'. This meaning follows when the suffix is added to roots referring to names of countries to indicate language, nationality or origin. For example, *Irish coffee* is coffee of a style which originates in Ireland, *Polish language* is language spoken in Poland, and *a Scottish dance* is a dance which originates in Scotland. A sample list of other adjectives with this meaning includes *British, Danish, Finnish, Spanish, Swedish,* etc. In addition to this use, the suffix can modify humans. For example, a *Finnish student* is a student who comes from Finland, and a *Swedish singer* is a singer who comes from Sweden.

d. 'having the quality specified by the root to some degree'. In these formations, the root describes approximation. This is used chiefly with adjectives referring to age, time, colour, size and weather. The suffix helps one to avoid sounding too strict about a matter. For example, *a purplish birthmark* is a birthmark that is slightly purple in colour, *a meeting around sevenish* takes place about 7 o'clock, and *a biggish backyard* is a backyard that is somewhat big. A sample list of other adjectives with this meaning includes *biggish, bluish, oldish, tallish, youngish*, etc.

Peripherally, the suffix *–ish* is attached to nouns denoting animate entities to form adjectives. In this case, the suffix means 'having the character of the thing specified by the nominal root'. The suffix stresses the undesirable quality of the thing referred to in the root. In some formations, the roots denote humans. For example, *a foolish person* is a person who is unwise, ridiculous or lacks in judgement, *a boorish bloke* is a bloke who is rude and does not consider other people's feelings, and *a wimpish climber* is a climber who is not strong, brave or confident. A sample list of other adjectives includes *fiendish, priggish, slavish, snobbish, thuggish*, etc. In other formations, the roots denote animals. For example, *a hawkish president* is a president who supports the use of force in settling political disputes, *a waspish tongue* is a tongue that makes sharp, cruel or unpleasant remarks, and *a mulish negotiator* is a negotiator who is unwilling to change his or her mind. A sample list of other adjectives includes *bearish, doggish, monkish, owlish, wolfish*, etc.

2.3.2.7 *–ly*

The suffix *–ly* is appended to nouns to derive adjectives. Prototypically, the suffix *–ly* is appended to nouns denoting inanimate entities to form adjectives. Affected by the nature of the root, the suffix bears the following shades of semantic senses:

a. 'having the manner of the thing specified by the nominal root'. This meaning emerges when the suffix is appended to roots denoting inanimate entities. For example, *a leisurely action* is an action that occurs in a relaxed way, *a timely meeting* is a meeting that happens at a suitable moment, *a courtly approach* is an approach that is polite in manner, and *a lively discussion* is a discussion that is energetic in manner.

b. 'moving towards or coming from the point specified by the nominal root'. This meaning emerges when the suffix is appended to roots denoting points of the compass and followed by types of wind. For example, *an easterly wind* is a wind that comes from the east, *a westerly gale* is a gale that comes from the west, and *a northerly breeze* is a breeze that comes from the north.

c. 'recurring with the regularity of the thing specified by the nominal root'. This meaning emerges when the suffix is appended to roots denoting periods of time. For example, *a daily shower* is a shower that recurs every day, *a weekly meeting* is a meeting that recurs every week, and *a yearly check-up* is a check-up that recurs every year. Similar adjectives include *hourly, quarterly, fortnightly, monthly*, etc.

d. 'bearing the character of the thing specified by the nominal root'. This meaning emerges when the suffix is appended to nouns denoting quality. For example, *a costly holiday* is a holiday that is expensive, *a chilly day* is a day that is cold, but not extremely cold, and *a homely hotel* is a hotel that is plain or ordinary but pleasant. Similar adjectives include *heavenly, orderly, shapely, stately, worldly*, etc.

e. 'having the nature of the thing specified by the adjectival root'. This meaning emerges when the suffix is appended to adjectives. For example, *a deadly conversation* is a conversation that is boring in content, *an elderly bike* is a bike that is old in age, and *a lowly job* is a job that is low in position or importance. Similar adjectives include *goodly, kindly, poorly, sickly, weakly*, etc.

Peripherally, the suffix *–ly* is attached to nouns denoting animate entities to form adjectives. In this case, the suffix *–ly* means 'befitting the thing specified by the nominal root'. Two types of root exist. Some roots imply praise. For example, *a motherly treatment* is a treatment that befits a mother, *queenly grace* is grace that befits a queen, and *a friendly offer* is an offer that befits a friend. Similar adjectives are *brotherly, fatherly, kingly, knightly, princely*, etc. Other roots imply blame. For example, *a cowardly retreat* is a retreat that befits a coward, *dastardly revenge* is revenge that befits a dastard, and *a beastly attitude* is an attitude that befits a beast. Similar adjectives are *beggarly, gangly, rascally, ruffianly, slovenly*, etc.

2.3.2.8 –ous

The suffix *–ous* is annexed to nouns to form adjectives. In its prototypical sense, the suffix *–ous* is attached to nouns denoting inanimate entities to form adjectives. Affected by the nature of the joining root, it evokes senses such as:

a. 'abounding in the thing denoted by the nominal root'. More precisely, the suffix might be glossed as 'copious', meaning there is a large supply of the thing named by the combining root. This meaning follows when the suffix is added to roots denoting inanimate entities. For example, *a dangerous mission* is a mission that abounds in potential harm or loss, *a riotous garden* is a garden that abounds in flowers, and *a mountainous countryside* is a countryside that abounds in mountains. Additional adjectives include *capacious, cavernous, numerous, perilous, voluminous*, etc.

b. 'having the element denoted by the nominal root to a low degree'. This meaning proceeds when the suffix is attached to roots denoting chemistry. In such formations, the suffix *–ous* denotes that the chemical element denoted by the nominal root has a valence lower than that denoted by the suffix *–ic*. For example, in *chlorous/chloric acid* the adjective ending in *–ous* contains a lower proportion of acid than the adjective ending in *–ic*. In *cuprous/cupric oxide*, the adjective ending in *–ous* contains oxide with a valence of one, whereas the adjective ending in *–ic* contains oxide with a valence of two. In *nitrous/nitric acid*, the termination *–ous* indicates a lesser quantity of acid, while the termination *–ic* indicates a greater quantity of acid. Additional adjectives include *sulphurous/sulphuric fume, ferrous/ferric salt, mercurous/mercuric chloride*, etc.

c. 'causing or inspiring the thing denoted by the nominal root'. In such formations, the root describes a quality. For example, *a contentious subject* is a subject that causes or is likely to cause disagreement, *a dolorous poem* is a poem that causes misery or grief, *a grievous loss* is a loss that causes pain, or sorrow, and *a hazardous journey* is a journey that causes loss or harm. Additional adjectives include *advantageous, arduous, disastrous, ruinous, slumberous*, etc.

Peripherally, the suffix *–ous* is attached to nouns denoting animate entities to form adjectives. The suffix conveys the following senses:

a. 'filled with the thing denoted by the nominal root'. For example, *an ambitious athlete* is an athlete who is filled with ambition, *an envious classmate* is a classmate who is filled with envy, and *a zealous campaigner* is a campaigner who is filled with zeal. Additional adjectives include *contemptuous, desirous, piteous, sensuous*, etc.

b. 'characterised by the thing denoted by the nominal root'. For example, *a courteous man* is a man who is characterised by polished manners, *a rebellious pupil* is a pupil who is characterised by stubborn resistance, and *virtuous people* are people who are characterised by moral qualities. Additional adjectives include *barbarous, courageous, malicious, traitorous, treacherous,* etc.

2.3.2.9 –some

The suffix *–some* is attached to nouns to produce adjectives. In its prototypical sense, the suffix *–some* is attached to nouns denoting inanimate entities to form adjectives. Relative to the nature of the joining root, it evokes these nuances of meanings:

a. 'having the thing denoted by the nominal root'. More precisely, the meaning might be glossed as 'considerable', meaning there is a noticeable supply of the quality stated in the combining root. For example, *toilsome efforts* are efforts that have toil, and *flavoursome wine* is wine that has flavour.

b. 'causing or inspiring the thing denoted by the joining root'. In some cases, the root is a noun. For example, *an awesome event* is an event that causes awe, *a burdensome responsibility* is a responsibility that causes a burden, and *a fearsome weapon* is a weapon that causes fear.

In some cases, the root is a verb. For example, *a worrisome affair* is an affair that makes people distressed or worried, *a tiresome job* is a job that causes tiredness, and *bothersome noise* is noise that causes annoyance. In some cases, the root is an adjective. For example, *a wearisome task* is a task that causes one to be weary, *a lonesome house* is a house that causes a feeling of loneliness, and *a loathsome business* is a business that causes feelings of hate.

c. 'willing to do the thing denoted by the joining root'. In some cases, the root is a noun. For example, *a quarrelsome kid* is a kid who is willing to quarrel, and *a venturesome traveller* is a traveller who is willing to venture. In some cases, the root is a verb. For example, *a meddlesome neighbour* is a neighbour who is willing to meddle.

Peripherally, the suffix *–some* is attached to nouns denoting animate entities to form adjectives. In such formations, the suffix *–some* means 'retaining the thing denoted by the nominal root'. For example, *a mettlesome team* is a team that retains mettle, i.e. energy and determination.

2.3.2.10 –y

The suffix *–y* is annexed to nouns to form adjectives. In its prototypical sense, the suffix *–y* is annexed to nouns denoting inanimate entities to form adjectives. It is used in a number of combinations, evoking each time a slightly different meaning.

a. 'full of the thing specified by the nominal root'. More precisely, the meaning might glossed as 'ample', meaning the quality is sufficient enough to satisfy a definite requirement. For example, *a sandy beach* is a beach that is full of sand, *a juicy orange* is an orange that is full of juice, and *an icy road* is a road that is covered with ice. A constellation of other adjectives includes *grassy, muddy, smoky, thorny, weedy,* etc.

b. 'having the content of the thing specified by the nominal root'. This is the case when the suffix is added to nouns denoting plants. For example, *a cottony pad* is a pad that contains cotton, *a peppery salad* is a salad that contains pepper, and *yeasty bread* is bread that contains yeast. In rare cases, the roots refer to substance. For example, *chalky soil* is soil that contains chalk, and *salty food* is food that contains salt.

c. 'having the appearance of the thing specified by the nominal root'. This is the case when the suffix is added to nouns denoting objects. For example, *baggy trousers* are trousers that have the appearance of bags in being loose, *a stony necklace* is a necklace that has the appearance of stone in being hard, *horny skin* is skin that has the appearance of horn in being tough. In rare cases, the roots refer to animals. For example, *a batty idea* is an idea that is crazy in a harmless way.

d. 'resembling the thing specified by the nominal root in quality'. This is the case when the suffix is added to nouns denoting substance. For example, *an oaky wine* is wine that resembles oak in taste, *a woolly picture* is a picture that resembles wool in lacking clearness, and *a waxy surface* is a surface that resembles wax in smoothness. Adjectives behaving similarly are *earthy, silky, woody*, etc.

e. 'producing or triggering the thing denoted by the verbal root'. This is the case when the suffix is added to verbs used transitively. The adjectives so formed are used to modify inanimate entities. For example, *a chilly pool* is a pool that produces a feeling of cold, *a teary story* is a story that triggers tears, and *a shady avenue* is an avenue that produces shade from the sunlight.

f. 'suggesting the colour denoted by the adjectival root'. This is the case when the suffix is added to roots denoting colour. The suffix *–y* describes something as being similar to the colour, while the suffix *–ish* describes something as having a small amount of the colour. For example, *greeny purple* is a shade of purple that is similar to green, and *yellowy black* is a shade of black that is similar to yellow. A constellation of other adjectives includes *greeny blue, bluey green, reddy brown*, and the like.

In its peripheral sense, the suffix *–y* is attached to other roots denoting animate entities to form adjectives. It is used in a number of combinations, evoking each time a slightly different meaning.

a. 'having the trait of the thing designated by the nominal root'. In these formations, the suffix is used with roots that apply to people, their body parts or their actions. For examples, *a witty remark* is a remark that is clever and funny, *a guilty look* is a look that is anxious and unhappy, and *a speedy reaction* is a reaction that is swift and hasty. A constellation of other adjectives includes *bossy, gloomy, greedy, moody, nosy*, etc. In rare cases, the roots apply to things. For example, *a bendy mast* is a mast that is pliable, and *a creaky economy* is an economy that is ineffective.

b. 'tending to do the action denoted by the root'. This is the case when the suffix is added to verbs used intransitively. The adjectives so formed are used to modify humans. For example, *a sleepy baby* is a baby who tends to sleep, *a chatty neighbour* is a neighbour who tends to chat, and *a sulky person* is a person who tends to sulk. A constellation of other adjectives includes *clingy, creepy, scary, shivery, weepy,* etc. In some cases, the roots apply to things. For example, *a sticky substance* is a substance that tends to stick, *floppy ears* are ears that tend to flop, and *a floaty scarf* is a scarf that tends to float.

2.3.3 De-nominal free suffixes[10]

A de-nominal suffix is a derivative morpheme that is added to a noun to form an adjective. It is free because it can stand on its own as a word, and can be used as a second part in a combination. For example, in *interest-free* the suffix *–free* is a free morpheme because it can be used in isolation in English. The combination is analysed as having two constituents: the root *interest* as an independent morpheme and the suffix *–free* as a derivational morpheme. Marchand (1969:356) treats such words as semi-suffixes because they stand midway between full words and suffixes. Huddleston & Pullum (2002:1711) take them to be roots forming compounds because they occur with the same form and meaning as separate words. Following Jespersen, I consider them to be suffixes because they meet the two requirements of derivation. First, they change the word class of the combined result in the same way as an affix does. Second, they add a specialised meaning to the combined result in the same way as an affix does. Furthermore, they are productive in the sense that they can be appended to almost any noun, including proper names, to form an adjective.

The meaning of a free suffix, I argue, is established in the idealised model of *concreteness*. This model is scalar in dimension in that the entity described falls into two classes: concrete and abstract. The dichotomy between the classes is borne out by the nature of the root. Let us take an example of the suffix *–free*. In a prototypical formation, *–free* is attached to a root denoting a concrete entity to form an adjective. The entity is undesirable, and so strongly unwelcome. In *a mud-free road*, the combination means 'a road that is free of mud'. Further is an extension in which the entity represented by the root is still concrete but desirable. Yet, the speaker prefers not to have it occasionally. In *a car-free zone*, the combination means 'a zone that is free of cars'. In a peripheral formation, the suffix *–free* is attached to a root denoting an abstract entity to form an adjective. The entity represented by the root is undesirable, and so firmly unwanted. In *a risk-free trip*, the combination means 'a trip that is free of risks'.

Below are the de-nominal free suffixes used to derive adjectives together with their synchronic descriptions.

2.3.3.1 –based

The suffix *–based* combines with nouns to form adjectives. Prototypically, the suffix is added to concrete nouns to form adjectives. Considering the nature of the root, it expresses two slightly different meanings:

a. 'the thing expressed by the nominal root forms the most important part of the noun it modifies'. This is the case when the roots refer to physical substances or raw materials. For example, *an oil-based economy* is an economy that relies heavily on oil, *rice-based food* is food that has rice as its vital ingredient, and *a petroleum-based detergent* is a detergent whose essential part is petroleum. Examples of other adjectives are *acid-based, coal-based, paper-based, rubber-based, water-based*, etc.

b. 'positioned in but moving around the place expressed by the nominal root'. This is the case when the roots refer to names of places. For example, *a land-based missile* is a missile that is fired from the ground but hits far-off places or objects, *a London-based news agency* is an agency that is based in London but its operations cover other places, and *a ground-based telescope* is a telescope that is installed on the ground but its range of activity extends beyond it. Examples of other such adjectives are *campus-based, farm-based, home-based, Swiss-based, village-based*, etc.

Peripherally, the suffix *–based* is attached to abstract nouns to form adjectives. In such formations, it means 'the thing expressed by the nominal root forms the most important feature of the noun it modifies'. For example, *insurance-based health* is health that has insurance as its typical feature, *a power-based organisation* is an organisation whose core feature is power, and *a rule-based system* is a system that takes rule as an important feature. Examples of other adjectives are *class-based, education-based, information-based, propaganda-based, science-based,* etc.

2.3.3.2 –bound

The suffix *–bound* combines with nouns to form adjectives. Prototypically, the suffix is added to concrete nouns to form adjectives. Relative to the nature of the root, it denotes three different meanings:

a. 'restricted or confined to the place or environment expressed by the nominal root'. Adjectives formed in this way describe someone or something as being limited by or caught in the locale referred to by the combining root. For example, *a fog-bound ship* is a ship whose movement is restricted because of fog, *a studio-bound programme* is a programme whose recording is restricted to the studio, and *a chair-bound patient* is a patient whose movement is confined to a chair. Examples of other adjectives are *desk-bound, earth-bound, house-bound, ice-bound, snow-bound,* etc.

b. 'leading towards the point expressed by the nominal root'. Adjectives formed in this way indicate the destination referred to by the combining root. This meaning emerges when the root refers to places or points of the sky. For example, *an eastbound train* is a train whose destination is the east, *a homebound ship* is a ship which is heading towards home, and *a Leeds-bound passenger* is a passenger whose end station is Leeds. Examples of other adjectives are *Dublin-bound, London-bound, northbound, southbound, westbound*, etc.

c. 'indicating the sort of covering expressed by the nominal root'. This meaning emerges when the root refers to names of material. For example, *a leather-bound book* is a book that is bound in leather, *a brass-bound handle* is a handle whose trim is covered with brass, and *a cloth-bound gift* is a gift that is covered with cloth. Examples of other adjectives are *metal-bound, cardboard-bound, paper-bound*, etc.

Peripherally, the suffix *–bound* combines with abstract nouns to form adjectives. In such formations, it means 'being held by or placed under the effect of the thing expressed by the nominal root'. For example, *a duty-bound official* is an official who is placed under legal obligation or moral restraint, *a spellbound audience* is an audience whose attention is held by a spell, and *a time-bound campaign* is a campaign whose activity is placed under time pressure. Examples of other adjectives are *class-bound, culture-bound, honour-bound, status-bound, tradition-bound*, etc.

2.3.3.3 –conscious

Prototypically, the suffix *–conscious* combines with concrete nouns to form adjectives, with the meaning of 'aware of the thing conveyed by the nominal root'. Adjectives formed in this way describe someone as being inwardly aware of or mentally awake to the thing referred to by the combining root. For example, *a dress-conscious teenager* is a teenager who takes an interest in clothes, *a camera-conscious person* is a person who feels nervous about having his photograph taken, and *a garden-conscious housewife* is a housewife who is too interested in her garden. The same description applies to adjectives like *body-conscious, complexion-conscious, diet-conscious, style-conscious, weight-conscious*, etc.

Peripherally, the suffix *–conscious* combines with abstract nouns to form adjectives, with the meaning of 'aware of the thing conveyed by the nominal root'. Adjectives formed in this way describe something one might be interested in or worried about, something that represents an important aspect of life. For example, *a budget-conscious businessman* is a man who is concerned or interested in a budget, *a cost-conscious businessman* is a man who is preoccupied with costs, and *a health-conscious person* is a person who is concerned about his health. The same description applies to adjectives like *age-conscious, class-conscious, duty-conscious, media-conscious, status-conscious*, etc.

2.3.3.4 –free

The suffix *–free* combines with nouns to form adjectives. Prototypically, the suffix attaches to concrete nouns to form adjectives. Relative to the nature of the root, the suffix has two meanings:

a. 'lacking the undesirable thing imparted by the nominal root'. This meaning emerges when the roots refer to something that one always dislikes. For example, *cloud-free sky* is sky that is empty of clouds, *queue-free check-in* is check-in that is free from queues, and *a weed-free garden* is a garden that lacks weed. Other adjectives are *dust-free, lead-free, mud-free, smoke-free, traffic-free*, etc.

b. 'lacking the desirable thing imparted by the nominal root'. This meaning emerges when the roots refer to something that one occasionally dislikes. For example, *a child-free gathering* is a gathering that is without children, *a meat-free diet* is a diet that is free from meat, and *sugar-free tea* is tea that lacks sugar. Other adjectives are *car-free, fence-free, ice-free, oil-free, tourist-free*, etc.

Peripherally, the suffix *–free* attaches to abstract nouns to form adjectives. In such formations, it means 'lacking the undesirable thing imparted by the nominal root'. The nominal roots refer to something that is categorically unwanted. For example, *a pain-free operation* is an operation that is without pain, *a duty-free car* is a car that is free from duty, and *a trouble-free journey* is a journey that lacks in trouble. Other adjectives are *accident-free, interest-free, risk-free, stress-free, tax-free*, etc.

2.3.3.5 –*less*

The suffix –*less* combines with nouns to coin adjectives. Prototypically, the suffix combines with concrete nouns to coin adjectives, expressing each time a slightly different shade of meaning:

a. 'devoid of the undesirable thing imparted by the nominal root'. This meaning emerges when the roots refer to something that one always dislikes. For example, *a flawless performance* is a performance that is devoid of mistakes, *a spotless house* is a house that is devoid of dirt, and *boneless fish* is fish that is devoid of skeleton. Similar coinages are *bloodless, cloudless, germless, rustless, seedless,* etc.

b. 'devoid of the desirable thing imparted by the nominal root'. This meaning emerges when the roots refer to something that one always wants. For example, *a characterless room* is a room that is without any character, *a fruitless tree* is a tree that is void of fruit, and *a motherless child* is a child that is without a mother. Similar coinages are *brainless, breathless, friendless, heartless, speechless*, etc.

Peripherally, the suffix –*less* is attached to other roots to coin adjectives, expressing each time a slightly different shade of meaning:

a. 'devoid of the quality imparted by the nominal root'. This meaning emerges when the suffix is attached to abstract nouns. In some coinages, the roots refer to something undesirable. For example, *harmless fun* is fun that is devoid of harm, *a fearless fighter* is a fighter who is devoid of fear, and *a faultless performance* is a performance that is devoid of fault. More coinages are *blameless, effortless, hasteless, needless, shameless*, etc. In other coinages, the roots refer to something desirable. For example, *a tactless remark* is a remark that is devoid of tact, *a profitless argument* is an argument that is devoid of profit, and *a merciless attack* is an attack that is devoid of mercy. More coinages are *goalless, hopeless, lawless, powerless, remorseless*, etc.

b. 'unable to perform or have performed the action imparted by the verbal root'. This meaning emerges when the suffix is attached to verbs. Adjectives coined in this way have a passive meaning in that the quality described cannot be measured in terms of whatever the root refers to. For example, *countless houses* are too many to be counted, and *a measureless ocean* is too big to be measured. On the analogy of these words, the suffix is appended to other words having the same form as a noun and as a verb. For example, *limitless possibilities* are without a limit or an end, i.e. very great. More coinages are *ceaseless, endless, numberless, timeless,* etc.

A graphical representation of the multiple senses of the de-nominal free suffix *–less* is offered in Figure 3:

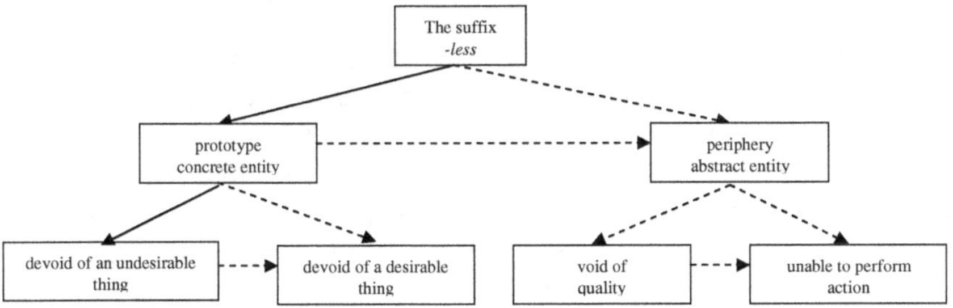

Figure 3: The semantic network of the de-nominal free suffix *–less*

The solid arrow represents the prototypical sense, whereas the dashed arrows represent the semantic extensions.

2.3.3.6 –like

The suffix *–like* combines with nouns to form adjectives. Prototypically, the suffix is attached to concrete nouns to form adjectives. Dependent on the combining root, the suffix evokes each time a different meaning:

a. 'having the character of the thing specified by the nominal root'. This meaning emerges when the roots refer mostly to people or animals. Although the suffix has neutral implications, the positive ones are predominant. For example, *godlike power* is power that has the character of god in being divine, *ladylike manner* is manner that has the character of a lady in being graceful, and *a catlike kid* is a kid who has the character of a cat in being stealthy, deliberate and secret in action. A sample list of other adjectives includes *clown-like, fox-like, model-like, owl-like, prince-like,* etc. Some of these combinations can also be used in describing appearance. For example, *a birdlike man* is a man who is like a bird perhaps in having a pointed nose and darting eyes.

b. 'having the peculiarity of the thing specified by nominal root'. This meaning emerges when the roots refer mostly to things or places. For example, *a dagger-like claw* is a claw that has the peculiarity of a dagger in being sharp and pointed, *a honey-like perfume* is a perfume that has the peculiarity of honey in smelling sweet, and *clocklike efficiency* is efficiency that has the peculiarity of a clock in being regular and precise. A sample list of other adjectives includes *ball-like, cage-like, desert-like, doll-like, prison-like*, etc.

Peripherally, the suffix *–like* combines with adjectives to form adjectives. This meaning emerges when the roots refer to mental qualities, conditions of temper, or the like. In such formations, it means 'having the characteristic of the thing specified by the adjectival root'. For example, *a grim-like smile* is a smile that has the characteristics of grimness in being ghastly or repellent, *sublime-like beauty* is beauty that has the characteristics of sublimity in being extremely good or admirable, and *a genteel-like lady* is a lady who has the characteristics of gentility in being polite or courteous. There is a reason why the speaker uses this form with the suffix rather than the adjective on its own. With the suffix, the adjective is used to indicate an imaginary existence of the quality, whereas without the suffix the adjective indicates its real existence.

2.3.3.7 –minded

The suffix *–minded* combines with nouns to form adjectives. Prototypically, the suffix is attached to roots referring to appearance with the meaning 'inclined towards the thing conveyed by the nominal root'. Adjectives formed in this way describe someone who is interested in something, knows its importance, supports it and aims to realise it. For example, *a chic-minded person* is a person who is inclined towards a fashion, *a fashion-minded buyer* is a buyer who is inclined towards a style, and *trend-minded people* are people who are inclined towards a trend. The same description can be applied to the following adjectives: *fad-minded, style-minded, vogue-minded,* etc.

Peripherally, the suffix *–minded* combines with other roots to form adjectives with similar or different meanings.

a. 'inclined towards the thing conveyed by the nominal root'. In these formations, the suffix is appended to roots referring to activity. For example, *a business-minded official* is a person who is inclined towards business, *an environment-minded activist* is a person who is inclined towards the environment, and *a peace-minded proponent* is a person who is inclined towards peace. The same description can be applied to the adjectives *economy-minded, future-minded, labour-minded, management-minded, security-minded,* etc.

b. 'having the tendency conveyed by the adjectival root'. This meaning emerges when the suffix is appended to two groups of adjectives. One group describes attitudes or ways of thinking. This meaning arises when the adjectives have positive implications. For example, *broad-minded parents* are parents who respect opinion and behaviour that are different from their own, *a fair-minded employer* is an employer who treats everyone equally, and *a high-minded person* is a person who has very high moral standards of behaviour and expects other people to follow them. Similar adjectives are *bright-minded, generous-minded, liberal-minded, open-minded, sharp-minded,* etc. Another group describes intellectual qualities. This meaning arises when the adjectives have negative implications. For example, *an empty-minded guy* is a guy who is unable to think or behave seriously, *a feeble-minded student* is a student who is unable to act or think in an intelligent way, and *a woolly-minded chatter* is a chatter who is unable to think clearly. Similar adjectives are *absent-minded, dirty-minded, evil-minded, mean-minded, narrow-minded,* etc.

2.3.3.8 –prone

The suffix *–prone* combines with nouns to form adjectives. Prototypically, the suffix is attached to concrete nouns to form adjectives. In each case, it has a different meaning:

a. 'disposed to the thing conveyed by the nominal root'. More often, the thing refers to something undesirable that one habitually does. In this formation, the person described has personality traits that make him or her likely to behave in an irritating way. For example, *a mischief-prone child* is a child who is disposed towards mischief, *a gaffe-prone person* is a person who is disposed towards gaffes, social mistakes, and *a quarrel-prone teenager* is a teenager who is disposed towards quarrels. Examples of other formations are *brawl-prone, feud-prone, squabble-prone,* etc.

b. 'susceptible to the thing conveyed by the nominal root'. This meaning arises in two cases. One case is when the root refers to something dangerous that a human is exposed to. For example, *an accident-prone child* is a child who is susceptible to accidents, *a failure-prone student* is a student whose is susceptible to failure, and *an injury-prone kid* is a kid who is susceptible to injuries. Examples of other formations are *casualty-prone, damage-prone, default-prone, mishap-prone*, etc. Another case is when the root refers to something adverse that a thing is subject to. For example, *an acne-prone skin* is a skin that is susceptible to acne, *fracture-prone glass* is glass that is susceptible to fracture, *an error-prone machine* is a machine that is susceptible to errors, and *a disease-prone garden* is a garden that is susceptible to diseases.

Peripherally, the suffix *–prone* combines with abstract nouns to form adjectives. In such formations, it means 'susceptible to the thing conveyed by the nominal root'. The thing refers to something undesriable that influences or is likely to influence an entity. For example, *a confusion-prone person* is a person who is susceptible to confusion, *an addiction-prone person* is a person who is susceptible to addiction, and *an erosion-prone soil* is a soil that is susceptible to erosion.

2.3.3.9 –related

The suffix *–related* combines with nouns to form adjectives. Prototypically, the suffix is attached to concrete nouns to form adjectives, spelling different meanings.

a. 'relating remotely to the thing named by the nominal root'. Adjectives formed in this way describe one thing as being connected with another. For example, *a school-related enquiry* is an enquiry that is related to school, *a performance-related reward* is a reward that is related to performance, and *a family-related dispute* is a dispute that is related to family. Examples of other adjectives are *animal-related, city-related, individual-related, industry-related, oil-related*, etc.

b. 'caused by the thing named by the nominal root'. Adjectives formed in this way are often used to describe the cause of an illness or accident. For example, *a drink-related fine* is a fine that is imposed because of drinking, *a smoking-related illness* is an illness that is caused by smoking, and *a drug-related crime* is a crime that is caused by drugs. Examples of other adjectives are *alcohol-related, injury-related, tobacco-related*, etc.

Peripherally, the suffix *–related* combines with abstract nouns to form adjectives. It means 'relating remotely to the thing named by the nominal root'. For example, *a work-related regulation* is a regulation that is related to work, *an age-related benefit* is a benefit that is related to age, and *a job-related advertisement* is an advertisement that is related to job. Examples of other adjectives are *career-related, earnings-related, income-related, race-related, tax-related*, etc.

2.3.3.10 –ridden

The suffix *–ridden* combines with nouns to form adjectives. Prototypically, the suffix is attached to concrete nouns to form adjectives triggering different meanings:

a. 'plagued by the thing imparted by the nominal root'. In these formations, the roots refer to calamities of incontrollable nature, which result in harm, damage or death. Adjectives formed in this way describe people or things that suffer from a large or excessive amount of something unpleasant or unwanted. For example, *cyclone-ridden terrain* is terrain that is plagued by cyclones, *a drought-ridden area* is an area that is plagued by drought, and *a mosquito-ridden swamp* is a swamp that is plagued by mosquitoes. The same description can be applied to the adjectives *flood-ridden, lice-ridden, litter-ridden, mouse-ridden, storm-ridden*, etc.

b. 'afflicted by the thing imparted by the nominal root'. In these formations, the roots name conditions or diseases. For example, *an acne-ridden face* is a face which is afflicted by acne, *an injury-ridden event* is an event that is afflicted by injury, and *a plague-ridden village* is a village that is afflicted by a plague.

Peripherally, the suffix *–ridden* combines with abstract nouns to form adjectives. In such formations, the roots refer to misfortunes of controllable nature. The suffix triggers two different meanings.

a. 'cursed by the thing imparted by the nominal root'. This meaning emerges when the suffix is attached to roots that describe actions which are against the law or actions of unacceptable behaviour. For example, *a crime-ridden city* is a city that is cursed by crimes, *a feud-ridden neighbourhood* is a neighbourhood that is cursed by feuds, and *a rumour-ridden community* is a community that is cursed by rumours. The same description can be applied to the adjectives *class-ridden, fraud-ridden, jargon-ridden, scandal-ridden, terror-ridden*, etc.

b. 'oppressed by the thing imparted by the nominal root'. This meaning emerges when the suffix is attached to roots that describe experiences resulting from unpleasant emotions. For example, *fear-ridden children* are children who are oppressed by fear, *a guilt-ridden man* is a man who is oppressed by guilt, and *a tension-ridden relationship* is a relationship that is oppressed by tension.

2.3.3.11 –stricken

The suffix *–stricken* combines with nouns to form adjectives. Prototypically, the suffix is attached to concrete nouns to form adjectives. Such nouns refer to disasters of incontrollable nature, which bring damage, loss or destruction. Adjectives formed in this way describe people or things that are very badly affected by such disasters. The suffix means 'hit by the thing imparted by the nominal root'. For example, *a famine-stricken region* is a region that is hit by shortage of food, *a hurricane-stricken coast* is a coast that is hit by a violent wind, and *a poverty-stricken area* is an area that is hit by destitution.

Peripherally, the suffix *–stricken* combines with abstract nouns to form adjectives. Such nouns refer to adversities of controllable nature. The majority of the nouns refer to unpleasant emotions. The suffix means 'overcome by the thing imparted by the nominal root'. For example, *a grief-stricken mother* is a mother who is overcome by grief, *a panic-stricken crowd* is a crowd which is overcome by panic, and *terror-stricken people* are people who are overcome by terror.

2.3.3.12 –style

Prototypically, the suffix *–style* combines with concrete nouns to form adjectives, showing some meaning variances:

a. 'resembling the thing designated by the nominal root in mode'. This meaning develops when the suffix is added to proper nouns. For example, *a Beatles-style band* is a band that resembles the Beatles in playing music, *European-style clothes* are clothes that resemble those worn by Europeans in fashion, and *a German-style car* is a car that resembles one made in Germany in design. The same description can be applied to the adjectives *African-style, British-style, French-style, Italian-style, Japanese-style,* etc.

b. 'akin to the thing designated by the nominal root'. This meaning develops when the suffix is added to common nouns. For example, *antique-style furniture* is furniture that is akin in beauty to antiques, *family-style food* is food that is akin in taste to that cooked in a family, and *a theatre-style ballroom* is a ballroom that is akin in architecture to a theatre. The same description can be applied to the adjectives *aircraft-style, bungalow-style, cafeteria-style, circus-style, factory-style*, etc.

Peripherally, the suffix *–style* combines with adjectives to form adjectives. In such formations, it means 'of the quality of the thing designated by the adjectival root'. For example, *an old-style suit* is a suit that is old in style, *modern-style technology* is technology that is modern in style, *new-style furniture* is furniture that is new in style, and *traditional-style customs* are customs that are traditional in style.

2.3.3.13 –type

Prototypically, the suffix *–type* combines with concrete nouns to form adjectives, causing some meaning extensions:

a. 'resembling the thing designated by the nominal root in specimen'. This meaning arises when the suffix combines with proper nouns. Adjectives formed in this way describe something as being imitative, or being typical in the sense of following a specified type of the thing referred to by the combining root. For example, *a California-type barbecue* is a barbecue that is typical of a barbecue people usually have in California, *a London-type jug* is a jug that is imitative of a jug commonly made in London, and *a Rome-type harrow* is a harrow that is emulative of a harrow used in Rome.

b. 'representative of the thing designated by the nominal root'. This meaning arises when the suffix combines with common nouns. For example, *a circus-type room* is a room that is as noisy as a circus, *a hospital-type bed* is a bed that is reminiscent of a bed generally used in hospitals, and *a military-type car* is a car that looks like a car in the military. The same description can be applied to the adjectives *arcade-type, bar-type, snack-type, umbrella-type, village-type*, etc.

Peripherally, the suffix *–type* combines with adjectives to form adjectives. In such formations, it means 'of the quality of the thing designated by the adjectival root'. For example, *domestic-type work* is work that is domestic in nature, *a national-type system* is a system that is national in nature, and *a wild-type tissue* is a tissue that grows in natural conditions.

2.3.3.14 –ward

Prototypically, the suffix *–ward* combines with concrete nouns to form adjectives, denoting some different but related meanings:

a. 'looking towards the point expressed by the nominal root'. For example, *a northward facade* is a facade that looks towards the north, *a seaward sign* is a sign that faces the sea, and *a skyward look* is a look that is directed towards the sky.

b. 'moving towards the region expressed by the nominal root'. For example, *ceiling-ward smoke* is smoke that moves upwards, *a homeward journey* is a journey that is on the way towards home, and *a southward walk* is a walk that moves in the direction of the south. Examples of other adjectives are *earthward, eastward, seaward, shoreward, westward,* etc. In some cases, the suffix combines with prepositions as in *downward, inward, onward, outward, upward,* etc. For example, *a downward trend* is a trend that moves towards a lower position, level or value, and *an upward trend* is a trend that moves towards a higher position, level or value.

Peripherally, the suffix *–ward* combines with the spatial prepositions *in-* and *out-* to form adjectives. In such formations, it means 'describing the inside or the outside of the thing expressed by the preposition'. It describes especially someone's thoughts and feelings or their appearance and expressions. For example, *inward interpretation* is interpretation that describes the mind or spirit, and *outward appearance* is appearance that describes the outside of something.

3 De-verbal domains

This chapter probes the role of domains in the semantic description of de-verbal suffixes. In the course of the investigation, it attempts to substantiate two principles of CS. One principle is that the meaning of an expression is described on the basis of the domain it evokes. Applying this principle to morphology, I argue that the meaning of a suffix can best be defined by comparing it with other suffixes located in the same domain. Another principle is that the syntax of an expression is a reflection of the construal imposed on its content. Applying this principle to morphology, I argue that the morphological form of a composite adjective is determined by the construal the speaker employs to structure its content. To that end, the chapter is organised as follows. Section 1 reviews the issue of meaning in the main theories of thought. Section 2 introduces the *domain* approach, highlights its essence and pinpoints its importance to the description of adjectival suffixes. Section 3 tackles the domain of *voice* and its morphological instantiations. Section 4 handles the domain of *aspect* and its morphological instantiations.

3.1 Introduction

Meaning is a basic notion used in the study of language. Meaning is employed to pick out some aspect of the non-linguistic world which is expressed by a linguistic form. Meaning is what the speaker conveys and what the receiver decodes. The meaning of a lexical item, word or morpheme, is so important that it has received attention in many approaches to language, but with differences in stance. The representational stances of the approaches follow from differences in their underlying assumptions. Taking my cue from Taylor (2002:186–204), I distinguish three approaches to the study of meaning. These are: the *language-world* approach proposed by Generative Linguistics, the *language-internal* approach advocated by Structural Linguistics, and the *conceptualist* approach defended by Cognitive Linguistics. In what follows, I present first the general observations made by each approach on the ways in which the topic of meaning is addressed. Then, I point out the relevance of each of the approaches to the analysis of adjectival suffixation.

In the *language-world* approach, the meaning of a lexical item resides in the relationship between the item and a state of affairs in the world. In this way, the meaning of a lexical item derives from the kind of thing it refers to in the world. Jackendoff (1983:29) asserts that the semantic value of a lexical item is reduced to the observable features of a situation. This stance stems from the *objectivist* theory of meaning, which views meaning in terms of correlation between what is said and what is seen. This approach is irrelevant to the concerns of the present analysis for various reasons. It applies only to linguistic items which designate concrete entities. It ignores extra-linguistic information in the definition of a lexical item. It disregards the speaker's role in construing a situation. Contrary to this, a lexical item involves a symbolic relationship between semantic and phonological structures. A lexical item refers to an entity in a mental space, be it actual or hypothetical. Its meaning includes knowledge that goes beyond its reference.

In the *language-internal* approach, the meaning of a lexical item is understood in terms of how it functions together with and in contrast to other related items. Namely, the meaning of a lexical item derives from the totality of relationships the item has with other items in the language. Lyons (1968:443) remarks that the meaning of a lexical item is internally determined by the set of relations which hold between the item in question and other items in the same linguistic system. A lexical item derives its meaning from syntagmatic and paradigmatic relations with other items in the language. This is indeed a valid technique of semantic enquiry, but it is not the whole story. It is true that one aspect of knowing a word is to know how that word is used in relation to other words. In this way, however, the semantic structure of a language becomes a vast calculus of internal relations, with no contact at all with the way speakers conceptualise the world. On the contrary, the context against which meanings are characterised is external to the linguistic system as such. Meanings are cognitive structures embedded in patterns of knowledge.

In the *conceptualist* approach, the meaning of a lexical item is a concept in the mind of the speaker using that item. The meaning of a lexical item derives, as Langacker (1987:147–166) stresses, from the domain to which it belongs. By *domain* is meant a context of background knowledge with respect to which lexical items are characterised. A domain includes a list of lexical items, where understanding the meaning of one item facilitates understanding the meaning of another. A domain provides motivation for the existence of lexical items in a language, sheds light on the interrelationships that hold between them, and explains how they are used in discourse. The meaning of a lexical item, as Langacker (1991a:294) asserts, reflects not only the content of a conceived situation, but also how that content is construed by the speaker. This stance originates as a result of the *subjectivist* or *empiricist* theory of meaning, which emphasises the importance of world experience to the representation of lexical items and recognises the speaker's capacity to construe a situation in alternative ways.

3.2 The domain approach to suffixation

In the preceding section, I argued against the *language-world* and *language-internal* approaches to meaning because their solutions can be regarded as symptomatic of meaning, not as meaning itself. Instead, I argued for the validity of a *conceptualist* approach to meaning. This is due to the stance it takes on meaning. On a general level, it considers the lexical items of a language as resources symbolising a speaker's construal of a state of affairs. On a specific level, it describes the meanings of lexical items in terms of the appropriate domains in which they are embedded. Accordingly, it justifies the existence of lexical pairs stemming from one root and helps to solve the riddles that blight their interpretation. As will be seen, each item describes a situation from a different angle, and so has a distinct meaning. It is time, now, to begin to fill in the details and to see how this approach can work in morphology. In this section, I focus on two things: the essence of the approach and its advantages to the area of adjectival suffixation.

3.2.1 Essence of the approach

The employment of a *domain* approach is of fundamental importance to the characterisation and understanding of suffixation. In CS, the meaning of an expression can be characterised relative to two aspects: *conceptual content* and *construal*. The conceptual content evoked by the expression is referred to by Langacker (1987:154) as a *cognitive domain*. A domain is any knowledge configuration which provides the basis for the characterisation of an expression. It subsumes a number of members which are linked not because they share the same features, but because they are similar to each other in some respects and different in others. It is a context where the relevant knowledge associated with an expression is coded. An expression is defined by recognising what domain it belongs to and how it differs from the other members of the same domain. Construal is a matter of how that content is conceptualised. It is a mental operation which allows the speaker to conceptualise a situation in alternative ways and choose the appropriate linguistic structures to represent them in language.

Adhering to the *domain* approach, I argue that a suffix does not exist in isolation in the mind of the speaker, but forms, together with other conceptually-related suffixes, a structured set. The set has some specific facets of meaning, which are profiled by the member suffixes. These facets represent semantic differences which are small but important. The essence of the approach is that to define a suffix it is best to compare it with the other suffixes that belong to the same domain. To understand the meanings of the suffixes *–able, –ible, –ive, –ory*, for example, we need to gather them in a domain which I refer to as *voice*. The first two form a subdomain which I refer to as *patientive*, whereas the last two form a subdomain which I refer to as *agentive*. The question then is: what difference exists between the members of each pair? Concerning the first pair, I argue that *–able* is restricted to computer uses as in *an accessable server*, whereas *–ible* is general in use as in *an accessible book*. Concerning the second pair, I argue that *–ive* describes an agent as initiating and imposing an action on the self as in *a regulative faculty*, whereas *–ory* describes an agent as initiating and imposing an action on others as in *a regulatory agency*.

In the examples given so far, it can be seen that an adjective has two structures: morphological and conceptual. The morphological structure is linguistic, which consists of a root plus a suffix. The conceptual structure is extra-linguistic, which consists of the particular construal imposed on its content. In this work, the construal chosen by the speaker is mapped onto the linguistic structure of the adjective via the use of an appropriate suffix. The construal is based on human experience in dealing with the world. The distinction, for instance, between self-imposition and other-imposition reflects human experience. Any variation in the meaning of an adjective pair is due to variation in the construal imposed on their common content. In each adjective, the construal is represented by an appropriate suffix. The meaning of any lexical item, including an adjective, does not contain only information about its part of speech or its obligatory and optional adjuncts. Rather, the meaning of a lexical item is something conceived in the mind. It is a mental entity that links up linguistic and extra-linguistic structures.

3.2.2 Advantages of the approach

In the discussion outlined previously, I argued that the meaning of a linguistic item, word or morpheme, can only be characterised relative to the cognitive domain to which it belongs. I defined the notion *domain* in two ways. At the conceptual level, a domain is a knowledge configuration which provides the basis for the description of concepts. It is a knowledge representation which organises concepts in a structured way. At the linguistic level, a domain is a set of lexical items which includes information not only about how they are related but also about how they are different. A domain is a device for unifying lexical items under a common concept rather than listing them in alphabetical order as dictionaries usually do. It accounts for the existence of lexical items in language and provides the contexts in which they are used. The employment of the *domain* approach to lexical meaning has, in addition to its descriptive and explanatory power, some practical advantages for the area of adjectival suffixation in English.

One advantage pertains to definition. A *domain* is an area of knowledge which contains information about lexical items, and so is a mechanism for defining their meanings. Extended to morphological units, a domain can serve to define the meanings of suffixes. To define a suffix, it is necessary to understand the entire domain and see which of its facets the suffix picks out. Although the suffixes unite under one domain, they move in different directions when it comes to details. For example, to define the meanings of the suffixes *–ous* and *–some*, we need to think of the domain of *possession* which they evoke. As shown in Chapter 4, the domain provides accurate descriptions of their features; *–ous* may or may not imply indiscretion, whereas *–some* implies only indiscretion. Accordingly, suffixes should not be defined on individual bases, as dictionaries usually do. Instead, suffixes should be defined in terms of their respective domains. When suffixes are joined together, they exhibit two qualities: comparison by sharing the main features of the domain and contrast by marking different aspects of it.

Another advantage concerns comparison. A *domain* is a sphere of knowledge within which a number of lexical items can be located, and so is a tool for comparing one item with another. Applied to morphological units, a domain can serve to explicate similarities and differences among its members, and so is a convenient way of coding information about the distributions of the suffixes and the patterns in which they occur. It shows the language user that understanding the meaning of a suffix facilitates understanding the meaning of a counterpart suffix in the domain. For example, to compare the suffixes *–ish* and *–like*, we need to think of the domain of *evaluation* which they evoke. As shown in Chapter 4, the domain highlights their contrastive structures; *–ish* is used when one evaluates somebody or something in a negative way, whereas *–like* is used when one evaluates somebody or something in a positive way. Accordingly, suffixes should not be tackled in isolation, as dictionaries usually do. Instead, they should be put in juxtaposition and tackled in terms of appropriate domains.

A further advantage belongs to construal. A *domain* is a realm of knowledge which provides the speaker with the lexical items required to construe a situation in different ways, and so is a means of symbolising conceptualisation. Related to morphological units, a domain can serve to show that the use of a particular suffix represents a particular construal of a content. The construal coded is based on experience that a human encounters, undergoes, or lives through. It is derived from direct observation of events or personal participation in activities. It is subjective in nature because it is gained, modified or affected by personal views or backgrounds. In construing a situation, two steps are thus involved. The first concerns the construal chosen which reflects the way the speaker conceptualises the situation. The second concerns the linguistic form which the speaker chooses to represent his or her conceptualisation. For example, in describing a feasible plan, the speaker chooses either *–able* or *–ed*. As shown in Chapter 5, the suffixes are not synonymous; the first refers to potentiality while the second refers to actuality.

In what follows, I apply the *domain* approach to the description of adjective-forming suffixes in English. The aim is to argue for the non-arbitrary quality of the mental lexicon and the highly creative nature of the human conceptual system. In describing a given situation or commenting on a special topic, the speaker selects the suffix that is appropriate. This means the suffix chosen correlates with the construal taken. Two suffixes can be attached to the same root, but they differ with respect to how they construe the same content. The method of description is as follows. First, I group the suffixes into different domains relative to their definitions that are provided in Chapter 2. Second, within each domain I pinpoint the peculiarity of each suffix which makes it different from the rest. Third, I compare suffixes that stand as rivals or make adjectival pairs. Fourth, I provide ample exemplification to support the comparison and describe the rivalry. Fifth, I confirm the analysis by means of evidence from the corpus, which is represented by discriminating collocations.

For the list of adjectival pairs, I rely on the data provided by the BNC. The lists of pairs compiled are not claimed to be exhaustive, but they are copious enough to reflect the meaning differences the suffixes represent. For the definitions of the common roots of the pairs, I rely on such major online English dictionaries as *Oxford English Dictionary*, *Cambridge Advanced Learner's Dictionary*, *Merriam-Webster Dictionary*, and a few others cited in the references. For the exemplification of the meanings diagnosed, I provide sentences based on the corpus. In most cases, I shorten the sentences by omitting elements that are not essential to meaning. For the sake of reinforcement, I check the characterisation of a few adjectival pairs against major manuals on English usage like Partridge (1961), Greenbaum & Whitcut (1988), Fowler (1996), and a few others mentioned in the references. One final note is in order. When an adjective is restricted to a certain position, i.e. attributive or predicative, this will be stated in the appropriate place. When no information is provided, this means the adjective can occur in both positions.

3.3 The domain of voice

Voice is an area of knowledge which expresses the mode of action of a verb. English has a two-way distinction of voice: active and passive. The difference between the two is accounted for by the construal of *prominence*, viz. the cognitive operation which assigns the quality of eminence to a substructure of a conception relative to its importance. One dimension of prominence that is at work in the domain of *voice* is *participant choice*. According to Langacker (1991a:330–335), the dimension of participant choice concerns the speaker's ability to confer subject or object status on a substructure within a base. Within an expression, one participant, termed the *trajector*, is analysed as the primary figure, and so associated with the function of subject. The other participant, termed *landmark*, is analysed as the secondary figure, and so associated with the function of object. When two expressions evoke the same content, the semantic contrast resides in the differential prominence accorded to the participants within them.

In CG, subject and object functions are characterised in terms of prominence and not in terms of semantic roles. In the active voice, prominence is conferred on the agent, while in the passive voice it is conferred on the patient. For example, in complement clauses as explained in Hamawand (2002:76), voice involves a change in the topic of the sentence. The use of either voice depends primarily on communicative considerations. In an active construction like *Nigel helped Kathy to make a presentation*, *Nigel* is the agent of the main event. He is the most important participant; consequently, he is chosen as subject. In a passive construction like *Kathy was helped to make a presentation*, the agent *Nigel* is bypassed in favour of the patient *Kathy*. She is the most important participant; therefore, she is chosen as subject. As is seen, the choice of a participant as subject arises from different conceptualisations. In the active *Nigel* receives prominence, whereas in the passive *Kathy* receives prominence.

Voice distinctions are relevant not only for syntactic forms of sentences but also for morphological forms of adjectives. The capacity of a de-verbal adjective to take a given suffix is determined by the construal imposed on its content. The construal of *participant choice* affects the morphology of an adjective and shows how the subject, represented by a noun, is related to the property designated by the adjective. To see how this works, we need to examine some sentences. In an active construction like *The writer is imaginative*, the subject is the entity performing the action of imagining[11]. In a passive construction like *The story is imaginable*, the subject is instead the entity undergoing the action of imagining. In the active, the subject acts to bring about a result expressed in the adjective, whereas in the passive it does not act although the same result occurs. In each case, the adjective ends in a different suffix and signals a different meaning. In the active, the adjective ends in the suffix *–ive*, whereas in the passive it ends in the suffix *–able*. In each case, the adjective profiles a property of the noun it modifies.

A graphical representation of the construal of *participant choice* in derived adjectives is sketched in Figure 4:

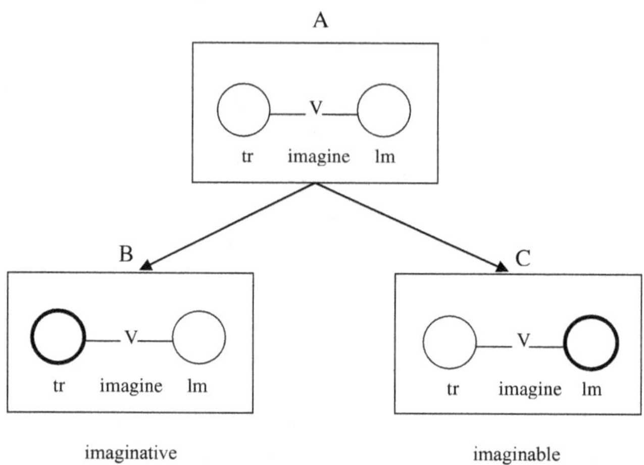

Figure 4: The construal of *participant choice* in derived adjectives

The box marked (A) represents a construction which includes the participants termed trajector (agent) and landmark (patient), which are linked by a relation (verb). The boxes marked (B) and (C) represent the construal of *participant choice* which the speaker imposes on the construction marked (A). In the box marked (B), the trajector participant is chosen, which is indicated in a bold circle. In the box marked (C), the landmark participant is chosen, which is indicated in a bold circle.

3.3.1 Morphological exponents

As noted earlier, the domain of *voice* comprises two subdomains: active and passive. Morphologically, each is indicated by rival types of suffixes, but with differences in meaning. The subdomain of active means acting to influence or change a situation. Morphologically, it is represented by the suffixes *–ive* and *–ory*, but with a difference in meaning. Both mean 'performing or tending to perform the action referred to in the verbal root', but with the former the agent acts on the self, whereas with the latter it acts on others (Section 3.3.2.2). The subdomain of passive means not acting to influence or change a situation. Morphologically, it is represented by the suffixes *–able* and *–ible*, but with a difference in meaning. Both mean 'capable of undergoing the action referred to in the verbal root', but with the former the action is restricted to specific contexts, whereas with the latter it is used in general ones (Section 3.3.2.3). A concomitant difference in *voice* is indicated by the suffixes *–ing* and *–ed*, but with a difference in meaning. The first represents the cause, while the second represents the effect (Section 3.3.2.4). In contrast to the suffixes *–ive* and *–ory* which describe a situation of permanent nature, the suffix *–ing* describes a situation of temporary nature. In contrast to the suffixes *–able* and *–ible* which describe a situation that changes through time, the suffix *–ed* describes a situation that goes on for some time.

3.3.2 Semantic distinctions

Adjectival suffixes belonging to the domain of *voice* can attach to the same root and form an adjective pair. The root has a kind of conceptual content, which includes more than one facet. The suffixes serve to shift the profile to each facet of the root's content. Each suffix imposes a certain construal on the content supplied by the root. Each adjective consisting of the root plus the suffix has, thus, meaning of its own. In spite of sharing the same root, the two adjectives do not mean the same, and so should be kept separate in use. In each case, the speaker imposes a different construal on the content, and so chooses a different suffix. This is in line with the cognitive premise that a particular situation can be construed in different ways, and that different ways of encoding a situation constitute different conceptualisations. Below are details of the semantic distinctions within the domain of *voice* and the rival suffixes that represent them.

3.3.2.1 The agentive-patientive distinction

As mentioned previously, *voice* involves two relations: agentivity and patientivity. *Agentivity* refers to a situation in which an entity performs a particular action to bring about an effect. Morphologically, the adjective ends in suffixes such as *–ive* or *–ory*. The difference between the two, which is detailed in 3.3.2.2, relates to the source and target of instigation. With the suffix *–ive*, it is self-instigated and self-targeted, whereas with the suffix *–ory* it is self-instigated but other-targeted. With both, the performer of the action, represented by human beings or their actions, is explicit in the sentence. By contrast, *patientivity* refers to a situation in which an entity undergoes a change or is affected in an event. Morphologically, the adjective ends in suffixes like *–able* or *–ible*. The difference between the two, which is detailed in 3.3.2.3, relates to their range of application. With the suffix *–able*, the range of application is definite, whereas with the suffix *–ible* it is indefinite. With both, the receiver of the action, represented by concrete or abstract objects, is explicit in the sentence. This distinction is represented by the following rival suffixes:

3.3.2.1.1 –ive vs. –able

The two suffixes have one thing in common: they belong to the domain of *voice*. Even so, they are not compatible for they fulfil separate functions. The suffix *–ive* focuses on agentivity, and means 'performing or tending to perform the action referred to in the verbal root'. By contrast, the suffix *–able* focuses on patientivity, and means 'capable of undergoing the action referred to in the verbal root'. A closer examination of the collocations in the corpus shows that there are distinct patterns discernible in the use of each suffix. Collocations of adjectives ending in *–ive* refer prototypically to humans and their actions or to entities that are metaphorically ascribed human properties, all of which confirm the agentivity that the suffix stands for. By contrast, collocations of adjectives ending in *–able* refer prototypically to objects that can be manipulated, hence confirming the non-agentivity that the suffix stands for. This distinction is borne out by adjective pairs such as the following:

(1) adaptive vs. adaptable
a. Adaptive behaviour is a necessary condition of existence.
b. The method is wonderfully adaptable to different needs.

The two adjectives are derived from the verb *adapt*, which means 'to change oneself or something to suit different conditions or uses'. Yet, each adjective represents a particular construal and so has a different use. In (1a), the adjective *adaptive* means 'tending to adapt'. Adaptive behaviour shows the tendency to change to suit different conditions. *Adaptive* tends to collocate with nouns referring to people such as *babysitter, father, mother, nurse, parent*; their actions such as *behaviour, demand, manner, reaction, response*; the machinery they use such as *appliance, equipment, instrument, mechanism, software*, etc. In (1b), the adjective *adaptable* means 'capable of being adapted'. An adaptable method has the capacity to be adjusted to suit different needs. *Adaptable* tends to collocate with nouns referring to tactics such as *method, policy, scheme, system, technique;* commerce such as *business, exchange, market, trade, transaction*; animals such as *bird, cow, dog, horse, monkey*, etc.

(2) communicative vs. communicable
a. She has become a lot more tolerant and communicative.
b. Her ideas were not easily communicable to her friends.

The two adjectives are derived from the verb *communicate*, which means 'to give thoughts, feelings, or information to others through speech, writing, bodily movements or signals'. Yet, each adjective represents a particular construal and so has a different use. In (2a), the adjective *communicative* means 'tending to communicate'. A communicative person is one who is willing to talk to people about his or her emotions and thoughts. *Communicative* shows the tendency to collocate with nouns referring to people such as *agent, coach, learner, researcher, teacher*; language such as *activity, competence, grammar, purpose, skill*, etc. In (2b), the adjective *communicable* means 'capable of being communicated'. A communicable idea is one that is capable of being transmitted or imparted to others. *Communicable* shows the tendency to collocate with nouns referring to sickness such as *ailment, disease, illness, infection, virus*; opinion such as *concept, idea, sentiment, thought, view*, etc.

(3) curative vs. curable
a. Do you believe in the curative powers of the local mineral water?
b. Tuberculosis which once killed many is today completely curable.

The two adjectives are derived from the verb *cure*, which means 'to make someone healthy again, or to make an illness disappear'. Yet, each adjective represents a particular construal and so has a different use. In (3a), the adjective *curative* means 'tending to heal disease'. A curative power is able to cure a disease or cause it to get better. *Curative* is associated with nouns referring to medication such as *medicament, medicine, drug, herb, flower*; treatment such as *care, healing, regimen, remedy, therapy*; natural means such as *powers of baths/hot springs/mineral water*, etc. In (3b), the adjective *curable* means 'capable of being healed'. A curable illness is able to be healed, i.e. remediable. *Curable* is associated with nouns referring to types of diseases such as *cancer, diabetes, measles, tuberculosis, whooping cough*; worried feelings such as *anxiety, concern, strain, stress, worry*; unreasonable interest in something such as *fascination, fetish, fixation, obsession, mania*; improper habits such as *addiction, dependence, gambling, stake, wager*, etc.

(4) demonstrative vs. demonstrable
a. He was more demonstrative of affection than his wife.
b. The new report contains demonstrable spelling errors.

The two adjectives are derived from the verb *demonstrate*, which means 'to make something clear, or to prove something as true'. Yet, each adjective represents a particular construal and so has a different use. In (4a), the adjective *demonstrative* means 'tending to demonstrate'. A person who is demonstrative of affection shows feelings of liking or love. The collocates of *demonstrative* show that it is most commonly used to describe people such as *father, man*, *mother, parent, person*; their emotions such as *affection, devotion, fondness, friendliness, love*; language functions such as *designation, identification, justification, reference, verification*, etc. In (4b), the adjective *demonstrable* means 'capable of being demonstrated'. A demonstrable error is capable of being shown or made obvious. The collocates of *demonstrable* show that it is most commonly used to describe symptoms of proof such as *evidence, example, fact, proof, sign*; consequences of action such as *conclusion, effect, outcome, result, upshot*; acts of advancement such as *development, improvement, progress, proliferation, superiority*; becoming smaller or larger in number or amount such as *drop, fall, growth, increase, rise*, etc.

(5) preventive vs. preventable
a. The therapist uses preventive medicine in the treatment.
b. Health upsets that spoil a holiday are easily preventable.

The two adjectives are derived from the verb *prevent*, which means 'to stop something from happening, or stop someone from doing something'. It implies taking advance measures against something possible or probable. Yet, each adjective represents a particular construal and so has a different use. In (5a), the adjective *preventive* means 'tending to prevent'. A preventive medicine has the power of keeping off or protecting against a disease. *Preventive* is followed by nouns referring to treatment of illnesses such as *injection, medicine, surgery, therapy, vaccine*; ways of preventing illnesses such as *approach, measure, precaution, procedure, step*; something that someone does to deal with a situation such as *act, action, deed, intervention, move*, etc. In (5b), the adjective *preventable* means 'capable of being prevented'. A preventable upset can be stopped from occurring. *Preventable* is followed by nouns referring to types of diseases such as *flu, heart attack, malaria, pneumonia, typhoid*; calamities such as *accident, death, incident, tragedy, upset*, etc.

3.3.2.1.2 –ive vs. –ible

The two suffixes evoke the domain of *voice*, yet each spins its own meaning and focuses on a different facet of it. The suffix *–ive* concentrates on agentivity, and means 'performing or tending to perform the action referred to in the verbal root'. In contrast, the suffix *–ible* concentrates on patientivity, and means 'capable of undergoing the action referred to in the verbal root'. A thorough examination of the concordances in the corpus shows that there are distinct patterns associated with each suffix. Adjectives ending in *–ive* tend to collocate with nouns referring to human beings and their deeds, or to substances on which human qualities are conferred. By contrast, adjectives ending in *–ible* tend to collocate with nouns referring to objects that undergo processes, or to human reactions that can be felt or seen. This distinction is illustrated by adjective pairs such as the following:

(6) digestive vs. digestible
 a. It takes two weeks for the baby's digestive system to recover.
 b. The meat I was served in the restaurant was easily digestible.

The two adjectives are derived from the verb *digest*, which means 'to assimilate food, or understand writing'. Still, the root is construed differently and so each adjective has its own sense. In (6a), the adjective *digestive* means 'performing digestion'. A digestive system is capable of digesting food. The majority of the noun collocates show that *digestive* describes digestion such as *mechanism, organ, process, system, tract*; substances aiding digestion such as *biscuit, cookie, enzyme, fluid, juice*; problems resulting from digestion such as *complication, disorder, disturbance, trouble, upset*, etc. In (6b), the adjective *digestible* means 'capable of being digested'. Digestible meat is capable of being assimilated. The majority of the noun collocates show that *digestible* describes types of food such as *beans, fruit, meat, sugar, vegetable*; discourse subjects such as *argument, matter, theme, thesis, topic*; books of different sizes such as *booklet, brochure, handout, leaflets, pamphlet*, etc.

(7) expressive vs. expressible
 a. The writer is innovative and his works are supremely expressive.
 b. Human thought is something essentially expressible in language.

The two adjectives are derived from the verb *express*, which means 'to show feelings or thoughts'. Still, the root is construed differently and so each adjective has its own sense. In (7a), the adjective *expressive* means 'tending to express'. An expressive work tends to show how the writer feels using words. The common noun collocates of *expressive* refer to works of art such as *drama, music, painting, poetry, prose*; the way in which they are presented such as *approach, manner, method, mode, style*; human body parts such as *eye, face, hand, mouth, voice,* etc. In (7b), the adjective *expressible* means 'capable of being expressed'. An expressible thought is capable of being expressed by means of words. The common noun collocates of *expressible* refer to beliefs such as *concept, idea, message, opinion, thought*; emotional responses that a work of art evokes such as *attitude, disposition, feeling, mood, spirit*; language such as *formula, illocution, locution, rule, skill*, etc.

(8) perceptive vs. perceptible
 a. She is the most realistic and perceptive scholar they had ever met.
 b. The past year has seen a perceptible decline in working standards.

The two adjectives are derived from the verb *perceive*, which means 'to understand or notice something'. Still, the root is construed differently and so each adjective has its own sense. In (8a), the adjective *perceptive* means 'tending to perceive'. If someone is perceptive, they are very good at understanding and noticing things that many people do not notice. Most of the noun collocates following *perceptive* concern people such as *campaigner, competitor, musician, scholar, scientist*; their reflections such as *comment, note, observation, remark, statement,* etc. In (8b), the adjective *perceptible* means 'capable of being perceived'. If something is perceptible, it can be seen, heard or noticed. Most of the noun collocates following *perceptible* belong to processes such as *decline, decrease, enlargement, fall, increase*; alterations such as *change, demarcation, difference, divergence, modification*; human physical reactions such as *beckon, nod, shrug, shake, wink*, etc[12].

(9) permissive vs. permissible
  a. The society has been too permissive towards drug use.
  b. Apparently, it is permissible for motorists to park here.

The two adjectives are derived from the verb *permit*, which means 'to allow something to happen, or make something possible'. Still, the root is construed differently and so each adjective has its own sense. In (9a), the adjective *permissive* means 'tending to permit'. A society that is permissive allows behaviour which other people might disapprove of. Many of the noun collocates that follow *permissive* concern people such as *community, father, mother, parent, society*; people who govern a place such as *administration, government, leadership, management, regime;* official rules such as *act, bylaw, law, legislation, statute*; period such as *age, days, epoch, era, time*, etc[13]. In (9b), the adjective *permissible* means 'capable of being permitted'. If something is permissible, it is allowed by law or by the rules. Many of the noun collocates that follow *permissible* concern proceedings such as *divorce, extradition, marriage, mortgage, ownership*; practices such as *drinking, fund-raising, photographing, selling, smoking*, etc. In a predicative position, *permissible* appears almost always in an *it*-construction and is followed by the preposition *to.*

(10) suggestive vs. suggestible
  a. The medical tests done show signs suggestive of cancer.
  b. The adverts prove that customers are highly suggestible.

The two adjectives are derived from the verb *suggest*, which means 'to propose an idea or a plan for other people to consider'. Still, the root is construed differently and so each adjective has its own sense. In (10a), the adjective *suggestive* means 'tending to suggest'. If something is suggestive of something else, it makes you think about it. Often, *suggestive* is used to describe something that makes people think about sex, as in *Some of his lyrics are rather suggestive*. *Suggestive* is used most commonly with noun collocates referring to objects of evidence such as *logo, mark, remark, sign, symbol*; events such as *development, happening, incident, occurrence, phenomenon*, etc. In a number of cases, *suggestive* is followed by the preposition *of*. In (10b), the adjective *suggestible* means 'capable of being suggested'. If someone is suggestible, he or she is easily influenced by other people's opinions. *Suggestible* is used most commonly with noun collocates referring to people such as *buyer, client, customer, person, shopper*, etc.

3.3.2.1.3 –ory vs. –able

The two suffixes are related by the domain of *voice*, but they are unrelated by definition. Each selects a different facet of the domain. The suffix *–ory* selects agentivity, and means 'performing or tending to perform the action referred to in the verbal root'. By contrast, the suffix *–able* selects patientivity, and means 'capable of undergoing the action referred to in the verbal root'. A careful examination of the concordance lines in the corpus shows that the behaviour of adjectives ending in the two suffixes is patterned in observable ways. Adjectives ending in the suffix *–ory* are often found with noun collocates that refer to human beings, individuals or groups, the work they do, or their products, oral or written. By contrast, adjectives ending in the suffix *–able* are often found with noun collocates that refer to objects, concrete or abstract, or intentions to perform tasks. This distinction is illuminated by adjective pairs such as the following:

(11) advisory vs. advisable
a. She set up an advisory council to improve the system.
b. It is always advisable to have regular medical checks.

The two adjectives are derived from the verb *advise*, which means 'to offer someone an opinion about what or how they should do in a particular situation'. Nevertheless, each adjective symbolises a certain construal and so has its individual sense. In (11a), the adjective *advisory* means 'tending to advise'. An advisory council has or exercises the power to advise. Most occurrences of *advisory* seem to refer to collective nouns of people such as *board, body, committee, council, panel*; individual people having special skills or knowledge such as *boffin, connoisseur, expert, pundit, specialist*; the work they do such as *capacity, job, role, service, work*, etc. In (11b), the adjective *advisable* means 'capable of being advised'. An advisable check is recommended to be done in order to avoid problems or risks. *Advisable* is almost exclusively predicative and occurs in *it*-constructions.

(12) explanatory vs. explainable
a. The book is well-presented with numerous explanatory notes at the end.
b. Their refusal to cooperate is explainable, considering the circumstances.

The two adjectives are derived from the verb *explain*, which means 'to make something clear or easy to understand'. Nevertheless, each adjective symbolises a certain construal and so has its individual sense. In (12a), the adjective *explanatory* means 'tending to explain'. An explanatory note is one that makes something easier to understand. The area that is associated with *explanatory* is parts of a book such as *appendix, foreword, glossary, index, reference*; features of a book such as *chart, diagram, drawing, figure, picture*, etc. When used predicatively, *explanatory* is preceded by the word *self* and becomes gradable as in *The aims are fairly self-explanatory*. In (12b), the adjective *explainable* means 'capable of being explained'. A situation that is explainable can be made clear or accounted for. *Explainable* is used nearly always in a predicative position.

(13) explicatory vs. explicable
a. They waited for the correspondent's full and explicatory account.
b. Under the circumstances, their mild reaction was quite explicable.

The two adjectives are derived from the verb *explicate*, which means 'to explain a work, especially of literature, or an idea in detail'. Nevertheless, each adjective symbolises a certain construal and so has its individual sense. In (13a), the adjective *explicatory* means 'tending to explicate'. An explicatory account has the function of explaining what is contained in a subject. *Explicatory* tends to co-occur with nouns referring to short pieces of writing such as *clause, excerpt, extract, passage, phrase*; long pieces of writing such as *account, analysis, article, commentary, survey*, etc. In (13b), the adjective *explicable* means 'capable of being explained'. An explicable reaction admits of being accounted for. *Explicable* tends to occur nearly always in a predicative position and is followed in some cases by the expression *in terms of*.

(14) inflammatory vs. inflammable
a. His inflammatory sermon produced a series of mob riots in the city.
b. Right of abortion has become a highly inflammable issue in politics.

The two adjectives are derived from the verb *inflame*, which means 'to make someone's feelings of anger or excitement much stronger'. Nevertheless, each adjective symbolises a certain construal and so has its individual sense. In (14a), the adjective *inflammatory* means 'tending to inflame'. An inflammatory sermon rouses passion or excites anger. The semantic preferences associated with *inflammatory* are spoken or written language such as *lecture, rhetoric, speech, sermon, talk*; illnesses or injuries such as *bowel disease, brain lesion, lung lesion, skin disease, spiral cord lesion* etc. In (14b), the adjective *inflammable* means 'capable of being inflamed'. An inflammable issue could easily be roused to passion or excited to anger. The semantic preferences associated with *inflammable* are substances such as *gas, liquid, nylon, petrol, plastic*; abstract nouns such as *issue, question, subject, theme, topic*, etc.

(15) laudatory vs. laudable
a. She was the subject of laudatory articles in many glossy magazines.
b. Laudable though the aim might be, the results have been criticised.

The two adjectives are derived from the verb *laud*, which means 'to praise actions and behaviour, even if there is little or no success'. Nevertheless, each adjective symbolises a certain construal and so has its individual sense. In (15a), the adjective *laudatory* means 'tending to laud'. A laudatory article is one that expresses praise or admiration. *Laudatory* is associated with a semantic preference for literary products such as *article, editorial, essay, report, treatise*, etc. In (15b), the adjective *laudable* means 'capable of being lauded'. A laudable aim is one that is praised or admired, even if it is not completely successful. *Laudable* is associated with a semantic preference for abstract nouns that refer to important pieces of work such as *errand, mission, project, task, undertaking*; plans to achieve them such as *plan, policy, programme, scheme, strategy*; intention such as *aim, end, goal, motive, objective*; qualities such as *attention, determination, persistence, resolution, steadfastness*, etc.

3.3.2.2 The self- vs. other-imposed distinction –ive vs. –ory

The two suffixes signify the subdomain of *agentivity*, but they do not mean exactly the same. Each has its own shade of meaning. The suffix *–ive* describes an action that an agent initiates and imposes on the self, which no one else has directed him or her to accept. Accordingly, the suffix *–ive* means 'performing an action at one's own discretion'. By contrast, the suffix *–ory* describes an action that an agent initiates and imposes on others, which they have to accept because it is a law or a rule. Accordingly, the suffix *–ory* means 'performing an action at someone else's discretion'. Briefly, with the suffix *–ive* the action imposed affects an individual, whereas with the *–ory* it affects a group of people. The database shows a striking difference in the head nouns which come directly after the adjectives. Nouns following adjectives ending in *–ive* refer most often to human beings, or their behaviour, abilities and passions. By contrast, nouns following adjectives ending in *–ory* refer most often to official rules, regulations at institutions and systems for organising activities. Consider this distinction in adjective pairs such as the ones below:

(16) compulsive vs. compulsory

a. He suffers from the addictive disease of compulsive gambling.

b. There are external exams at the end of compulsory schooling.

The two adjectives are derived from the verb *compel*, which means 'to force someone to do something'. Nonetheless, a difference in construal keeps the two adjectives apart. In (16a), the adjective *compulsive* means 'tending to compel'. Compulsive gambling is behaviour that is difficult to stop or control; the compulsion is due to internal urges. The majority of the collocates of *compulsive* relate to the field of behaviour such as *drinking, (over)eating, gambling, shopping, (over)spending*; agent nouns derived from such behaviour such as *drinker, (over)eater, gambler*, *shopper, (over)spender*; simple nouns implying an inner drive such as *ambition, desire, longing, need, urge*, etc. In (16b), the adjective *compulsory* means 'tending to compel'. Compulsory schooling is something people are obliged to do because it is a law; the compulsion is due to external urges. The majority of the collocates of *compulsory* relate to the field of education such as *classes, courses, exams, schooling, subjects*; regulations at workplaces such as *back protector, safety checks, safety measures, safety precautions, seat belts*; forcing workers to leave their jobs such as *dismissal, lay off, redundancy, sacking, suspension*, etc. In a predicative position, *compulsory* occurs in an *it*-construction.

(17) contributive vs. contributory

a. The charity's contributive nature is to aid victims of natural disasters.

b. The workers oppose the government's contributory pension scheme.

The two adjectives are derived from the verb *contribute*, which means 'to give or do something to help something be successful'. Nonetheless, a difference in construal keeps the two adjectives apart. In (17a), the adjective *contributive* means 'tending to contribute'. A charity that is contributive gives people money or offers them help; the contribution is of its own accord. Collocates of *contributive* have to do with nouns implying essential qualities of something such as *attribute, character, feature, nature, trait*; variation such as *change, difference, differentiation, disparity, diversity*, etc. In a predicative use, *contributive* is followed by the preposition *to*. In (17b), the adjective *contributory* means 'tending to contribute'. A contributory pension scheme is an insurance plan that is paid for by the workers as well as by the company; the contribution is of someone else's accord. Collocates of *contributory* have to do with nouns referring to things that cause or influence something such as *cause, factor, impetus, reason, stimulus*; a system for achieving something important such as *blueprint, plan, programme, scheme, strategy*, etc.

(18) discriminative vs. discriminatory
a. She showed a discriminative taste in choosing her clothes for the occasions.
b. The court outlawed the party because of its grossly discriminatory practices.

The two adjectives are derived from the verb *discriminate*, which means 'to recognise a difference between things, or treat people differently in an unfair way'. Nonetheless, a difference in construal keeps the two adjectives apart. In (18a), the adjective *discriminative* means 'tending to discriminate'. A discriminative taste is one that shows discernment in art, music or style; the discrimination is of one's own will. The context in which *discriminative* occurs is the ability to judge the quality of something such as *connoisseurship, discernment, judgement, sagacity, taste*; what someone says or does when reacting to something such as *answer, feedback, reaction, reply, response*, etc. In (18b), the adjective *discriminatory* means 'tending to discriminate'. A discriminatory practice is one that is unjust because it treats one group of people worse than other groups; the discrimination is of someone else's will. The context in which *discriminatory* occurs is official rules such as *act, bill, law, legislation, regulation*; official actions such as *conditions, measures, practices, procedures, requirements*, etc.

(19) innovative vs. innovatory
a. As to manner and diction, the writer is the most innovative of all.
b. The new universities are considered innovatory places to study at.

The two adjectives are derived from the verb *innovate*, which means 'to use new ideas, or introduce changes'. Nonetheless, a difference in construal keeps the two adjectives apart. In (19a), the adjective *innovative* means 'tending to innovate'. An innovative writer is one who introduces new methods and original ideas; the innovation is on one's own initiative. *Innovative* is used most commonly to qualify people such as *administrator, designer*, *novelist, organiser, writer*; things related to them such as *ability, design, mind, plan, view*, etc. In (19b), the adjective *innovatory* means 'tending to innovate'. An innovatory place is a place that is surprisingly useful, results in marvels, and that people admire very much; the innovation is on someone else's initiative. *Innovatory* is used most commonly to qualify educational institutions such as *academy, college, faculty, institute, university*; things related to them such as *course, project, method, model, research*; music such as *melody, notes, rhythm, synthesis, tune*, etc.

(20) participative vs. participatory
a. The new manager practises a genuinely participative style of management.
b. The government promised to uphold principles of participatory democracy.

The two adjectives are derived from the verb *participate*, which means 'to take part in an activity or event'. Nonetheless, a difference in construal keeps the two adjectives apart. In (20a), the adjective *participative* means 'tending to participate'. A participative style is one in which one is certainly engaged in an activity; the participation is at one's own request. The common collocates of *participative* describe people such as *client, leader, manager, staff, worker*; ways of doing things or dealing with other people such as *leadership, management, manner, role, style*, etc. In (20b), the adjective *participatory* means 'tending to participate'. A participatory democracy is a system which involves the participation of all the people in making decisions; the participation is at someone else's request. The common collocates of *participatory* describe systems such as *decision-making, democracy, enterprise, politics, sports*, etc.

3.3.2.3 The narrow-broad distinction –able vs. –ible

The two suffixes signal the subdomain of *patientivity*, but each is used in a differing context. Although the pattern is rare, I managed to locate a relatively small number of adjective pairs derived by means of these suffixes, some of which are also mentioned in Fowler (1996:4–7,395) and Huddleston & Pullum (2002:1706). Most dictionaries either ignore the existence of such pairs or cite them, when they exist, as spelling variants with no difference in meaning or usage. However, the database reveals a difference in their distributions and their collocations. That is, in spite of the overlap in the use of such adjective pairs, there are cases in which their behavioural patterns are different. The difference resides in terms of the application within which the suffix is used, which can be either *narrow* or *broad*. A narrow application is one in which the adjective has a more restricted sense. Morphologically, it is represented by the suffix *–able*. A broad application is one in which the adjective has a more general sense. Morphologically, it is represented by the suffix *–ible*. Interestingly, adjectives ending in *–able* are mostly negated with *un-*, whereas adjectives ending in *–ible* are mostly negated with *in-* and its variants *il-, im-, ir-*, etc. Notice this distinction in adjective pairs such as the ones below:

(21) accessable vs. accessible
a. The computer file is readily accessable to all.
b. The town is easily accessible by rail network.

The two adjectives are derived from the root *access*. Even so, construal separates the two adjectives from each other. In (21a), the adjective *accessable* is derived from the verb *access* and means 'capable of being accessed'. An accessable file is one that can be obtained or used by the users. *Accessable* has a restricted sense in that it is most often associated with the field of computing such as *internet, search engine, server, web page, website,* etc. In (21b), the adjective *accessible* is derived from the noun *access* and means 'capable of being accessed'. An accessible town is one that is easy to reach or get into. *Accessible* has a more general sense in that it appears before nouns denoting places such as *city, destination, forest, site, town*; objects such as *book, dictionary, material, pattern, style*; people such as *author, caregiver, lecturer, novelist, therapist*, etc.

(22) collectable vs. collectible
  a. The bill for the repairs is collectable before August.
  b. Works of art are increasingly collectible these days.

The two adjectives are derived from the verb *collect*, which means 'to get things of the same type from different places and bring them together'. Even so, construal separates the two adjectives from each other. In (22a), the adjective *collectable* means 'capable of being collected'. A collectable bill is one that is liable to be paid. Apart from its use with souvenirs, only *collectable* is used when the context is that of collecting money such as *bill, costs, debt, € 100, tax*, or that of picking up vehicles. In (22b), the adjective *collectible* means 'capable of being collected'. Collectible works of art can be brought together, especially because they might increase in value. *Collectible* is used most often in the context of physical objects such as *CDs, dolls, gifts, stamps, toys,* etc.

(23) contractable vs. contractible
  a. Diseases are contractable by contact.
  b. The heart is rhythmically contractible.

The two adjectives are derived from the two different meanings of the verb *contract*. Even so, construal separates the two adjectives from each other. In (23a), the adjective *contractable* means 'capable of being contracted', acquired as a disease. A contractable disease is one that can be transmitted by infection. *Contractable* has a more restricted sense in that most frequently it modifies nouns denoting diseases. In (23b), the adjective *contractible* means 'capable of being contracted', drawn together so as to become diminished in size. A contractible heart is a body organ that can be made smaller. *Contractible* has a more general sense in that it modifies nouns denoting body organs as well as metals such as *gold, iron, steel*, etc.

(24) defendable vs. defendible
  a. It was a defendable site, raising above the surrounding landscape.
  b. Most of the theories Richard presents are not morally defendible.

The two adjectives are derived from the verb *defend*, which means 'to do something in order to protect someone or something from being attacked'. Even so, construal separates the two adjectives from each other. In (24a), the adjective *defendable* or *defensible* means 'capable of being defended'. A defendable site is one that can be protected against attack. *Defendable* is preferable in military contexts such as *boundaries, fortress, frontier, site, territory*, etc. In (24b), the adjective *defendible* means 'capable of being defended'. A defendible theory is one that can be supported, i.e. reasonable. *Defendible* is preferable in other general contexts including suggestions such as *concept, hypothesis, idea, premise, theory*; actions such as *choice, pattern, practice, solution, strategy*; nouns dealing with law or disease, etc.

(25) extendable vs. extendible
a. They took the dog out for a walk on an extendable leash.
b. The implication of the law is extendible to all businesses.

The two adjectives are derived from the verb *extend*, which means 'to continue to happen for a period of time, cover a particular distance, or increase the range of operation'. Even so, construal separates the two adjectives from each other. In (25a), the adjective *extendable* means 'capable of being extended'. An extendable leash is one that can be lengthened or stretched out. *Extendable* applies to units of measurement including time such as *hour, day, week, month* and *year*, which modify nouns such as *contract, deadline, holiday, sojourn, visa*; distance such as *inch, feet, yard, metre* and *kilometre*, which modify physical objects such as *hood, ladder, leash, lid, pole*, etc. In (25b), the adjective *extendible* means 'capable of being extended'. An extendible implication is one whose effect extends to cover other sectors of the society. *Extendible* applies to general contexts including the effect that an action or a situation has on the way people behave such as *effect, impact, implication, influence, power;* social happenings such as *condolences, greetings, invitations, thanks, welcome*, etc[14].

3.3.2.4 The cause-effect distinction –ing vs. –ed

Two events may be related in a way that the first produces, brings about, or necessitates the second. The first event describes the cause or the reason that produces an effect. Morphologically, when the de-verbal adjective is the cause for triggering an action, it takes the *–ing* suffix, which means 'causing the action referred to in the verbal root'. The second event describes the effect or the result towards which the cause is directed. Morphologically, when the de-verbal adjective is the effect ensuing from an action, it takes the *–ed* suffix, which means 'affected by the action referred to in the verbal root'. This shows that both the *–ing* present participle and the *–ed* past participle can be used as adjectives. Most often, the de-verbal adjectives come from verbs of emotion. They imply both positive and negative emotion. Adjectives expressing positive emotion, like the ones in (26), (29) and (30), have good or useful effects. Adjectives expressing negative emotion, like the ones in (27) and (28), have bad or harmful effects.

From the concordance listings in the corpus, one can draw a number of conclusions, some of which are also mentioned in Collins COBUILD English Grammar (1992:76–82). These adjectives are called *qualitative* or *descriptive* because they link an attribute to the referent of the noun. They have the following characteristics. First, they are related to transitive verbs. The present participle suffix *–ing* has an active meaning in the sense that it is the cause that is triggered by an agent. The past participle suffix *–ed* has a passive meaning in the sense that it is the effect that is absorbed by some patient. Second, they are gradable in that they (i) have comparatives as in *It was a more stimulating discussion*, (ii) have superlatives as in *It was one of the most thrilling championships*, (iii) can be preceded by intensifiers as in *His views are very alarming*, and (iv) can be modified by adverbs as in *The news is extremely startling*. Third, they can be used in attributive or predicative positions, as in *It is a frustrating loss/The loss is frustrating*.

Emotional adjectives ending in the suffixes *–ing* and *–ed* pattern differently. Most frequently, the collocates of the suffix *–ing* deal with things, concrete or abstract, human habits and actions, general events and names of places. By comparison, the collocates of the suffix *–ed* deal with human beings, which come in the form of proper nouns, personal pronouns or common nouns, their body parts, and their reactions whether oral or written. When emotional adjectives are used in predicative positions, they assume different patterns. Adjectives ending in the *–ing* suffix occur in such a pattern as *it+be+adjective+ to-infinitive*. Adjectives ending in the *–ed* suffix occur in such patterns as *S+linking verb+adjective*, *S+adjective+to+infinitive*, *S+be+adjective+by+agent*, and *Agent+made+person+adjective*. This type of distinction is highlighted by adjective pairs like the ones below:

(26) amusing vs. amused
a. The story is greatly amusing for the child.
b. The child is greatly amused by the story.

The two adjectives are derived from the verb *amuse*, which means ‘to make someone laugh or smile’. However, construal draws a distinction between them. In (26a), the present participle *amusing* means ‘causing amusement’. An amusing story is pleasantly entertaining or diverting, exciting the risible faculty or tickling the fancy. The concordances of *amusing* show that it is used with concrete nouns such as *book, film, manual, portrait, shop*; abstract nouns such as *criticism, custom, incident, life, situation*; spoken or written language such as *gag, joke, pun, story, tale*; people but rarely, etc. In (26b), the past participle *amused* means 'affected by amusement'. An amused child is diverted, entertained or made happy. The concordances of *amused* show that it is used with people such as *companion, founder, husband, observer, queen*; human facial reactions such as *expression, glance, grin, look, smile*, etc.

(27) annoying vs. annoyed

a. The commercial breaks were so annoying to the viewers.

b. The viewers were so annoyed by the commercial breaks.

The two adjectives are derived from the verb *annoy*, which means 'to make someone feel slightly angry about something'. However, construal draws a distinction between them. In (27a), the present participle *annoying* means 'causing annoyance'. An annoying commercial break is bothering or disturbing for the viewers. *Annoying* accepts the company of nouns denoting habits such as *custom, habit, institution, mannerism, tradition*; tedious actions such as *change, calculation, delay, distraction, repetition*; weather conditions such as *climate, season, summer, weather, winter*; part of a situation or subject such as *aspect, dimension, element, feature, side*; people but rarely, etc. In (27b), the past participle *annoyed* means 'affected by annoyance'. Annoyed viewers are troubled or disturbed by the commercials. *Annoyed* accepts the company of nouns referring to people such as *commentator, inspector, parents, solicitor, traveller*, etc.

(28) disappointing vs. disappointed

a. The match was bitterly disappointing for us.

b. We were bitterly disappointed with the match.

The two adjectives are derived from the verb *disappoint*, which means 'to make someone feel sad because something they hoped for did not happen'. However, construal draws a distinction between them. In (28a), the present participle *disappointing* means 'causing disappointment'. A disappointing match foils expectation and makes one sad because it is not so good as one hoped it would be. Collocates of *disappointing* refer to trade such as *economic figures, financial results, price index, profits, retail sales*; football such as *championship, defeat, match, season, start*; actions such as *adventure, campaign, display, performance, reply*; people but rarely, etc. In (28b), the past participle *disappointed* means 'affected by disappointment'. Disappointed people are unhappy because of having their expectations foiled. Collocates of *disappointed* refer to people such as *buyer, customer, fan, investor; trader*, etc.

(29) exciting vs. excited

a. The experience is enormously exciting for her.

b. She is enormously excited by the experience.

The two adjectives are derived from the verb *excite*, which means 'to make someone feel a particular emotion, especially of happiness'. However, construal draws a distinction between them. The present participle *exciting* in (29a) means 'causing excitement'. An exciting experience is stimulating and makes one happy. The nouns with which *exciting* is associated include sports such as *competition, contest, game, match, race*; actions such as *development, discovery, experience, exploration, performance*; jobs such as *career, occupation, profession, trade, vacation*; people but rarely. The past participle *excited* in (29b) means 'affected by excitement'. An excited person is stirred by strong emotion, full of energy and feels happy. The nouns with which *excited* is associated include people such as *children, citizens, fans, girls, supporters*; human spoken reactions such as *cheer, roar, scream, shout, yell*, etc.

(30) fascinating vs. fascinated
a. The tale is really fascinating for her.
b. She is really fascinated by the tale.

The two adjectives are derived from the verb *fascinate*, which means 'to make someone think of and watch something because it is interesting'. However, construal draws a distinction between them. In (30a), the present participle *fascinating* means 'causing fascination'. A fascinating tale is capable of capturing one's interest and attention. The patterns of collocation in which *fascinating* occurs include names of places such as *building, city, country, region, town;* places where art is shown such as *exhibition, gallery, museum, show*; nouns meaning a large group of things such as *array, chain, collection, mix, selection*; events such as *anecdote, epic, saga, story, tale*; abstract nouns such as *account, experience, glimpse, history, period*; people but rarely etc. In (30b), the past participle *fascinated* means 'affected by fascination'. A fascinated person is one whose interest is aroused or attention is held. The patterns of collocation in which *fascinated* occurs include people such as *listener, observer, onlooker, spectator, visitor*; human body parts such as *eye, eyebrow, expression, face, voice*; nouns having unfavourable denotation such as *awe, disgust, fear, horror, repulsion*, etc[15].

3.4 The domain of aspect

Aspect is an area of knowledge which describes how a situation develops through time. The semantic nature of the verb often has something to do with the aspect it expresses. As Huddleston & Pullum (2002:118–125) explain, English has two main aspectual types: *states* (stative) and *occurrences* (dynamic). *States* exist or obtain, while *occurrences* happen or take place. *States* do not involve change, while *occurrences* do. *States* stay the same throughout their duration; they have no distinguishable phases. In *She likes him*, the situation is viewed as denoting a condition that exists. *Occurrences* include *processes* (durative) and *achievements* (punctual). *Processes* include *activities* (continuative) and *accomplishments* (terminative). *Activities* are unbounded; the situation can continue for a period of time. In *She is playing golf*, the situation is viewed as a process extending over time, without regard to beginning or end. *Accomplishments* are bounded; the situation must necessarily come to an end. In *She walks to the post office*, the situation is viewed as a process tending towards an end. *Achievements* are conceived of as being instantaneous or occurring at a point in time. In *She found the key*, the situation is viewed as being punctual, with the endpoint of the action occurring promptly[16].

Aspectual distinctions are relevant not only for verbs but also for adjectives. In this regard, *aspect* refers to the temporal structure of a situation on which the speaker can take different views. The ability of an adjective to represent any of the aspectual types is a matter of the construal of *prominence* that the speaker imposes on a situation. Recall that *prominence* is the quality of eminence given to a substructure of an expression relative to its importance. One dimension of prominence which is at work here pertains to *profiling.* According to Langacker (1988b:68–69), a *profile* is a substructure within an expression that functions as the focal point of attention. Profiling explains the way the speaker confers prominence on the different substructures within an expression. This is the consequence of the way the speaker construes a scene, not an inherent property of a scene. In CS, the realisation of a linguistic expression represents the speaker's choice to express what is most important depending on the communicative needs of the discourse.

Applied to suffixation, profiling accounts for the different ways the speaker views a situation represented by a de-verbal adjective. Adjectives denoting *state* end in *–ed*. In *He made a determined effort to change the situation*, the speaker views the effort as having a stable influence vis-à-vis a situation. Adjectives denoting *activity* end in *–ing*. In *Heavy snow is a determining factor in accidents*, the speaker views snow as steadily influencing accidents. Adjectives denoting *accomplishment* end in *–ive* or *–ant*. In *Educational qualifications play a determinative function*, the speaker views qualifications as having influence leading to an end. Adjectives denoting *achievement* end in *–ant* or *–ive*. In *The medicine works a determinant force upon the patient*, the speaker views the medicine as having influence within a brief instant. What the examples show is that the construal of *profiling* affects the morphology of the derived adjective. In each case, the adjective ends in a different suffix and signals a different shade of meaning.

A graphical representation of the different types of aspectual situations is sketched in Figure 5:

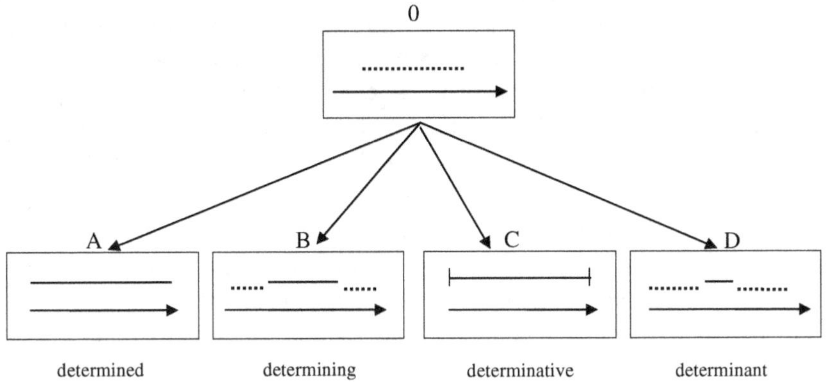

Figure 5: The construal of *profiling* in derived adjectives

The box marked (0) represents a situation, be it an occurrence or a state. The dotted line represents its unspecified duration. The arrow represents a time line. The box marked (A) represents a state, where a lasting condition is in profile. The box marked (B) represents an occurrence, where a segment of an activity is in profile. The box marked (C) represents an occurrence, where the whole action is in profile. The box marked (D) represents an occurrence, where a momentary act is in profile.

3.4.1 Morphological exponents

As noted earlier, the domain of *aspect* consists of different situation types. Morphologically, they are indicated by rival types of suffixes, but with subtle meaning differences. A situation denoting a process going on for a period of time is expressed by an adjective ending in an *–ing* suffix, whereas a situation denoting a process leading to a terminus is expressed by an adjective ending in an *–ive* or *–ant* suffix (Section 3.4.2.1). Likewise, a situation denoting a state that is stable or lasting is expressed by an adjective ending in an *–ed* suffix, whereas a situation denoting an act that has an immediate result is expressed by an adjective ending in an *–ive* or *–ant* suffix (Section 3.4.2.2). The difference between *–ing* and *–ed* is that the former describes an activity that continues over a period of time, whereas the latter describes a state that has existed at a particular time (Section 3.4.2.3). The difference between *–ive* and *–ant* is that the former is favoured in ordinary contexts, whereas the latter is favoured in technical contexts (Section 3.4.2.4).

3.4.2 Semantic distinctions

Adjectival suffixes belonging to the domain of *aspect* can attach to the same root and form an adjective pair. The root has a conceptual content, which includes more than one facet. The suffixes profile each facet of the root's content. Each suffix imposes a particular construal on the content supplied by the root. On the surface, the two adjectives appear to be interchangeable. A closer look, however, shows they are not. Each has its own distinct meaning, which is contributed partly by the attached suffix. A firm grasp of that meaning can make a difference in how each adjective is correctly used. The choice of an adjective relies on the way the situation is conceptualised, which is morphologically reflected by the choice of the appropriate suffix. This is compatible with the cognitive norm that a particular situation can be construed alternatively and that the alternative ways can be encoded linguistically in different ways. Below are details of the semantic distinctions within the domain of *aspect* and the rival suffixes that represent them.

3.4.2.1 The continuative-terminative distinction

Continuative aspect, also known as *atelic*, expresses a process that is perceived as lasting for a certain length of time, and so is unbounded. In this construal, the speaker takes an internal perspective of a situation and gets only a partial view of it. This meaning is symbolised by the suffix *–ing* which describes the ongoing activity represented by the root, but its nature is temporary. *Terminative* aspect, also known as *telic*, expresses an action that is conceptualised as lasting for some time, but it is bounded. In this construal, the speaker adopts an external perspective of the situation and sees it in its entirety. The speaker views the situation as being directed towards a definite end or purpose. This meaning is symbolised by the suffixes *–ive* and *–ant*, which describe the entire action represented by the root, but its nature is lasting. The difference between them (Section 3.4.2.4) is that the suffix *–ive* applies to contexts of an ordinary nature, while the suffix *–ant* applies to contexts of a technical nature. This distinction is represented by the following rival suffixes:

3.4.2.1.1 –ing vs. –ive

Despite conveying the domain of *aspect*, the two suffixes are dissimilar. Each suffix has its own nugget of meaning. The suffix *–ing* represents *continuative* aspect, and means 'keep on the activity signified by the verbal root'. It allows one to perceive part of the activity. By contrast, the suffix *–ive* represents *terminative* aspect, and means 'apt to do the action signified by the verbal root'. It allows one to perceive the whole action. With both suffixes, duration is implied. However, with *–ing* it is unbounded, whereas with *–ive* it is bounded. A detailed analysis of data from the corpus should suffice to identify the typical environment in which each suffix occurs. Adjectives ending in *–ing* refer to human beings, their ways of doing things, location, construction and parts of a building. Adjectives ending in *–ive* refer to human beings, individual or groups, their mood and character, things, specialised or general, networks and forms of entertainment. This distinction is manifested in terms of the following adjective pairs:

(31) acting vs. active
a. He's the acting manager of the shop whenever the owner is away.
b. He is an active campaigner against poverty and for welfare rights.

The two adjectives are derived from the verb *act*, which means 'to do something for a particular purpose, or to behave in the stated way'. The two adjectives, nevertheless, represent different construals of the root and so have individual meanings. In (31a), the adjective *acting* means 'keep on acting'. An acting manager is someone who keeps on doing a temporary job, while the usual person is not there, or until a new person is chosen for the job. *Acting* tends to collocate with nouns referring to people such as *chairman, commander, manager, officer, secretary*; nouns related to drama such as *basis*, *capacity, career, part, school,* etc. In (31b), the adjective *active* means 'apt to act'. An active campaigner is someone who is apt to change something in society by taking part in organised activities. *Active* tends to collocate with nouns referring to people such *campaigner, children, crew, kids, maker*; or nouns denoting things such as *crime, exercise, fighting*, *life, work*, etc.

(32) contrasting vs. contrastive
a. The book explores contrasting views of the poet's early work.
b. It is a grammar with a complex system of contrastive patterns.

The two adjectives are derived from the verb *contrast*, which means 'to compare two people or things to show how different they are'. The two adjectives, nevertheless, represent different construals of the root and so have individual meanings. In (32a), the adjective *contrasting* means 'keep on contrasting'. Contrasting views are views which keep on being different in style or attitude, especially in an interesting way. *Contrasting* collocates with nouns referring to a person's mode of looking at things such as *attitude, conviction, feeling, opinion, view*; a person's natural disposition such as *disposition, mood, nature, spirit, temperament*; location such as *areas, countryside, pitches, places, venues*; abstract nouns such as *aspect, colour, flavour, play, tale,* etc. In (32b), the adjective *contrastive* means 'apt to contrast'. Contrastive patterns are patterns which are apt to show contrast for the sake of achieving clarity. *Contrastive* collocates with nouns used in language and linguistics such as *analysis, phoneme, patterns, stress, syllables*, etc.

(33) interacting vs. interactive
a. Many interacting factors may trigger the fatal disease.
b. This is an interactive video game for children to enjoy.

The two adjectives are derived from the verb *interact*, which means 'to communicate with or react to'. The two adjectives, nevertheless, represent different construals of the root and so have individual meanings. In (33a), the adjective *interacting* means 'keep on interacting'. Interacting factors are factors which keep on acting upon one another to produce a state of affairs. Collocations of *interacting* revolve around nouns referring to parts of a combination which influence the result of something such as *components, constituents, elements, factors, ingredients*; people such as *actors, groups, individuals, partakers, participants*, etc. In (33b), the adjective *interactive* means 'apt to interact'. An interactive videogame is a game that is apt to interact between a user's orders and the responses from TV. It is a programme in which the player controls moving pictures on a screen by pressing buttons. Collocations of *interactive* revolve around nouns standing for networks such as *computer, movie, radio, telephone, TV*; forms of media entertainment such as *broadcast, game, programme, software, web page*, etc.

(34) projecting vs. projective
a. A particular feature of the church is the projecting porch.
b. A projective test is one method of measuring personality.

The two adjectives are derived from the verb *project*, which means 'to stick out from a surface, or calculate something based on information'. The two adjectives, nevertheless, represent different construals of the root and so have individual meanings. In (34a), the adjective *projecting* means 'keep on projecting'. A projecting porch is a porch that keeps on jutting out from the surrounding. It is a covered structure in front of the entrance to a building. Nouns which collocate with *projecting* centre around areas of a building such as *balcony, porch, stairway, terrace, wing*; hard points such as *bone, brink, corner, edge, stone*, etc. In (34b), the adjective *projective* means 'apt to project'. A projective test is a test that is apt to project by making something known. It is a test which indicates the psychodynamic constitution of an individual. Nouns which collocate with *projective* are *geometry, test, theorem, zone* (in the context of neuron), etc.

(35) supporting vs. supportive
a. The new cathedral roof is held up by supporting pillars.
b. When she is in trouble, her husband is most supportive.

The two adjectives are derived from the verb *support*, which means 'to hold the weight of something, or help someone during a difficult time'. The two adjectives, nevertheless, represent different construals of the root and so have individual meanings. In (35a), the adjective *supporting* means 'keep on supporting'. A supporting pillar is a pillar that keeps on supporting something in place to stop it from falling. *Supporting* collocates with a variety of nouns used in the fields of theatre such as *actor, actress, cast, player, role*; construction such as *beam, leg, pillar, prop, tower*; means of illustration such as *example, mark, sign, specimen, token*, etc. In (35b), the adjective *supportive* means 'apt to support'. A supportive person is a person who is apt to support someone in a difficult situation. *Supportive* collocates with nouns referring to people, individuals such as *brother, countryman, husband, partner, relative*, or groups such as *administration, committee, council, crowd, department*; or the character or mood of a place or a situation such as *atmosphere, climate, environment, milieu, surroundings*, etc. In a predicative position, the adjective *supportive* is followed by the preposition *of*.

3.4.2.1.2 –ing vs. –ant

Although the two suffixes indicate the domain of *aspect*, they are not alike in meaning. Each describes a different situation. The suffix *–ing* represents *continuative* aspect, and means 'keep on the activity signified by the verbal root'. It gives a partial view of the activity. By contrast, the suffix *–ant* represents *terminative* aspect, and means 'apt to do the action signified by the verbal root'. It gives a holistic view of the action. With both suffixes, duration is implied. However, with *–ing* it is unbounded, whereas with *–ant* it is bounded. A research into data from the corpus is sufficient to draw a distinction between the two suffixes. Nouns following adjectives ending in *–ing* refer to human beings, means of expressing their feelings, actions and their outcomes, and physical objects that are set for continuity. Nouns following adjectives ending in *–ant* refer to specialised contexts such as law, sports, cooking, colours and science. This distinction is shown in terms of the following adjective pairs:

(36) complaining vs. complainant
a. Relatives were responsive to his complaining voice of sorrow.
b. The complainant party could not come up with enough proofs.

The two adjectives are derived from the verb *complain*, which means 'to say that something is wrong, or not satisfactory'. The speaker, however, imposes a different construal on the root and so each adjective has its own meaning. In (36a), the adjective *complaining* means 'keep on complaining'. A complaining voice is a voice which keeps on lamenting or murmuring and so expresses dissatisfaction or grief. *Complaining* tends to collocate with nouns referring to people in general such as *customer, neighbour, patient, student, visitor*; means of expressing their complaints such as *expression, language, speech, tone, voice,* etc. In (36b), the adjective *complainant* means 'apt to complain'. A complainant party is a party that is apt to complain by making a formal charge in a court of law. *Complainant* is a legal term used to describe people in a court of law.

(37) discriminating vs. discriminant
a. He shows a discriminating interest in any musical instrument he gets hold of.
b. A discriminant analysis was run to test the differences between the products.

The two adjectives are derived from the verb *discriminate*, which means 'to judge the difference between two things or people'. The speaker, however, imposes a different construal on the root and so each adjective has its own meaning. In (37a), the adjective *discriminating* means 'keep on discriminating'. A discriminating person is a person who keeps on making a difference between good and bad quality. Most occurrences of *discriminating* include common nouns referring to people such as *audience, collector, filmgoer, observer, reader*; abstract nouns denoting a mental position or act of choosing such as *attitude, choice, interest, selection, taste, etc.* In a predicative position, *discriminating* is followed by the prepositions *about* and *against*. In (37b), the adjective *discriminant* means 'apt to discriminate'. A discriminant analysis is an analysis which is apt to discriminate by examining something in detail to discover more about it. Most occurrences of *discriminant* include words used in science such as *analysis* and *function*.

(38) hesitating vs. hesitant
a. The woman sat down on her own chair in a hesitating manner.
b. The player recovered from his slightly hesitant start to the match.

The two adjectives are derived from the verb *hesitate*, which means 'to pause before doing or saying something because you are uncertain or nervous'. The speaker, however, imposes a different construal on the root and so each adjective has its own meaning. In (38a), the adjective *hesitating* means 'keep on hesitating'. A hesitating manner is a manner which keeps on not knowing what to do, or is unable to decide about something. *Hesitating* has a tendency to collocate with nouns indicating manner such as *approach, fashion, mode, style, way*, etc. In (38b), the adjective *hesitant* means 'apt to hesitate'. A hesitant player is a player who keeps on vacillating because he pauses before doing something or does it slowly. *Hesitant* has a tendency to collocate with nouns referring to people such as *doctor, leader, parent, player, sprinter*; their body parts such as *fingers, hand, legs, lips, voice*; their actions such as *answer, decision, recovery, smile, speech,* etc. With people, *hesitant* is used in a predicative position and sometimes followed by the preposition *about* plus *–ing* or *to*+infinitive. With things, it is used in an attributive position.

(39) resulting vs. resultant
a. The resulting report is of significant value in defining their plan of action.
b. The economy was hit by high inflation with its resultant impact on profit.

The two adjectives are derived from the verb *result*, which means 'to happen or exist because of something else'. The speaker, however, imposes a different construal on the root and so each adjective has its own meaning. In (39a), the adjective *resulting* means 'keep on resulting'. A resulting report is a report which arises as the outcome of action which happens because of something else. Collocates of *resulting* refer to nouns meaning outcome of action or event such as (negative) *damage, havoc, injury, jumble, loss,* (positive) *benefits, gains, profits, returns, revenues*; outcome of investigation or meeting such as *announcement, communiqué, declaration, report, statement*; change of state such as *change, combination, decline, development, movement*, etc. In (39b), the adjective *resultant* means 'apt to result'. A resultant impact is an impact which is apt to result from an action just mentioned. Collocates of *resultant* refer to nouns meaning output of cooking such as *juice, paste, powder, sauce, soup*; effect that a situation has such as *difference, gap, gulf, impact, influence*; situation in which people are found such as *bewilderment, confusion, misunderstanding, perplexity, recrimination*; etc.

(40) vibrating vs. vibrant
a. The vibrating alarm clock is one of the latest technological breakthroughs.
b. The city is vibrant with affordable accommodation and excellent restaurants.

The two adjectives are derived from the verb *vibrate*, which means 'to make something shake continuously with fast movements'. The speaker, however, imposes a different construal on the root and so each adjective has its own meaning. In (40a), the adjective *vibrating* means 'keep on vibrating'. A vibrating clock is a clock which keeps on moving. Collocations of *vibrating* deal with concrete nouns of physical entities such as *alarm clock, belt, kite, ribbon, string*; oral entities such as *air, message, signal, sound, wave*, etc. In (40b), the adjective *vibrant* means 'apt to vibrate'. A vibrant city is a city which is apt to excite people. Collocations of *vibrant* deal with places such as *city, place, room, scene, street*; colour terms such as *colour, hue, orange, red, shade*; distinctive personal features such as *clothes, eyes, talk, tone, voice*; group collectives such as *community, faction, movement, organisation, team*; general feelings given by an event or place such as *ambience, atmosphere, aura, climate, semblance*, etc.

3.4.2.2 The stative-punctual distinction

Stative aspect, also known as *atelic*, refers to a condition or way of being that exists at a particular time. It refers to the way something is in essence and implies no change. This meaning is symbolised by the suffix *–ed* which describes someone or something as being in the condition represented by the root. *Punctual* aspect, also known as *telic*, refers to an act that is done at once and without delay. It refers to a momentary act and implies a change. This meaning is symbolised by the suffixes *–ive* and *–ant*, which describe someone or something as being inclined to the act represented by the root. The two suffixes differ (Section 3.4.2.4) in that *–ive* stands for the act, whereas *–ant* stands for an embodied attribute or trait. This distinction is represented by the following rival suffixes:

3.4.2.2.1 –ed vs. –ive

The two suffixes belong to the domain of *aspect*, but they are not synonyms. The meaning of each has a slant of its own. The suffix *–ed* refers to *stative* aspect and means 'having been in the state signified by the verbal root'. By contrast, the suffix *–ive* refers to *punctual* aspect and means 'liable to do the act signified by the verbal root'. With the suffix *–ed*, there is duration, whereas with the suffix *–ive* there is no duration. Close scrutiny of the collocational patterns in the corpus helps us to draw some conclusions about the two suffixes. Nouns following adjectives ending in *–ed* refer to human beings, their beliefs and acts, (un)favourable conditions, places and merchandise. Nouns following adjectives ending in *–ive* refer to human beings, processes, operations, oral arrangements and turning points. To comprehend the distinction, consider the following pairs of adjectives:

(41) aborted vs. abortive

a. The passenger expressed bitterness at the aborted flight.

b. Although it took ages, the negotiations proved abortive.

The two adjectives are derived from the verb *abort*, which means 'to stop an activity before it begins or before it is complete'. The construal of the root in each adjective is, nonetheless, different and so causes a distinction in use. In (41a), the adjective *aborted* means 'having been aborted'. An aborted flight is a flight that has been cancelled. The majority of the collocational instances of the adjective *aborted* refer to (un)born animal or human beings such as *baby, child, embryo, foetus*; intention such as *aim, attempt, mission, plan, scheme*; acts such as *coup, flight, gathering, purchase, robbery*, etc. In (41b), the adjective *abortive* means 'liable to abort'. An abortive negotiation is a negotiation that is liable to fail. The majority of the collocational instances of the adjective *abortive* refer to nouns denoting military operations such as *assault, battle, incursion, invasion, occupation*; oral arrangements such as *bargaining, debate, discussion, negotiation, talk,* etc.

(42) adopted vs. adoptive
 a. They've got two adopted children and one of their own.
 b. Her adoptive parents are tolerant of her choice of music.

The two adjectives are derived from the verb *adopt*, which means 'to legally make another person's child part of your family'. The construal of the root in each adjective is, nonetheless, different and so causes a distinction in use. In (42a), the adjective *adopted* means 'having been adopted'. An adopted child is a child who has been legally admitted into a family that he or she was not born into. Most collocational occurrences of the adjective *adopted* refer to people such as *athlete, brother, child(ren), daughter, infant*; places such as *city, country, home, homeland, town*; ways of performing something such as *means, method, procedure, technique, system*, etc. In (42b), the adjective *adoptive* means 'liable to adopt'. An adoptive parent is a parent who has adopted a child not related to him biologically. Most collocational occurrences of the adjective *adoptive* include nouns referring to people such as *family, father, mother, parent, relative*, etc.

(43) decided vs. decisive
 a. His weight gave him a decided advantage over his opponents.
 b. The clues were decisive in establishing the criminal's identity.

The two adjectives are derived from the verb *decide*, which means 'to choose something after careful thought, especially among several possibilities'. The construal of the root in each adjective is, nonetheless, different and so causes a distinction in use. In (43a), the adjective *decided* means 'having been decided'. A decided advantage is an advantage that has been clear or certain. Most collocates of the adjective *decided* have to do with nouns denoting beliefs such as *conviction, opinion, position, principle, view*; subjects for thought or feeling such as *case, issue, matter, subject, topic*; favourable conditions such as *advantage, asset, avail, benefit, plus*, unfavourable conditions such as *defect, disadvantage, drawback, fault, snag*, etc. In (43b), the adjective *decisive* means 'liable to decide'. A decisive clue is a clue that is liable to conclude by having the character to end disputes. Most collocates of the adjective *decisive* have to do with military nouns such as *battle, breakthrough, clash, defeat, victory*; nouns denoting the point at which a change takes place such as *critical point, crossroads, crucial point, turning-point, watershed*; nouns denoting effect on the way something develops such as *factor, importance, influence, role, significance*; nouns referring to people such as *judge, leader, politician, prime minister, teacher*, etc[17].

(44) extended vs. extensive

a. Because of its extended coastline, the country is ideal for tourism.

b. The royal wedding received extensive coverage in the mass media.

The two adjectives are derived from the verb *extend*, which means 'to continue to cover a large area or contain a lot of information'. The construal of the root in each adjective is, nonetheless, different and so causes a distinction in use. In (44a), the adjective *extended* means 'having been extended'. An extended line is a line that has been drawn out in length or width. The semantic preference associated with the adjective *extended* is location at sea such as *beach, coastline, seaside, shore, strand*; location at mountains such as *area, chain, row, series, string*; a pursuit of knowledge such as *course, programme, schedule, study, training*; a portion of time such as *break, interval, period, span, spell*, etc. In (44b), the adjective *extensive* means 'liable to extend'. An extensive coverage is a coverage that is liable to be thorough in scope. The semantic preference associated with the adjective *extensive* is an account of a particular subject or event such as *coverage, discussion, interview, recording, review*; remains of destruction such as *damage, debris, ruins, shambles, wastes*; processes such as *collection, consideration, inspection, integration, interaction*; large areas such as *gallery, library, museum, park, woodland*, etc.

(45) restricted vs. restrictive

a. The manufacturer was licensed to export only restricted items.

b. They found life in the village overly restrictive and repressive.

The two adjectives are derived from the verb *restrict*, which means 'to limit the size, amount, or range of something, or the actions or movements of someone'. The construal of the root in each adjective is, nonetheless, different and so causes a distinction in use. In (45a), the adjective *restricted* means 'having been restricted'. A restricted item is an item that has been limited or confined, especially by laws or rules. The semantic context preferred by the adjective *restricted* is merchandise such as *commodities, equipment, goods, items, wares*; money such as *assets, budget, funds, resources, finances*; situation such as *climate, competition, credit, distribution, market*; people involved such as *dealer, exporter, importer, manufacturer, seller*; secrecy such as *data, document, information, message, news*, etc. In (45b), the adjective *restrictive* means 'liable to restrict'. Restrictive life is life that is liable to confine by setting bounds to one's activity. The semantic context preferred by the adjective *restrictive* is a set of rules such as *laws, legislation, norms, practices, rules*; a kind of life that someone has such as *attitude, life, manner, nature, style*, etc.

3.4.2.2.2 –*ed* vs. –*ant*

The two suffixes refer to the domain of *aspect*, but they are not interchangeable. Each has its own individual meaning. The suffix *–ed* refers to *stative* aspect, and means 'having been in the state signified by the verbal root'. By contrast, the suffix *–ant* refers to *punctual* aspect, and means 'liable to do the act signified by the verbal root'. With the suffix *–ed*, there is duration, whereas with the suffix *–ant* there is no duration. Intense scrutiny of the collocations in the corpus demonstrates the discrepancy between the two suffixes. Nouns following adjectives ending in *–ed* refer to (un)proven theories, established customs, official instructions, acts of cautioning and processes. Nouns following adjectives ending in *–ant* refer to specialised contexts such as phonetics, language, body movements, human beings, their work and inclination, and prevalent fashion. To understand the distinction, consider the following pairs of adjectives:

(46) accepted vs. acceptant
  a. There is no generally accepted definition of life.
  b. After some time, she made an acceptant gesture.

The two words are derived from the verb *accept*, which means 'to agree to take something as satisfactory or reasonable'. In each adjective, nevertheless, the speaker construes the root differently and so uses the adjectives discriminately. In (46a), the adjective *accepted* means 'having been accepted'. An accepted definition is a definition that has been approved or regarded as normal. Collocates following *accepted* belong to ideology such as *credo, creed, precept, principle, tenet*; unproven theory such as *assumption, hypothesis, premise, presumption, surmise*; proven theory such as *axiom, fact, maxim, proverb, truth*; established customs such as *norms, practices, rules, standards, tradition*; way of doing things such as *fashion, form, method, methodology, pattern*; people such as *applicants, candidates, members, newcomers, outsiders*, etc. In (46b), the adjective *acceptant* means 'liable to accept'. An acceptant gesture is a gesture that is liable to receive something offered willingly. Collocates following *acceptant* include body movements in token of assent such as *gesture, nod, sign, signal, wave*, etc.

(47) continued vs. continuant
  a. The continued failure of the police caused a public outcry.
  b. In English, all vowels and fricatives are continuant sounds.

The two adjectives are derived from the verb *continue*, which means 'to keep doing something for some time without stopping'. In each adjective, nevertheless, the speaker construes the root differently and so uses the adjectives discriminately.

In (47a), the adjective *continued* means 'having been continued'. A continued failure is a failure that has been carried on for a long time. *Continued* is followed by collocates of derived nouns denoting processes such as *ascendancy, dominance, failure, involvement, seizure*; simple nouns such as *growth, reform, progress, success, support*, etc. In (47b), the adjective *continuant* means 'liable to continue'. A continuant sound is a sound that is liable to be prolonged. It is a sound that is produced with an incomplete closure of the vocal tract. *Continuant* is followed by collocates related to the field of phonetics.

(48) dominated vs. dominant
a. They argued against the male-dominated department.
b. She was a dominant figure in the French film industry.

The two adjectives are derived from the verb *dominate*, which means 'to have control over a place or a person, or be the most important person or thing'. In each adjective, nevertheless, the speaker construes the root differently and so uses the adjectives discriminately. In (48a), the adjective *dominated* means 'having been dominated'. A dominated department is a department that has been governed by certain people. *Dominated* occurs in the pattern *Noun+dominated+Noun* such as *communist-dominated organisation, labour-dominated authorities, male-dominated workplace, protestant-dominated school, Tory-dominated committee*, etc. Occasionally, the adjective is followed by words such as *countries, groups, markets*, etc. In (48b), the adjective *dominant* means 'liable to dominate'. A dominant person is a person who is liable to prevail over all others. *Dominant* is followed by words referring to people such as *class, figure, mother, partner, person*; parts they are called upon to perform such as *function, part, position, post, role*; general inclination such as *bent, interest, tendency, tradition, trend*; prevalent fashion such as *craze, fad, model, style, vogue*; a distinctive quality such as *aspect, facet, feature, mark, property*; subjects on which a person speaks or writes such as *argument, issue, theme, thesis, topic*, etc[18].

(49) ignored vs. ignorant
a. Most road accidents are due to the ignored safety regulations.
b. Many people are ignorant of the facts about global warming.

The two adjectives are derived from the verb *ignore*, which means 'to behave as if you had not heard or seen someone or something'. In each adjective, nevertheless, the speaker construes the root differently and so uses the adjectives discriminately. In (49a), the adjective *ignored* means 'having been ignored'. An ignored regulation is a regulation that has been disregarded or not been taken notice of. *Ignored* collocates with nouns denoting official instructions such as *directives, guidelines, instructions, ordinances, regulations*; acts of cautioning such as *advice, admonition, caution, premonition, warning*, etc. In (49b), the adjective *ignorant* means 'liable to ignore'. Ignorant people are people who are liable to lack knowledge either in general or with respect to a particular subject. *Ignorant* collocates with nouns referring to people such as *man, pupil, traveller, woman, worker*, etc. In a predicative position, *ignorant* is followed by the preposition *of* or *about*.

(50) varied vs. variant
a. Before his retirement, he had enjoyed a long and varied career.
b. There are cases where variant readings of a single poem exist.

The two adjectives are derived from the verb *vary*, which means 'to be different from one thing to another within a group, or from the usual form of something'. In each adjective, nevertheless, the speaker construes the root differently and so uses the adjectives discriminately. In (50a), the adjective *varied* means 'having been varied'. A varied career is a career that has been different in forms or kinds. *Varied* collocates with almost any noun, people, things and activities. In (50b), the adjective *variant* means 'liable to vary'. A variant reading is a reading that is liable to be slightly different from another reading. *Variant* collocates with vocabulary used generally in language such as *forms, pronunciations, readings, spellings, words*, etc[19].

3.4.2.3 The continuative-stative distinction –ing vs. –ed

Even though both suffixes express *aspect*, they cannot be interchanged. The suffix *–ing* means 'keep on the activity signified by the verbal root'. It describes an activity that continues over a period of time. By contrast, the suffix *–ed* means 'having been in the state signified by the verbal root'. It expresses a state that has existed at a particular time. From concordance listings in the corpus, some conclusions can be drawn, some of which are also mentioned in Collins COBUILD English Grammar (1992:77,80). These adjectives are called *classifying* or *categorising* because they refer the noun to a certain category. They have the following characteristics. First, they are related to intransitive verbs. The present participle suffix *–ing* has a durative meaning in the sense that it refers to an ongoing process, whereas the past participle suffix *–ed* has a stative meaning in the sense that it refers to a finished result. Second, they are non-gradable in that they (i) have no comparatives, (ii) have no superlatives, (iii) cannot be preceded by intensifiers, but (iv) can be modified by adverbs of manner or degree, as in *They recorded a rapidly rising productivity*, and *She rented a pleasantly furnished room*. Third, they can only be used attributively.

Collocates of *–ing* tend to refer to nouns representing processes, measurement and the capacity to operate. Collocates of *–ed* tend to refer to nouns representing money, time, products, skills and public services. The following adjective pairs will serve to illustrate this distinction:

(51) diminishing vs. diminished

a. To revive diminishing aid, the government safeguards all human rights.

b. The accused pleaded not guilty on grounds of diminished responsibility.

The two adjectives are derived from the verb *diminish*, which means 'to make something smaller in size or importance'. Although they derive from the same root, the adjectives are certainly distinctive. In (51a), the adjective *diminishing* means 'keep on diminishing'. Diminishing aid is aid that keeps on becoming less in size or intensity. Collocates that combine frequently with *diminishing* relate to economics such as *aid, budget, investment, profit, return*; abstract nouns such as *echo, effect, impact, implication, importance*; count nouns such as *choices, initiatives, numbers, opportunities, populations*; etc. In (51b), the adjective *diminished* means 'having been diminished'. Diminished responsibility is a state in which someone has not been considered responsible for their actions because they are mentally ill. Collocates that combine frequently with *diminished* relate to law such as *responsibility*; music intervals such as *fourth*; skills such as *ability, capability, capacity, competence, might*, etc.

(52) improving vs. improved

a. The new students have shown an improving level of musical ability.

b. Industry developments are facilitated by improved communications.

The two adjectives are derived from the verb *improve*, which means 'to make something better'. Although they derive from the same root, the adjectives are certainly distinctive. In (52a), the adjective *improving* means 'keep on improving'. An improving level is a level that keeps on advancing in performance or increasing in excellence. Collocates that frequently neighbour *improving* contain nouns denoting measurement such as *grade, level, notch, rate, standard*; the capacity to function well such as *efficiency, fitness, flexibility, management, performance*; the position that the economy is in such as *condition, outlook, quality, situation, status*, etc. In (52b), the adjective *improved* means 'having been improved'. An improved communication is a communication that has been brought to a higher or more desirable condition as a result of changes. Collocates that frequently neighbour *improved* contain nouns referring to systems of public services such as *communication, education, health, housing, sanitation*; a type of product made by a company such as *brand, logo, make, model, trademark*; the way things are arranged such as *arrangement, formation, layout, order, setup*, etc.

(53) increasing vs. increased

a. There is an increasing demand for highly qualified staff.

b. The resolution endorses increased expenditure on research.

The two adjectives are derived from the verb *increase*, which means 'to become larger in amount or size'. Although they derive from the same root, the adjectives are certainly distinctive. In (53a), the adjective *increasing* means 'keep on increasing'. An increasing demand is a demand that keeps on growing or enlarging in amount or degree. Collocates that are frequently used with *increasing* include abstract nouns such as *confidence, dependence, difficulty, pressure, stability*; processes such as *concern, delay, demand, request, use*, etc. In (53b), the adjective *increased* means 'having been increased'. An increased expenditure is an expenditure that has been made greater in amount or degree. Collocates that are frequently used with *increased* include nouns implying money such as *charge, cost, expenditure, fund, price*; importance such as *emphasis, importance, influence, significance, weight*; other nouns such as *burden, chance, control, support, use*, etc.

(54) reviving vs. revived

a. After her work, she met him for a reviving cup of coffee.

b. There is no scope for success in the revived negotiations.

The two adjectives are derived from the verb *revive*, which means 'to make someone strong again, or bring something back to use'. Although they derive from the same root, the adjectives are certainly distinctive. In (54a), the adjective *reviving* means 'keep on reviving'. A reviving cup of coffee is one that keeps on restoring activity by bringing one back from an inactive state. Frequent collocates of *reviving* include names of drinks such as *coffee* or *tea* preceded by their containers such as *cup, espresso cup, glass, mug*, etc. In (54b), the adjective *revived* means 'having been revived'. A revived negotiation is a negotiation that has been renewed or brought back into use. Frequent collocates of *revived* include planned actions such as *campaign, investigation, movement, negotiation, resistance*; politics such as *congress, empire, kingdom, parliament, power*; names of political parties; beliefs such as *liberalism, nationalism, patriotism, realism, socialism*, etc.

(55) wasting vs. wasted

a. For the wasting muscles, massage should be employed.

b. No worry, you will be recompensed for the wasted time.

The two adjectives are derived from the verb *waste*, which means 'to destroy something progressively, or use something inefficiently'. Although they derive from the same root, the adjectives are certainly distinctive. In (55a), the adjective *wasting* means 'keep on wasting'. Wasting muscles are muscles that keep on decaying, waning or weakening. *Wasting* collocates almost always with the noun *muscles*. In (55b), the adjective *wasted* means 'having been wasted'. Wasted time is time that has been inefficiently used or unprofitably expended. *Wasted* collocates with nouns denoting time such as *day, hour, time, week, year*; natural abilities such as *aptitude, faculty, gift, skill, talent*; money such as *cost, expenditure, outlay, payment, tariff*; exertion of physical or mental power such as *campaign, effort, energy, force, power*; types of journeys such as *cruise, expedition, journey, tour, trip*, etc[20].

3.4.2.4 The ordinary-technical distinction –ive vs. –ant

As defined earlier, these suffixes mean either 'apt to do the action signified by the verbal root', or 'liable to do the act signified by the verbal root'. Yet, each has its own individual usage. On the basis of the various collocations provided in the corpus, one can deduce that the suffix *–ive* is used more in ordinary contexts and stresses acts that apply to both animate and inanimate entities. The suffix *–ant* is used more in technical contexts and focuses on embodied traits expressed in names of professions or substances. When applied to professionals, the trait is studied, which means it is learned in a course or acquired in training. When applied to substances, the trait is inherent, which means it exists as a natural or basic part of the thing described. The suffix *–ive* is used before or after nouns, whereas the suffix *–ant* is used before nouns only. Nouns following adjectives ending in *–ive* refer to human beings, materials of language and ways of expressing them, or establishments and places operated by human beings. Nouns following adjectives ending in *–ant* refer to specialised contexts such as architecture, music, psychology, physics, pharmacy or the military. The following adjective pairs will serve to clarify this distinction:

(56) combative vs. combatant
a. The boss conducted the monthly meeting in an intensely combative style.
b. Many combatant units were destroyed in the battle for control of the city.

The two adjectives are derived from the verb *combat*, which means 'to fight in a war'. Even though the adjectives belong to the same root, there is a clear distinction between them. In (56a), the adjective *combative* means 'apt to combat'. A combative style is a style that is apt to fight or argue. Among the collocates that *combative* co-occurs with, some refer to oral and script material of language such as *expression, prose, rhetoric, speech, verse*; ways of expressing them such as *approach, form, manner, mode, style*; people such as *boss, minister, official, speaker, spokesman*, their disposition such as *attitude, mood, spirit, temper, urge*, etc. In (56b), the adjective *combatant* means 'apt to combat'. A combatant unit is a unit that is apt to take part in active fighting, as distinguished from the non-combatant units of the medical or the commissariat staff. *Combatant* is reserved for military contexts such as *armies, battalions, forces, troops, units*, etc.

(57) executive vs. executant
 a. Charles became the executive dean of the medical school in 1985.
 b. Burn began his career as an executant architect of country houses.

The two adjectives are derived from the verb *execute*, which means 'to do something, especially in a planned way'. Even though the adjectives belong to the same root, there is a clear distinction between them. In (57a), the adjective *executive* means 'apt to execute'. An executive dean is a dean who is apt to make or charged with making decisions, especially within an institution, a company or a government. *Executive* collocates with common nouns referring to people holding important jobs such as *dean, director, producer, officer, secretary*; the type of work they do such as *agreement, business, power, role, search*; group of people such as *agency, board, branch, committee, council*, etc. In (57b), the adjective *executant* means 'apt to execute'. An executant architect is an architecture who is apt to design or charged with designing new buildings. *Executant* collocates with nouns referring to people working in the fields of architecture and music, such as *accompanist, architect, musician, planner, soloist*, etc.

(58) operative vs. operant
 a. The commercial television service will be fully operative again in September.
 b. In operant learning, unlike instrumental learning, the animal is free to respond.

The two adjectives are derived from the verb *operate*, which means 'to make something work so as to have an effect'. Even though the adjectives belong to the same root, there is a clear distinction between them. In (58a), the adjective *operative* means 'apt to operate'. An operative service is a service that is apt to work anew. *Operative* prefers nouns referring to establishments where radio or TV programmes are transmitted such as *broadcaster, channel, programme, service, station*; places where passengers get on and off such as *depot, garage, terminal, terminus, station*; forms of agreement such as *accord, agreement, contract, pact, treaty*; official rules such as *act, bill, law, legislation, statute*, etc. In (58b), the adjective *operant* means 'apt to operate'. Operant learning is learning that is apt to produce effect. In operant learning, an item or sequence of behaviour is strengthened or weakened by its consequences. *Operant* prefers nouns that relate to psychology such as *behaviour, conditioning, learning, task, terminology*, etc[12].

(59) reflective vs. reflectant

a. After hearing the news, she lay on the sofa in a reflective attitude of mind.

b. In the wall, there is a window made from a single pane of reflectant glass.

The two adjectives are derived from the verb *reflect*, which means 'to think carefully about opinions, or to send back light, heat, etc'. Even though the adjectives belong to the same root, there is a clear distinction between them. In (59a), the adjective *reflective* means 'apt to reflect'. A reflective attitude is an attitude that is apt to think deeply about something. *Reflective* collocates with nouns referring to types of writing such as *article, chronicle, narrative, prose, verse*; ways of thinking such as *attitude, conception, thinking, thought, reasoning*; people, preferably in a predicative position, such as *girl, man, policeman, student, troubleshooter*; their body parts or features such as *head, mind, soul, tone, voice*, etc. In (59b), the adjective *reflectant* means 'apt to reflect'. Reflectant glass is glass that is apt to mirror something. It throws back something that hits it such as light, heat, sound, or an image of an object. *Reflectant* co-occurs with words related to physics, especially the word *glass*.

(60) stimulative vs. stimulant

a. It is possible that a tax cut may have some stimulative effect.

b. The patient was prescribed a drug with a stimulant property.

The two adjectives are derived from the verb *stimulate*, which means 'to encourage something to develop or someone to become active'. Even though the adjectives belong to the same root, there is a clear distinction between them. In (60a), the adjective *stimulative* means 'apt to stimulate'. A stimulative effect is an effect that is apt to encourage activity. It is a policy that helps the economy grow or develop further. *Stimulative* is used most often in the fields of education and economy such as *development grant, foreign investment, government funding, state subsidy, tax cut*, etc. In (60b), the adjective *stimulant* means 'apt to stimulate'. A stimulant drug is a drug that is apt to give power. It makes one more active and full of energy. *Stimulant* is used most often in the fields of medicine and pharmacy such as *drug, laxative, medicament, panacea, solution*, etc[22].

4 De-nominal domains

This chapter examines the role of domains in the semantic description of de-nominal suffixes. In the course of the investigation, it strives to substantiate two principles of CS. One principle is that the meaning of a lexical item can best be described relative to the domain to which it belongs. Applying this principle to morphology, I argue that the meaning of a suffix can best be defined by comparing it with other suffixes located in the same domain. Another principle is that the syntactic form of a lexical item is determined by the particular construal imposed on its conceptual content. Applying this principle to morphology, I argue that the morphological form of a composite adjective is determined by the particular way the speaker construes its scene. To that end, the chapter is organised as follows. Section 1 explicates the impact of the construal of *perspective* on the morphological forms of composite adjectives derived by means of suffixes. Sections 2–8 present the domains under which de-nominal suffixes are grouped, namely *evaluation, possession, relation, resemblance, motion, trouble* and *disposition.*

4.1 Introduction

By the assumptions of CS, the meaning of an expression involves not only the properties inherent in the scene conceptualised, but also the way the conceptualiser chooses to construe its conceptual content. In morphology, conceptual content is the property inherent in the components of an adjective, which includes that of the root and that of the suffix. Their combination is governed by the semantic compatibility that exists between them, which in turn determines the distribution of the adjective. Construal is the way in which the speaker handles the conceptual content or gears it up to the needs of the discourse, which in turn determines the form of the adjective. Because the root has a multiple facet of content, the speaker has the option to construe it alternatively. In each alternative, the speaker uses a different suffix to highlight a different facet within the root's content. That is, making use of the suffixes the speaker realises the alternative construals in different morphological forms. Each morphological form describes the same content but does so in a particular way. Two adjectives may have the same conceptual content, yet they differ by virtue of the construals imposed on their content.

One dimension of construal which is responsible for perceiving the content of a situation is referred to by Langacker (1987:491) as *perspective*, defined as the way in which a situation is construed, which changes according to the requirements of the discourse. *Perspective* relates to the ability of the speaker to view a situation in alternative ways and choose the appropriate linguistic resources to represent them. Phrased differently, the very wording that the speaker chooses to linguistically encode a situation rests on the manner in which the situation is mentally viewed. To make this clear, let us take some examples. On a conceptual content like *tiger*, the speaker can take two perspectives. When s/he describes a person as cruel, s/he uses *tigerish*, for the suffix *–ish* profiles a negative feature. In *Nobody stands her tigerish heart*, the adjective *tigerish* means like a tiger in being bloodthirsty, fierce and relentless. When s/he describes a person as eager, s/he uses *tiger-like*, for the suffix *–like* profiles a positive feature. In *She has a tiger-like thirst for knowledge*, the adjective *tiger-like* means like a tiger in being eager for knowledge. In each example, the speaker selects a different construal, the suffix signals a distinct quality of the animal, and the adjective has a different meaning.

A graphical representation of the construal of *perspective* in derived adjectives is sketched in Figure 6:

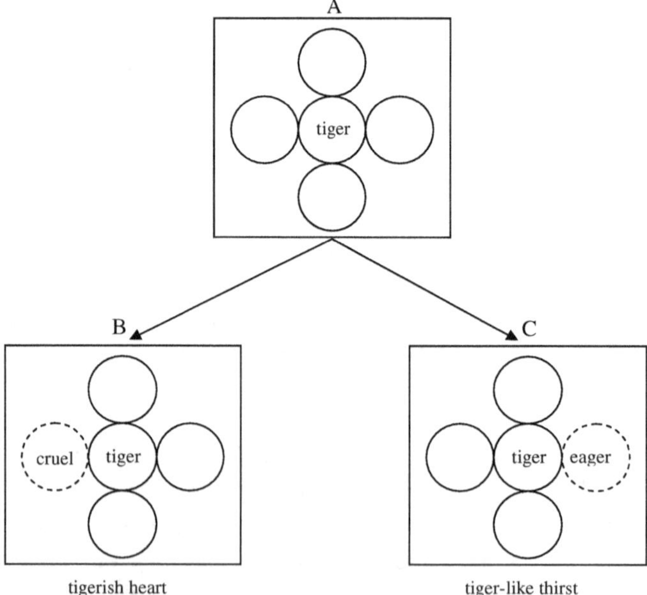

Figure 6: The construal of *perspective* in derived adjectives

The circles in the box marked (A) represent different facets of the conceptual content of *tiger*. The boxes marked (B) and (C) represent the construal of *perspective*, which the speaker imposes on the conceptual content of *tiger*. In the box marked (B), a negative facet of the conceptual content of *tiger*, that of *cruel*, is chosen, which is indicated in a dashed circle. In the box marked (C), a positive facet of the conceptual content of *tiger*, that of *eager*, is chosen, which is indicated in a dashed circle.

4.2 The domain of evaluation

Evaluation or assessment is an area of knowledge which refers to the process of making a judgement, approving or disapproving, about whatever aspect of a person or a situation. It refers to the act of forming an opinion after thinking carefully about someone or something. In *Evaluation of the new treatment cannot take place until all the data has been collected*, the speaker states that a value judgement or a quality calculation of the subject in question can be made only when the data is available.

4.2.1 Morphological exponents

In morphology, the domain of evaluation is expressed by rival suffixes, but with subtle differences in meaning. Evaluation can be neutral, favourable and unfavourable. Neutral evaluation shows that you describe someone or something as having both positive and negative characteristics. Favourable evaluation shows that you approve of someone or something. Unfavourable evaluation shows that you disapprove of someone or something. Morphologically, neutral evaluation is represented by the suffixes *–ly* and *–y*. The suffix *–ly* highlights manner attributes relative to the noun to which it is attached (Section 4.2.2.1). The suffix *–y* emphasises negative physical appearance of an animal which serves as a root, or natural qualities of a thing which serves as a root (Section 4.2.2.2). Favourable evaluation is represented by *–like*, whereas unfavourable evaluation is represented by *–ish*. The suffix *–like* focuses on character attributes that are positive, whereas the suffix *–ish* describes character in derogatory ways by making someone or something seem less important or less good (Section 4.2.2.3).

4.2.2 Semantic distinctions

Adjectival suffixes belonging to the domain of *evaluation* can attach to the same root and form an adjective pair. The root has more than one facet of content, with each suffix focusing on one particular facet. Despite sharing the same root, the adjectives are not interchangeable. The meaning of each adjective has a slant of its own that should not be confused with the other. The disparity in meaning, which is often overlooked, has to do with the way in which their conceptual content is construed. In each case, the speaker imposes a different construal on the content, and so chooses a different suffix. The choice of each suffix depends on the perspective the speaker takes of the situation. Each adjective has, thus, a meaning of its own. Below are details of the semantic distinctions within the domain of *evaluation* and the rival suffixes that represent them.

4.2.2.1 The character-manner distinction

Character refers to the particular qualities in someone that makes him or her different from others, whereas *manner* refers to the way in which someone behaves, or to the way in which something is done. Description of character is conveyed by the suffixes *–ish* and *–like*, but with a difference in use. The suffix *–ish* lays emphasis on the negative side of the character, whereas the suffix *–like* lays emphasis on the positive side of the character. Description of manner is conveyed by the suffix *–ly*. This distinction is represented by the following rival suffixes:

4.2.2.1.1 –ish vs. –ly

Both suffixes refer to the domain of *evaluation*, but they are distinct in use. The suffix *–ish* means 'having the character of the thing specified by the nominal root'. It symbolises the negative qualities of the thing specified by the root. By contrast, the suffix *–ly* means 'having the manner of the thing specified by the nominal root'. It symbolises the manner qualities of the thing specified by the root. A trawl through the concordance lines in the corpus leads to the following key remarks. Adjectives ending in *–ish* apply to people and the things they wear such as clothes and accessories. Adjectives ending in *–ly* apply to people, their abilities, actions, qualities, responsibilities and body parts. By way of illustration, consider the following pairs of adjectives:

(1) mannish vs. manly
  a. Clara is well-known for her mannish clothes.
  b. Mike's manly strength is behind his success.

The two adjectives are derived from the noun *man*, 'an adult male human being'. Nonetheless, a difference in construal gives each adjective a specific mission to carry out in the language. In (1a), the adjective *mannish* means 'having the character of a man'. When applied to women, it refers to negative qualities. Mannish clothes are clothes worn by a woman, which make her look unattractive. *Mannish* collocates with nouns referring to females such as *dame, figure, girl, lass, woman*; clothes such as *blouse, headgear, jacket, suit, trousers*, etc. In (1b), the adjective *manly* means 'having the manner of a man'. It refers to positive qualities proper to men. Manly strength is the ability to deal with difficult situations. *Manly* collocates with nouns referring to males such as *bloke, chap, guy, lad, man*; their body parts such as *arms, chest, heart, shoulders, skull*; natural power such as *ability, aptitude, faculty, flair, skill*; features or qualities such as *attraction, charm, firmness, strength, virtue*; responsibility such as *assignment, chore, duty, job, task*, etc[23].

(2) wifish vs. wifely

a. We used to wonder at Jim's being so wifish.

b. Helen sets an example of wifely tenderness.

The two adjectives are derived from the noun *wife*, 'the woman to whom a man is married'. Nonetheless, a difference in construal gives each adjective a specific mission to carry out in the language. In (1a), the adjective *wifish* means 'having the character of a wife'. When applied to men, it refers to negative qualities. A wifish man is a man who has the character that is stereotypical of a wife, especially in being too devoted or submissive to their partner. *Wifish* collocates with nouns referring to males. In (1b), the adjective *wifely* means 'having the manner of a wife'. It refers to attractive qualities typical of a wife. Wifely tenderness is tenderness that subsumes such features as gentleness, care or sympathy. *Wifely* collocates with nouns referring to females; features or qualities such as *countenance, forbearance, loyalty, patience, tenderness*; responsibility such as *chore, duty, labour, role, task*, etc.

(3) womanish vs. womanly

a. Tom wears a T-shirt with a womanish necklace.

b. Mary uses her womanly maturity to win people.

The two adjectives are derived from the noun *woman*, 'an adult female human being'. Nonetheless, a difference in construal gives each adjective a specific mission to carry out in the language. In (3a), the adjective *womanish* means 'having the character of a woman'. It refers to things that are suitable for a woman. If you describe a man as womanish you mean that his appearance or character is like that of a woman. *Womanish* collocates with nouns referring to males; accessories such as *chain, necklace, perfume, ring, watch*, etc. In (3b), the adjective *womanly* means 'having the manner of a woman'. It refers to virtues generally considered suitable for a woman. If you describe a person as womanly you mean that she uses the virtues of compassion, devotion and sympathy in dealing with others. *Womanly* collocates with nouns referring to females; their body parts such as *breasts, hips, shape, skin, thighs*; features or qualities such as *gentleness, maturity, prudence, tenderness, wisdom*, etc.

4.2.2.1.2 –*like* vs. –*ly*

The two suffixes share the domain of *evaluation*, but they symbolise different meanings. The suffix *–like* means 'having the character of the thing specified by the nominal root'. It symbolises the character attributes specified by the root, used chiefly in a positive sense. For its part, the suffix *–ly* means 'having the manner of the thing specified by the nominal root'. It symbolises the manner attributes of the thing specified by the root, used chiefly in a good sense. A perusal of the concordance lines in the corpus produces the following main points. Adjectives ending in *–like* describe people, with emphasis placed on the qualities they have or the standing they enjoy. Adjectives ending in *–ly* describe people's behaviour, with stress laid on the actions they take or the methods they adopt to do them. Consider, by way of illustration, the following pairs of adjectives:

(4) godlike vs. godly
  a. He is a noble figure of godlike magnanimity.
  b. He gave his son-in-law some godly guidance.

The two adjectives are derived from the noun *god*, 'a being believed to control the universe or life'. Nevertheless, each adjective is distinct in construal and so has a specific role to play in the language. In (4a), the adjective *godlike* means 'having the character of god'. A person who is godlike in magnanimity is very kind and generous towards others. *Godlike* collocates with nouns referring to people such as *banker, chieftain, figure, maker, ruler*; charitable qualities such as *benevolence, clemency, compassion, generosity, magnanimity*; social standings such as *position, prestige, rank, stature, status*, etc. In (4b), the adjective *godly* means 'having the manner of god'. Godly guidance is help and advice about how to deal with problems in all walks of life. *Godly* collocates with nouns referring to opinions as to a course of action such as *admonition, advice, counsel, directive, guidance*; ways of doing it such as *approach, attitude, fashion, manner, method*, etc.

(5) sisterlike vs. sisterly
  a. The dancers' sisterlike compatibility is unparalleled on the stage.
  b. Frank greeted her very warmly, and she gave him a sisterly kiss.

The two adjectives are derived from the noun *sister*, 'a girl or woman who has the same parents as another person'. Nevertheless, each adjective is distinct in construal and so has a specific role to play in the language. In (5a), the adjective *sisterlike* means 'having the character of a sister'. Sisterlike compatibility is compatibility which reflects the ability of people to exist, live together, or work successfully together. *Sisterlike* collocates with nouns referring to people such as *companion, creature, figure, friend, roommate*; nature of a relationship such as *affinity, closeness, compatibility, harmony, intimacy*, etc. In (5b), the adjective *sisterly* means 'having the manner of a sister'. A sisterly kiss is a kiss that is affectionate, kind and caring. *Sisterly* collocates with nouns referring to strong feelings such as *affection, devotion, fondness, kindness, love*; ways of showing them such as *embrace, hug, kiss, peck, squeeze*, etc.

(6) statesmanlike vs. statesmanly
  a. He takes a statesmanlike stance on nuclear disarmament.
  b. Johnson made some statesmanly reflections on the issue.

The two adjectives are derived from the noun *statesman*, 'an experienced politician who is respected for making good judgements'. Nevertheless, each adjective is distinct in construal and so has a specific role to play in the language. In (6a), the adjective *statesmanlike* means 'having the character of a statesman'. A statesmanlike stance is a stance that befits a statesman, in which opinion is exercised wisely and without narrow partisanship. *Statesmanlike* collocates with nouns referring to people; acts of performance such as *comment, decision, remark, speech, utterance*; a mental position such as *attitude, pose, position, stance, stand*, etc. In (6b), the adjective *statesmanly* means 'having the manner of a statesman'. A statesmanly reflection is a reflection that is serious and careful. *Statesmanly* collocates with nouns referring to brainwork such as *cerebration, cogitation, deliberation, reflection, speculation*, etc.

4.2.2.2 The character-appearance distinction

Character refers to the particular qualities in someone that shows the type of person he or she is, whereas *appearance* refers to the way a person or thing looks to other people. As mentioned earlier, character is described by the suffixes *–ish* and *–like*, but with a difference in meaning. The suffix *–ish* indicates a negative evaluation, whereas the suffix *–like* indicates a positive evaluation. Appearance is described by the suffix *–y*. It can be used to evoke both a negative appearance of the noun when it is an animal and a natural appearance of the noun when it is a thing. This distinction is represented by the following rival suffixes:

4.2.2.2.1 –ish vs. –y[24]

These suffixes point to the domain of *evaluation*, but they emphasise different facets of it. The suffix *–ish* means 'having the character of the thing specified by the nominal root'. In using animals for comparison, it refers to the negative attributes that pertain to the character of the animal in question. By contrast, the suffix *–y* means 'having the appearance of the thing specified by the nominal root'. It describes the negative attributes that pertain to the physical form of the animal in question. Scanning through the concordance lists in the corpus presents the following core notes. Adjectives ending in *–ish* state the main qualities of people's character. Adjectives ending in *–y* identify the main characteristics of people's appearance. By way of example, examine the following pairs of adjectives[25]:

(7) doggish vs. doggy
a. He's doggish, spiteful and treacherous by nature.
b. The sheep farmer in the field had a doggy voice.

The two adjectives are derived from the noun *dog*, 'an animal kept as a pet or for hunting or guarding things'. Even so, each adjective receives a specific construal that describes its function in the language. In (7a), the adjective *doggish* means 'having the character of a dog'. A doggish person is a person who has the character qualities of a dog like malice or ill-naturedness. *Doggish* collocates with nouns referring to people. In (7b), the adjective *doggy* means 'having the appearance of a dog'. A doggy voice is a voice that is loud, like a dog's. *Doggy* collocates with nouns referring to people; their body parts such as *ears, eyes, grin, smile, voice*, etc In *She is dog-like in fidelity*, the adjective *dog-like* strikes positive values. The sentence means that she is faithful to her friends and refrains from doing anything that is against her beliefs.

(8) piggish vs. piggy
a. He did not mean his neighbours were piggish or coarse.
b. She sued the paper for saying she had little piggy eyes.

The two adjectives are derived from the noun *pig*, 'a farm animal kept for its meat'. Even so, each adjective receives a specific construal that describes its function in the language. In (8a), the adjective *piggish* means 'having the character of a pig'. A piggish person is a person who has the character qualities of a pig like greediness, meanness or stubbornness. *Piggish* collocates with nouns referring to people. In (8b), the adjective *piggy* means 'having the appearance of a pig'. Piggy eyes are eyes that are unpleasantly small, like those of a pig. *Piggy* collocates with nouns referring to people, with a frequent reference to the body part *eyes*.

(9) waspish vs. waspy
  a. Carter appears everywhere, he's really waspish.
  b. Although he is waspy, he is generally dominant.

The two adjectives are derived from the noun *wasp*, 'a black and yellow flying insect which can sting'. Even so, each adjective receives a specific construal that describes its function in the language. In (9a), the adjective *waspish* means 'having the character of a wasp'. A waspish person is a person who has the character qualities of a wasp like virulence or petulance. *Waspish* collocates with nouns referring to people; their mental attitude such as *mood, outlook, sentiment, spirit, temperament*, etc. In (9b), the adjective *waspy* means 'having the appearance of a wasp'. A waspy person is a person who is slightly built, like a wasp. *Waspy* collocates with nouns referring to people, with an intense concentration on their size or stature[26].

4.2.2.2.2 –like vs. –y

The two suffixes deal with the domain of *evaluation*, but they have their own discrete identity. The suffix *–like* means 'having the character of the thing specified by the nominal root'. In using things for comparison, it refers to something fanciful or imagined, i.e. not based on reality. In comparing something to something else, the speaker strikes a vague and imaginary resemblance. The suffix *–y* means 'having the content of the thing specified by the nominal root'. It refers to something that is authentic or genuine, i.e. based on reality. Whereas the suffix *–like* stands for the imaginary quality of the thing denoted in the root, the suffix *–y* stands for the genuine quality of the thing denoted in the root. Skimming through the concordance lists in the corpus reveals the following prime facts. In using adjectives ending in *–like*, the speaker expounds on properties of things related to human beings. In using adjectives ending in *–y*, the speaker imparts on properties of objects. Examine, by way of example, the following pairs of adjectives:

(10) flower-like vs. flowery
  a. We were amazed at Linda's flower-like freshness.
  b. She is wearing a brown skirt and a flowery blouse.

The two adjectives are derived from the noun *flower*, 'the part of a plant which is brightly coloured with a pleasant smell'. Still, each adjective represents a different construal and so has a special task to perform in the language. In (10a), the adjective *flower-like* means 'having the character of a flower'. Flower-like freshness is as new or vigorous as a flower. *Flower-like* collocates with nouns referring to qualities of things such as *attractiveness, beauty, energy, freshness, serenity*; physical appearances of objects such as *design, form, pattern, shape, structure*, etc. In (10b), the adjective *flowery* means 'having the content of a flower'. A flowery blouse is a blouse that contains pictures of flowers. *Flowery* collocates with nouns referring to clothing such as *apron, blouse, dress, sweater, overall*; means of decoration such as *curtain, drapery, tapestry, wallpaper, wrapping-paper*; features of land such as *field, hill, lane, meadow, slope*, etc.

(11) rock-like vs. rocky

a. They rely on her rock-like determination to see the project through.

b. The beach might be regarded romantic, but it is very rocky indeed.

The two adjectives are derived from the noun *rock*, 'the dry solid part of the Earth's surface, or any large piece of this which sticks up out of the ground or the sea'. Still, each adjective represents a different construal and so has a special task to perform in the language. In (11a), the adjective *rock-like* means 'having the character of a rock'. Rock-like determination is hard or firm as rock. *Rock-like* collocates with nouns implying strength of character such as *certainty, determination, endurance, firmness, steadfastness*, etc. In (11b), the adjective *rocky* means 'having the content of rock'. A rocky beach is a beach that contains rocks. *Rocky* collocates with nouns referring to ground such as *beach, coast, landscape, mountain, path*; valleys such as *canyon, defile, gorge, gulley, valley*; rocks sticking out from the ground such as *bluff, buttress, crag, edge, outcrop*, etc.

(12) spring-like vs. springy

a. Their plan has a spring-like elasticity to suit changes.

b. She was stepping down upon a springy cushion of air.

The two adjectives are derived from the noun *spring*, 'a piece of curved or bent metal that can be pressed into a smaller space but then returns to its usual shape'. Still, each adjective represents a different construal and so has a special task to perform in the language. In (12a), the adjective *spring-like* means 'having the character of a spring'. A spring-like plan is as elastic or resilient as a spring. *Spring-like* collocates with nouns referring to qualities of things such as *buoyancy, elasticity, flexibility, pliability, resilience*, etc. In (12b), the adjective *springy* means 'having the content of a spring'. A springy cushion is a cushion that functions like a spring, which returns to its normal shape after being pressed down. *Springy* collocates with nouns referring to objects such as *cushion, pillow, tightrope, turf, upholstery*; their shapes such as *coil, curl, loop, twine, twist*, etc[27].

4.2.2.3 The vice-virtue distinction –ish vs. –like

Both *–ish* and *–like* have to do with character, but with a difference seen in terms of vice vs. virtue. *Vice* refers to a bad quality in someone's character, whereas *virtue* refers to a good quality in someone's character. The suffix *–ish* picks out the vicious characteristics of the thing denoted in the root. It is used to designate ugly qualities. The suffix *–like* picks out the virtuous characteristics of the thing denoted in the root. It is used to designate attractive qualities. A review of the concordance occurrences in the corpus results in the following findings. Adjectives ending in *–ish* characterise people with attention attracted to their misdemeanour and uneasy feelings. As evidence, such adjectives can only combine with other adjectives having negative denotations, as in *Stop being silly and childish.* Also, such adjectives may co-occur with *rather*. By contrast, adjectives ending in *–like* characterise people, highlighting their general qualities of goodness. As evidence, such adjectives can only combine with other adjectives having positive denotations, as in *She is honest and childlike.* The following pairs of adjectives will serve to illustrate this:

(13) childish vs. childlike
a. None of his friends tolerates his childish outbreaks of temper.
b. At 85, she retains a childlike curiosity about her environment.

The two adjectives are derived from the noun *child*, 'a boy or girl from the time of birth until he or she is an adult'. Yet, each adjective signifies a particular construal that earmarks its use in the language. In (13a), the adjective *childish* means 'having the character of a child'. A person who is childish is immature, irrational and impatient. *Childish* collocates with nouns referring to people; vices such as *bewilderment, hostility, impatience, spite, temper*; misdemeanour such as *bickering, gestures, giggling, prank, tantrum*; activities such as *drawings, games, handwriting, stunts, writing*, etc. In (13b), the adjective *childlike* means 'having the character of a child'. A person who is childlike is innocent, fresh and honest. *Childlike* collocates with nouns referring to people; virtues such as *curiosity, delight, energy, enthusiasm, frankness*, etc.

(14) owlish vs. owl-like
a. The rapist is owlish, he stalks his victims at night.
b. He is owl-like, sitting in the corner of the library.

The two adjectives are derived from *owl*, 'a bird with a flat face, large eyes, a hook-shaped beak and strong curved talons, which hunts small mammals at night'. Yet, each adjective signifies a particular construal that earmarks its use in the language. In (14a), the adjective *owlish* means 'having the character of an owl'. A person who is owlish is wicked and hunts a victim at night, by following him or her over a period of time in order for example to kill him or rape her. *Owlish* collocates with nouns referring to people; their body parts such as *eyes, face, fingers, head, nails*, etc. In (14b), the adjective *owl-like* means 'having the character of an owl'. A person who is owl-like is wise or serious. *Owl-like* collocates with nouns referring to people; qualities such as *cleverness, seriousness, shrewdness, solemnity, wisdom*, etc.

(15) sheepish vs. sheep-like
a. The hostess admitted her fault with a sheepish chuckle.
b. She is sheep-like; everybody wants her companionship.

The two adjectives are derived from the noun *sheep*, 'a farm animal, with thick whitish-coloured hair, which eats grass and is kept for its wool, skin and meat'. Yet, each adjective signifies a particular construal that earmarks its use in the language. In (15a), the adjective *sheepish* means 'having the character of a sheep'. A person who is sheepish is timid, shy or nervous and feels embarrassed because of doing something silly. *Sheepish* collocates with nouns referring to people; types of laughter such as *chuckle, giggle, grin, snigger, titter*; feelings such as *bashfulness, embarrassment, humiliation, shyness, timidity*, etc. Most often, the adjective occurs in the pattern: S+linking verbs+adj. In (15b), the adjective *sheep-like* means 'having the character of a sheep'. A person who is sheep-like is meek, gentle or flexible because s/he is quiet and easy to influence. *Sheep-like* collocates with nouns referring to people; qualities of character such as *amenability, compliance, modesty, obedience, tameness*, etc.

4.3 The domain of possession

Possession is an area of knowledge which refers to the state of owning something, especially a valuable object, or to the state of having a particular quality. As the definition makes clear, the thing possessed could be either an object or a quality. In *I have in my possession a painting which may be of interest to you*, the thing possessed is an object, and the sentence means having the painting after buying it or taking it from someone else. In *The possession of autonomy is something they will never give up*, the thing possessed is a quality, and the sentence means having freedom from being influenced by someone else.

4.3.1 Morphological exponents

In morphology, the domain of *possession* is expressed by rival suffixes, but with subtle meaning differences. Possession is represented by the suffixes *–ful*, *–y*, *–ous* and *–some* (Section 4.3.2.1). Both *–ful* and *–y* refer to an extremely large amount of the quality possessed to the extent of exhibiting or manifesting it. That is, they put the emphasis on form, i.e. the shape or appearance of something. However, with *–ful* the quality possessed is natural, whereas with *–y* it is affected (Section 4.3.2.2). Both *–ous* and *–some* refer to a fairly large amount of the quality possessed to the extent of inducing or producing it. That is, they point to function, i.e. the process of doing something and its implications. However, with *–ous* the quality possessed is conducive to a proper action, whereas with *–some* it is conducive to improper action (Section 4.3.2.3).

4.3.2 Semantic distinctions

Adjectival suffixes belonging to the domain of *possession* can attach to the same root and form an adjective pair. The root's content is polysemous by nature, with each suffix focusing on one particular facet of it. Even though the adjectives are related in derivation, they are of course different in meaning. The difference in meaning can be ascribed to the particular perspective imposed by the speaker on their common content. Under influence from the respective suffix, each adjective develops a meaning of its own. In each adjective, the speaker imposes a different construal on the content, and so opts for a different suffix. The two adjectives thus encode different conceptualisations of the same situation. Below are details of the semantic distinctions within the domain of *possession* and the rival suffixes that represent them.

4.3.2.1 The exhibitive-inducive distinction

Exhibitive refers to the act of manifesting or demonstrating something clearly through signs. *Inducive* refers to the act of causing or leading something to happen. The first meaning is indicated by the suffixes *–ful* and *–y*, but with a difference in meaning. With *–ful*, the thing possessed seems natural, whereas with *–y* it seems affected. The second meaning is indicated by the suffixes *–ous* and *–some*, but with a difference in meaning. With *–ous*, the thing possessed is expressive of discretion, whereas with *–some* it is expressive of indiscretion. This distinction is represented by the following rival suffixes:

4.3.2.1.1 –ful vs. –ous

The two suffixes elicit the domain of *possession*, but they identify different properties of it. The suffix *–ful* means 'full of the thing denoted by the nominal root'. By contrast, its rival suffix *–ous* means 'causing or inspiring the thing denoted by the nominal root'. Careful scrutiny of the concordances in the corpus shows that adjectives in *–ful* collocate mostly with nouns standing for material objects of different nature, whereas adjectives in *–ous* collocate mostly with nouns referring to actions performed by people or machines. To elucidate the contrast, we need to probe some adjective pairs:

(16) graceful vs. gracious
a. She won the competition because she has a graceful body.
b. The speaker delivered a gracious speech on human rights.

The two adjectives are derived from the noun *grace*, 'the quality of beauty in appearance or kindness in behaviour'. The disparity between the adjectives in usage is due to the discrete ways of construing the root. In (16a), the adjective *graceful* means 'full of grace'. A graceful body is one that shows elegance, beauty and smoothness of form. *Graceful* collocates with nouns referring to body parts such as *arms, body, feet, hands, legs*; buildings and their parts such as *bridge, curves, house, steeple, windows*; things additional to the main item such as *frills, railings, ridges, trappings, trimmings*; types of writing such as *acknowledgement, epilogue, foreword, preface, tribute*, etc. In (16b), the adjective *gracious* means 'causing or inspiring grace'. A gracious speech is one that inspires kindness and courtesy. *Gracious* collocates with nouns referring to people and their actions such as *offer, reply, response, smile, speech*, etc.

(17) joyful vs. joyous
a. She spread the joyful news about Tina and Tom.
b. She suddenly let out a shriek of joyous laughter.

The two adjectives are derived from the noun *joy*, 'the feeling of great happiness'. The disparity between the adjectives in usage is due to the discrete ways of construing the root. In (17a), the adjective *joyful* means 'full of joy'. Joyful news is news that exhibits a lively sense of pleasure or satisfaction. *Joyful* collocates with nouns referring to communication whether oral or written such as *information, message, news, report, tidings*; states such as *awareness, elation, freedom, reality, renaissance*, etc. In (17b), the adjective *joyous* means 'causing or inspiring joy'. A joyous laughter is one that produces a powerful emotion because of realising some good thing or event. *Joyous* collocates with nouns referring to people and their actions such as *bouncing, laughter, skating, swaying, wagging*; events such as *celebration, gala, occasion, parade, show*, etc.

(18) wonderful vs. wondrous
a. My father took a lot of wonderful photographs of us when we were young.
b. The world changed rapidly after the wondrous invention of the telephone.

The two adjectives are derived from the noun *wonder*, 'a feeling of surprise for something very beautiful or new'. The disparity between the adjectives in usage is due to the discrete ways of construing the root. In (18a), the adjective *wonderful* means 'full of wonder'. A wonderful photograph is one that is amazing in content and admirable in appearance. *Wonderful* collocates with nouns referring to objects such as *car, gift, photograph, picture, shirt*; works of art such as *article, drama, poetry, story, tale*; arrangement such as *configuration, design, ornament, pattern, shape*; people and their body parts such as *arms, figure, hair, lips, voice*; foods; vegetables, etc. In (18b), the adjective *wondrous* means 'causing or inspiring wonder'. A wondrous invention is one that excites wonder because it is so admirable in application. *Wondrous* collocates with nouns referring to processes and their results such as *concoction, creation, discovery, innovation, invention*; tools for producing desired effects such as *appliance, device, drug, gadget, weapon*, etc[28].

4.3.2.1.2 –ful vs. –some

The two suffixes exemplify the domain of *possession*; however, they differ in use. The suffix *–ful* means 'full of thing denoted by the nominal root'. By contrast, the suffix *–some* means 'causing or inspiring the thing denoted by the root'. Close scrutiny of the concordances in the corpus illustrates that adjectives in *–ful* tend to take nouns referring to things, which collocate with form of injuries, products of art or mistakes. By contrast, adjectives in *–some* tend to collocate with nouns referring to actions performed by people and the equipment at their disposal to achieve certain purposes. To illuminate the contrast, we need to examine some adjective pairs:

(19) awful vs. awesome

a. Several of the passengers sustained awful injuries in the train crash.

b. We have an awesome responsibility for protecting the environment.

The two adjectives are derived from the noun *awe*, 'a feeling of shock or respect usually mixed with fear or surprise'. The adjectives differ in terms of construal, notwithstanding the identical root. In (19a), the adjective *awful* means 'full of awe'. An awful injury is one that is full of shock because it is extremely bad. *Awful* collocates with nouns denoting harm to health such as *cough, cramp, headache, injury, wound*; products of art such as *book, composition, film, story, symphony*; mistakes such as *blunder, error, gaffe, mistake, oversight*, etc. In a predicative position, it occurs in the patterns: *it+be+adj+-ing* and *S+linking verbs+adj*. In (19b), the adjective *awesome* means 'causing or inspiring awe'. An awesome responsibility is one that causes dread because of its size or difficulty. *Awesome* collocates mainly with nouns referring to works to be done such as *burden, duty, onus, responsibility, task*; disadvantages such as *complexity, debts, losses, notoriety, problem*; happenings such as *event, experi-*

ence, incident, occasion, occurrence, etc. In a predicative position, it occurs in the patterns: *it+be+adj+to* and *it+be+adj*[29].

(20) fearful vs. fearsome

a. She is fearful that she may lose custody of her children.

b. They objected to the use of such fearsome instruments.

The two adjectives are derived from the noun *fear*, 'an unpleasant feeling of being frightened or worried that something bad might happen'. The adjectives differ in terms of construal, notwithstanding the identical root. In (20a), the adjective *fearful* means 'full of fear'. A fearful person is a person who shows fright about something. *Fearful* occurs mainly in a predicative position and is preceded by nouns referring to people such as *businessman, figure, man, resident, woman*. It occurs in the patterns: *S+linking verbs+adj and it+be+adj+for/of/that*. In (20b), the adjective *fearsome* means 'causing or inspiring fear'. A fearsome instrument is one that causes anxiety or alarm in others. *Fearsome* collocates with nouns referring to people such as *competitor, creature, enemy, fighter, figure*; their actions or style such as *attack, noise, punch, style, yell*; creatures such as *beast, bully, dinosaur, dog, dragon*; their body parts such as *beak, claws, horns, tail, teeth*; equipment such as *device, gear, instrument, tensile, tool*, etc.

(21) flavourful vs. flavoursome

a. The white wine they serve is flavourful.

b. The meat nearest the bone is flavoursome.

The two adjectives are derived from the noun *flavour*, 'the particular taste of a food or drink'. The adjectives differ in terms of construal, notwithstanding the identical root. In (21a), the adjective *flavourful* means 'full of flavour'. Flavourful wine is wine that has the quality of pleasant taste. *Flavourful* collocates with nouns referring to drinks such as *beer, juice, liquor, whisky, wine*, etc. In (21b), the adjective *flavoursome* means 'causing or inspiring flavour'. Flavoursome meat is meat that gives a real or strong taste. *Flavoursome* collocates with nouns referring to meat such as *beef, chicken, fish, mutton, pork*; vegetables such as *carrots, lettuce, parsnips, potato, tomato*, etc.

4.3.2.1.3 –y vs. –ous

These suffixes are concerned with the domain of *possession*, but they are dissimilar in use. The suffix *–y* means 'full of the thing denoted by the nominal root'. By contrast, its rival suffix *–ous* means 'causing or inspiring the thing denoted by the nominal root'. Intense scrutiny of the concordances in the corpus demonstrates that adjectives ending in *–y* neighbour nouns denoting form, whereas adjectives ending in *–ous* co-occur with nouns involving function. To depict the contrast, we need to investigate some adjective pairs:

(22) gassy vs. gaseous
   a. The beer served at this pub is a bit too gassy for my taste.
   b. Environmentalists call for a reduction in gaseous emission.

The two adjectives are derived from the noun *gas*, 'a substance like air, which is not solid or liquid, and usually cannot be seen'. The semantic discrepancy between the adjectives is explainable in terms of construal. In (22a), the adjective *gassy* means 'full of gas'. Gassy beer is beer that is full of bubbles, a negative description for drinks with unexpected carbonation produced by bottle fermentation. *Gassy* collocates with nouns referring to alcoholic beverages such as *ale, beer, champagne, lager, wine*; space such as *air, atmosphere, cloud, planets, protostar*, etc. In (22b), the adjective *gaseous* means 'causing or inspiring gas'. A gaseous emission is one that involves sending out material made up of gases. *Gaseous* collocates with nouns referring to names of gases or their components such as *carbon, chlorine, hydrogen, ion, oxygen*; processes such as *diffusion, discharge, distension, emission, reaction*; material such as *make-up, material, matter, substance, stuff,* etc.

(23) nervy vs. nervous
   a. The teams looked nervy in the closing stages.
   b. The student gave her paper a nervous shuffle.

The two adjectives are derived from the noun *nerve*, 'a group of long thin fibres that carry instructions between the brain and other parts of the body'. The semantic discrepancy between the adjectives is explainable in terms of construal. In (23a), the adjective *nervy* means 'full of nerve'. A nervy team is one that exhibits anxiety and tension. *Nervy* collocates with nouns referring to people such as *companion, mother, patient, team, youth*; the word *horse*, etc. In (23b), the adjective *nervous* means 'causing or inspiring nerve'. A nervous shuffle is one that involves moving something from one position to another with no particular purpose. *Nervous* collocates mainly with the word *system* and its disorders/breakdown; nouns referring to people such as *child, man, performer, presenter, student*; restless movements such as *fiddle, fidget, shuffle, tremor, twiddle,* states such as *exhaustion, frenzy, strain, temperament, wariness*, etc.

(24) thundery vs. thunderous
   a. There will be thundery rain all over the country.
   b. They took curtain calls to thunderous applause.

The two adjectives are derived from the noun *thunder,* 'the sudden loud noise which comes after a flash of lightning especially during a storm'. The semantic discrepancy between the adjectives is explainable in terms of construal. In (24a), the adjective *thundery* means 'full of thunder'. Thundery rain is rain that contains a large amount of water falling heavily. *Thundery* collocates mainly with nouns referring to weather such as *heat, rain, shower, sky, weather*, etc. In (24b), the adjective *thunderous* means 'causing or inspiring thunder'. Thunderous applause is one that causes a noise like thunder because it is extremely loud. *Thunderous* collocates with nouns denoting noise such as *applause, crash, ovation, outcry, sneeze*; actions such as *approval, greeting, reaction, reception, welcome*, etc.

4.3.2.2 The natural vs. affected distinction –ful vs. –y

Both *–ful* and *–y* mean 'full of', but there is a difference in meaning which stems from whether it is natural vs. affected. *Natural* refers to something that is expected or usual, whereas *affected* refers to something that is artificial or insincere. The first meaning is conveyed by the suffix *–ful*, which expresses the quality possessed in a genuine way. The second meaning is conveyed by the suffix *–y*, which expresses the quality possessed in a pretentious way. A searching examination of the occurrences in the corpus indicates that adjectives ending in *–ful* prefer nouns referring to people's character, forms of communication and the results of their actions. For their part, adjectives ending in *–y* prefer nouns referring to people's greetings, different kinds of stuff and their qualities. This is evidenced by contrasting pairs of adjectives such as the following:

(25) artful vs. arty
a. The parties reached an artful agreement over the price.
b. Their house was filled with arty, not artistic, furniture.

The two adjectives are derived from the noun *art*, 'the use of a work of art to express ideas, or the skill involved in doing or making something'. The contrast between the adjectives is caused by construal. In (25a), the adjective *artful* means 'full of art'. An artful agreement is one that abounds in genuine art or skill in performance. *Artful* collocates with nouns referring to people such as *asset-stripper, dodger, mediator, negotiator, trader*; results of their actions such as *agreement, arrangement, contribution, definition, ventriloquism*, etc. In (25b), the adjective *arty* means 'full of art'. Arty furniture is furniture that abounds in artistic phoniness or pretension. *Arty* collocates with nouns referring to various stuff such as *drawings, furniture, jewelry, photos, paintings*, etc. In describing people, it means connected with art and artists, as in *She hangs out with a lot of arty types.*

(26) cheerful vs. cheery
a. The manager of the project is in a cheerful mood today.
b. The public is wary of the cheery smile of salespersons.

The two adjectives are derived from the noun *cheer,* 'a shout of happiness, approval or encouragement'. The contrast between the adjectives is caused by construal. In (26a), the adjective *cheerful* means 'full of cheer'. A cheerful mood is a mood that is genuinely happy. *Cheerful* collocates with nouns referring to people such as *girl, pilgrim, serviceman, sponsor, student*; their character such as *disposition, humour, mood, nature, temperament*, etc. In (26b), the adjective *cheery* means 'full of cheer'. A cheery smile is a smile that is forced or intrusive, which is intended to persuade one to do things one does not really want to do. *Cheery* collocates with nouns referring to people such as *lockkeeper, owner, porter, salesperson, walker*; ways of greetings such as *greet, nod, salute, wave, welcome*; verbal communication such as *beam, chat, grin, smile, talk*, etc.

(27) fruitful vs. fruity
a. There has been a fruitful dialogue between the two sides.
b. It was a delicious dish served with a bottle of fruity wine.

The two adjectives are derived form the noun *fruit*, 'something that grows on a tree or other plant and tastes sweet'. The contrast between the adjectives is caused by construal. In (27a), the adjective *fruitful* means 'full of fruit'. A fruitful dialogue is one that abounds in genuine profits or yields good results. *Fruitful* collocates with nouns referring to forms of communication such as *conversation, dialogue, discussion, interaction, interchange*; means of examination such as *approach, enquiry, method, research, survey*; sphere of examination such as *area, domain, field, realm, sphere*, etc. In some cases, the adjective is used in *it*-constructions. In (27b), the adjective *fruity* means 'full of fruit'. Fruity wine is wine that has the taste or smell of ripe fruit, made in such a way as if it was fruit. *Fruity* collocates with nouns referring to drinks; quality of any substance which affects the taste such as *aromas, flavour, odour, savour, scent*, etc[30].

4.3.2.3 The circumspect-imprudent distinction –ous vs. –some

Both *–ous* and *–some* mean 'causing or inspiring', but they differ in terms of circumspect vs. imprudent. *Circumspection* refers to a condition in which a person considers the circumstances and consequences of own actions. This meaning is carried by the suffix *–ous*, which stresses the nature, character or state of the thing expressed in the root. It may or may not imply indiscretion.

Imprudence refers to a condition in which the person fails to consider the likely results of his or her own actions. This meaning is carried by the suffix *–some*, which emphasises an action, behaviour or tendency towards the thing expressed in the root. It implies only indiscretion. An investigation of the occurrences in the corpus tells us that adjectives ending in *–ous* accept nouns denoting exciting but dangerous undertakings, whereas adjectives ending in *–some* accept nouns denoting perilous and improper activities. As evidence, adjectives ending in *–ous* can combine with adjectives having positive denotation, as in *He is active, keen and adventurous*, whereas adjectives ending in *–some* can combine with adjectives having negative denotation, as in *He is rash, reckless and adventuresome*. Furthermore, only *adventuresome* takes *rather*. This is shown by comparing pairs of adjectives such as the following:

(28) adventurous vs. adventuresome
a. The adventurous manoeuvre of the staff secured the firm profits.
b. They don't like drivers to be so adventuresome as to wreck cars.

The two adjectives are derived from the noun *adventure*, 'an exciting experience in which dangerous or unusual things happen'. The divide between the adjectives is accounted for by construal. In (28a), the adjective *adventurous* means 'causing or inspiring adventure'. An adventurous manoeuvre is one that is difficult but exciting, so cleverly planned as to obtain an advantage. *Adventurous* collocates with nouns referring to people such as *consultant, journalist, manager, staff, tourist*; a proposed method of doing something such as *approach, design, manoeuvre, plot, scheme*; mental attitude such as *bent, inclination, mood, outlook, spirit*, etc. In (28b), the adjective *adventuresome* means 'causing or inspiring adventure'. An adventuresome driver is a driver who tends to take excessive risks, so daring as s/he lacks discretion. *Adventuresome* collocates with nouns referring to people such as *climber, diver, driver, hunter, soldier* or their activities.

(29) troublous vs. troublesome
a. We went through troublous times before matters came to a settlement.
b. He is growing particularly troublesome because of his drinking sprees.

The two adjectives are derived from the noun *trouble*, 'problems that make something difficult or spoil plans'. The divide between the adjectives is accounted for by construal. In (29a), the adjective *troublous* means 'causing or inspiring trouble'. A troublous time is a time that is fraught with difficulty and problems. *Troublous* collocates with nouns referring to time such as *period, span, spell, term, time*, and the word *world*. In (29b), the adjective *troublesome* means 'causing or inspiring trouble'. A troublesome person is a person who causes problems for others. *Troublesome* collocates with nouns referring to people such as *bandboys, foreigners, inmates, interviewee, prisoners*; improper deeds such as *brawling, drinking, quarrelling, rioting, wrangling*; subjects such as *cause, issue, matter, problem, question*, etc. In a predicative position, the adjective takes the pattern: *S+linking verb+adjective+to+O*[31].

(30) venturous vs. venturesome
a. They set out on a venturous journey across the mountains.
b. He is a venturesome hunter chasing prey in all conditions.

The two adjectives are derived from the noun *venture,* 'an activity that involves taking risks'. The divide between the adjectives is accounted for by construal. In (30a), the adjective *venturous* means 'causing or inspiring venture'. A venturous journey is a journey that is difficult but exciting, in which a person is eager for challenging undertakings. *Venturous* collocates with nouns referring to people such as *fellow, prince, tourist, traveller, woman*; any journey for some definite object *excursion, expedition, outing, tour, trip*, etc. In (30b), the adjective *venturesome* means 'causing or inspiring venture'. A venturesome hunter is a hunter who disregards danger or takes risks, one who is led by a spirit of boldness. *Venturesome* collocates with nouns referring to people or their activities.

4.4 The domain of relation

Relation is an area of knowledge in which two or more things or parts are seen as belonging or working together, or as being of the same kind. It refers to the connection that a thing has, or the reference an idea makes, to other things or ideas. In *The relation between smoking and cancer is well-known,* the speaker wants to show that the connection between the two things is known by a lot of people.

4.4.1 Morphological exponents

In morphology, the domain of *relation* is expressed by rival suffixes, but with differences in meaning. *Relation* can be of two types: internal and external. In internal relation, the two things standing in connection with each other are closely related in identity and nature. In external relation, the two things standing in association with each other are remotely related. The two types of relation are represented by the suffixes *–al*, *–ary* and *–related* (Section 4.4.2.1). Both *–al* and *–ary* represent internal relation, but they differ in meaning. The suffix *–al* singles out the essential characteristics of the thing described, whereas the suffix *–ary* points out only its peripheral characteristics (Section 4.4.2.2). The suffix *–related* represents external relation by striking only a vague relation because it does not give enough details, or does not show exactly how the two things are linked. Additionally, *relation* is represented by the suffixes *–ic* and *–ical*, but with a difference in meaning. The suffix *–ic* sheds light on a core property drawn from the combining root, whereas its rival suffix *–ical* connects the noun described to the field of knowledge borne by the combining root (Section 4.4.2.3).

4.4.2 Semantic distinctions

A pair of adjectives can be derived from the same root by means of suffixes belonging to the domain of *relation*. This is due to the polysemous nature of the root. Such adjectives, even though they look alike, have different meanings. In fact, they are distinct when one considers the perspective that the speaker imposes on them, which is lexicalised by the different suffixes. Each adjective has its distinctive meaning and its own mission to carry out. To place their meanings in proper contexts, the speaker should keep in mind the effect of the perspective taken and the role of the suffix employed. Such adjectives are good examples of how the meanings of words can change when discrete elements are added to their final positions. Below are details of the semantic distinctions within the domain of *relation* and the rival suffixes that represent them.

4.4.2.1 The internal-external distinction

Internal refers to the inside part of something, whereas *external* refers to the outside part of it. The first meaning is signified by the suffix *–al* which connects the noun modified to the combining root with focus on its principal characteristics, and by the suffix *–ary* which connects the noun modified to the combining root with focus on its secondary characteristics. With both suffixes, the relation is based on a fact. The second meaning is signified by the suffix *–related* which connects the noun modified to the combining root with focus on its outer characteristics. With this suffix, the connection is a matter of supposition or presumption why something happens. This distinction is represented by the following rival suffixes:

4.4.2.1.1 –al vs. –related

These suffixes are affiliated with the domain of *relation*, but they designate different meanings. The suffix *–al* picks out internal characteristics. It means 'relating closely to the thing named by the nominal root'. By contrast, the suffix *–related* picks out external characteristics. It means 'relating remotely to the thing named by the nominal root'. Trawling through concordances in the corpus and pages on the internet gives the impression that nouns collocating with adjectives ending in *–al* refer to people whether individuals or groups, things that they actually do, and the places where they are done. By contrast, nouns collocating with adjectives ending in *–related* deal with subjects of discourse or things that people theoretically do, which come in the form of information, enquiry or data. This contrast can be grasped by means of the following adjective pairs:

(31) professional vs. profession-related
a. The player sought professional guidance on the contract details.
b. I dislike discussing profession-related matters at private parties.

The two adjectives are derived from the noun *profession*, 'any type of work which needs special training or a particular skill', but they are contrastive. What lies behind the contrast is construal. In (31a), the adjective *professional* means 'relating closely to profession'. Professional guidance is guidance that relates closely to a profession, work people do as part of a job which needs training or study. *Professional* collocates with nouns referring to people such as *photographer, player, swimmer, staff, therapist*; their actions such as *advice, counselling, direction, guidance, instruction*; names of sports such as *cricket, football, golf, rugby, tennis*; organised body or society such as *aircraft corporation, building society, consulting firm, football association, industry confederation*, etc. In (31b), the adjective *profession-related* means 'relating remotely to profession'. Profession-related matters are matters that are remotely associated with a profession. *Profession-related* collocates with nouns referring to a subject of discourse or conversation such as *issue, matter, subject, theme, topic*, etc.

(32) regional vs. region-related
a. All attempts to ease regional tensions have failed.
b. They surfed the net for some region-related pages.

The two adjectives are derived from the noun *region*, 'a fairly large area of a country or the world, usually without exact limits', but they are contrastive. What lies behind the contrast is construal. In (32a), the adjective *regional* means 'relating closely to region'. Regional tensions are tensions that relate closely to a region, a situation in which countries do not trust each other and may suddenly attack each other. *Regional* collocates with nouns referring to people such as *commander, director, entrant, investor, maker*; assemblies such as *board, committee, congregation, council, panel*; work places such as *agency, airlines, bureau, headquarters, office*; political states such as *conflict, development, growth, stability, tension*, etc. In (32b), the adjective *region-related* means 'relating remotely to region'. Region-related pages are pages that are remotely linked to a region. *Region-related* collocates with nouns used mostly in the field of computing such as *data, internet sites, pages, web links, web sites*, etc.

(33) traditional vs. tradition-related
a. The villagers retain a strong attachment to their traditional values.
b. The attendees raised many tradition-related questions at the forum.

The two adjectives are derived from the noun *tradition*, 'a belief or way of doing something which people have continued to follow for a long time', but they are contrastive. What lies behind the contrast is construal. In (33a), the adjective *traditional* means 'relating closely to tradition'. Traditional values are values that relate closely to tradition, an established or a customary pattern of thought, action, or behaviour. *Traditional* collocates with nouns referring to habitual actions such as *practice, observance, policy, procedure, ritual*; things practised such as *beer, breakfast, dress, music, pie*; people such as *client, critic, friend, society, vendor*; immobile objects such as *building, garden, house, restaurant, school*, etc. In (33b), the adjective *tradition-related* means 'relating remotely to tradition'. Tradition-related questions are questions that are remotely connected with tradition. *Tradition-related* collocates with nouns referring to a subject of argument such as *enquiry, issue, point, query, question*, etc[32].

4.4.2.1.2 –ary vs. –related

These suffixes are associated with the domain of *relation*, but they have different uses. The suffix *–ary* places emphasis on secondary characteristics. It means 'relating closely to the thing named by the nominal root'. By contrast, the suffix *–related* focuses on outer characteristics. It means 'relating remotely to the thing named by the nominal root'. Poring over concordances in the corpus and pages on the internet gives the following results. Adjectives ending in *–ary* collocate with nouns used in the technical fields, such as law and economy, together with the actions involved and the results obtained. By comparison, adjectives ending in *–related* collocate with nouns referring to material, taking the form of either oral or written composition. This contrast can be comprehended through the following adjective pairs:

(34) customary vs. custom-related
a. It is customary for the most important person to sit at the end of the table.
b. The participants discuss only custom-related topics in their conversation.

The two adjectives are derived from the noun *custom*, 'something that is done by people in a particular society because it is traditional', but they are distinct. What accounts for the distinction is construal. In (34a), the adjective *customary* means 'relating closely to custom'. A customary act is an act that relates closely to custom, something that is really practised. *Customary* collocates with nouns referring to conduct such as *behaviour, fashion, habit, manners, practice*; qualities such as *allegiance, elegance, excellence, frankness, warmth*, etc. The adjective is most often used in *it*-constructions. In (34b), the adjective *custom-related* means 'relating remotely to custom'. Custom-related topics are topics that deal remotely with custom, something that is considered theoretically. *Custom-related* collocates with nouns referring to a subject of discourse such as *issue, matter, subject, theme, topic*; printed material such as *information, literature, publication, text, writing*, etc.

(35) disciplinary vs. discipline-related
  a. Following the elbowing incident, the player faced a disciplinary enquiry.
  b. The book contains some new discipline-related material used in schools.

The two adjectives are derived from the noun *discipline*, 'the practice of training people to obey rules and orders', but they are distinct. What accounts for the distinction is construal. In (35a), the adjective *disciplinary* means 'relating closely to discipline'. Disciplinary enquiry is enquiry that relates closely to discipline, a factual observance of rules. *Disciplinary* collocates with nouns referring to a judicial investigation such as *examination, hearing, inquest, enquiry, trial*; a legal action taken against someone such as *arrangements, measures, procedures, proceedings, steps*; a collection of people such as *committee, panel, regime, team, society*, etc. In (35b), the adjective *discipline-related* means 'relating remotely to discipline'. Discipline-related material is material that is remotely linked to discipline, a theoretical observance of rules. *Discipline-related* collocates with nouns referring to ideas in a written or oral composition such as *data, facts, ideas, material, notes*, etc.

(36) inflationary vs. inflation-related
  a. The bank is worried about the mounting inflationary pressures.
  b. The trade union insists on inflation-related payroll adjustments.

The two adjectives are derived from the noun *inflation*, 'a continuing increase in prices', but they are distinct. What accounts for the distinction is construal. In (36a), the adjective *inflationary* means 'relating closely to inflation'. Inflationary pressures are pressures that relate closely to inflation, price increases that are a fact. *Inflationary* collocates with nouns referring to the economy such as *currency, policy, propensity, situation, tendency*; resulting detriments such as *damage, disarray, disintegration, pressure, shock*; processes such as *growth, increase, rise, spiral, surge*, etc. In (36b), the adjective *inflation-related* means 'relating remotely to inflation'. Inflation-related adjustments are adjustments that are remotely linked to inflation, payments of wages that are a demand. *Inflation-related* collocates with nouns referring to money such as *clothing allowances, future increments, payroll adjustments, salary increases, wage offers*, etc.

4.4.2.2 The essential-peripheral distinction –al vs. –ary

Both *–al* and *–ary* emphasise the closeness of the relationship between the noun modified and the root, but they differ in terms of essential vs. peripheral. *Essential* refers to the important parts of something, whereas *peripheral* refers to the less important parts of something. The first meaning is signalled by the suffix *–al*, which connects the noun modified to the combining root by pinpointing its crucial, fundamental or indispensable constituents. The second meaning is signalled by the suffix *–ary*, which connects the noun modified to the combining root by pinpointing its introductory, simple or extra constituents. The difference can be described as one of value. The constituents of the first have more importance than those of the second. As evidence, adjectives ending in *–al* combine with adjectives denoting essence or necessity, whereas adjectives ending in *–ary* combine with adjectives denoting simplicity or incompletion. For example, one can say *elemental and fundamental diet*, but not *elemental and simple diet*. Scouring the concordance instances for evidence helps one to draw some significant conclusions. Nouns following adjectives in *–al* revolve around things that are primary for human existence like nourishment, proof of identity and natural phenomena. Nouns following adjectives in *–ary* revolve around things that are secondary for human existence like education, entertainment and money. To clarify the contrast, the following are given as adjective pairs:

(37) documental vs. documentary
a. They have not produced documental proof of their identity.
b. We watched a documentary film on gold miners in Africa.

The two adjectives are derived from the noun *document*, 'a piece of paper that gives official written information about something', but they are discrete. What is responsible for the discrepancy is construal. In (37a), the adjective *documental* means 'relating closely to document'. Documental proof is proof that provides a crucial piece of information about the truth of something. *Documental* collocates with nouns implying confirmation such as *attestation, evidence, proof, validation, verification*. In (37b), the adjective *documentary* means 'relating closely to document'. A documentary film is a film that provides simple or general information about something. *Documentary* collocates with nouns referring to media broadcasts such as *feature, film, news, programme, show*; supporting material such as *citations, extracts, quotations, references, sources*, etc. When used in literature or art, the adjective *documentary* means giving a record of the facts about something as in *a documentary account of the war*.

(38) elemental vs. elementary

a. At the time of surgery, patients receive elemental diet.

b. The entrant has an elementary knowledge of physics.

The two adjectives are derived from the noun *element*, 'a part of a system, plan or piece of writing', but they are discrete. What is responsible for the discrepancy is construal. In (38a), the adjective *elemental* means 'relating closely to element'. An elemental diet is a diet that is taken by a person at the most fundamental level. *Elemental* collocates with nouns referring to nourishment such as *diet, drink, food, sustenance, nutrition*; theory such as *analysis, changes, functions, principles, stimuli*; uncontrollable phenomena of nature such as *earth, air, fire and water*, and its physical powers such as *dynamism, energy, force, impulse, momentum*, etc. In (38b), the adjective *elementary* means 'relating closely to element'. Elementary knowledge is knowledge that suggests simplicity or self-evidence. *Elementary* collocates with nouns used in the field of education including assessment such as *formula, knowledge, level, mistake, test*; mental exercises to develop skills such as *exercise, drill, lesson, problem, task*; demands such as *needs, necessity, preconditions, prerequisites, requirements*, etc.

(39) fragmental vs. fragmentary

a. The last volcano threw fragmental material into the air.

b. We received only fragmentary accounts of the incident.

The two adjectives are derived from the noun *fragment*, 'a small piece of something which comes from something larger', but they are discrete. What is responsible for the discrepancy is construal. In (39a), the adjective *fragmental* means 'relating closely to fragment'. Fragmental material is material that consists of disconnected or disjoined pieces of key nature, broken off from something large. *Fragmental* collocates predominantly with the noun *material*. In (39b), the adjective *fragmentary* means 'relating closely to fragment'. Fragmentary accounts are accounts made of separate or scattered pieces of insignificant nature. *Fragmentary* collocates with nouns referring to written description of an event such as *account, annals, version, record, report*; acts of meditation such as *consideration, deliberations, discussions, observations, recollections*, etc.

(40) supplemental vs. supplementary

a. The money I get from teaching extra classes is supplemental to my main income.

b. She was receiving a supplementary benefit from the figure awarded as damages.

The two adjectives are derived from the noun *supplement*, 'something which is added to something else to improve it or complete it', but they are discrete. What is responsible for the discrepancy is construal. In (40a), the adjective *supplemental* means 'relating closely to supplement'. A supplemental income is income that is vitally added to an already-existing income so as to improve it or make it complete. *Supplemental* collocates with nouns referring to money such as *earnings, funds, income, resources, wages*; nourishment such as *diet, drink, food, sustenance, nutrition,* etc. In (40b), the adjective *supplementary* means 'relating closely to supplement'. A supplementary benefit is extra money provided to people with low income so as to buy things they need. *Supplementary* collocates with nouns referring to a sum of money such as *allowance, benefit, deposit, grant, payment*; schooling such as *assignment, information, questions, reading, skills*, etc.

4.4.2.3 The hallmark-speciality distinction *–ic* vs. *–ical*

Both *–ic* and *–ical* describe the noun as pertaining to the thing named by the nominal root, but there is a semantic difference understood in terms of hallmark vs. speciality. *Hallmark* refers to a typical characteristic of a person or thing, whereas *speciality* refers to a particular area of knowledge. The first meaning is communicated by the suffix *–ic*, which pertains to the important or excellent trait of the combining root. It means 'pertaining to the typical feature of the thing named by the nominal root'. It is used in figurative senses derived from or produced by the root. The second meaning is communicated by the suffix *–ical*, which pertains to the field of knowledge or subject of study expressed by the combining noun. It means 'pertaining to the area of the thing named by the nominal root'. It is confined almost entirely to the technical sense of 'concerned with'. Combing the concordance instances for evidence helps one to arrive at some important findings. Nouns that follow adjectives in *–ic* describe people plus their achievements, or events plus their results. Nouns that follow adjectives in *–ical* describe fields of knowledge, works of art, or portions of time[33]. To make the contrast clear, the following are cited as adjective pairs:

(41) classic vs. classical
a. Paul scored a classic goal in the 90th minute.
b. He has little knowledge of classical literature.

The two adjectives are derived from the noun *class*, 'a group into which people or things are divided according to their quality', but they are disparate. What explicates the disparity is construal. In (41a), the adjective *classic* means 'pertaining to the typical feature of class'. A classic goal is a goal that is of the first class, highest rank or importance. *Classic* collocates with nouns referring to achievements such as *design, essay, goal, performance, study*; objects such as *album, car, dress, film, picture*; a specimen such as *case, example, instance, model, sample*, etc. In (41b), the adjective *classical* means 'pertaining to the area of class'. Classical literature is literature that belongs to the ancient Greek and Roman world. *Classical* collocates with nouns used in the domain of music such as *ballet, concert, guitar, music, musician*; ancient arts of *Greece* and *Rome* such as *civilisation, culture, drama, literature, myth*; objects of historic interest such as *artefacts, building, city, relic, souvenir*, etc.

(42) historic vs. historical
   a. More money is needed for the preservation of historic monuments.
   b. Doreen specialises in historical novels set in 18th-century England.

The two adjectives are derived from the noun *history*, 'a record of past events of a particular period, country or subject', but they are disparate. What explicates the disparity is construal. In (42a), the adjective *historic* means 'pertaining to the typical feature of history'. A historic monument is one that is famous, important or celebrated in history. *Historic* collocates with nouns referring to actions such as *agreement, change, decision, election, victory*; places such as *building, house, landmark, monument, site*, etc. In (42b), the adjective *historical* means 'pertaining to the area of history'. A historical novel is one that is connected with the study or representation of things from the past. *Historical* collocates with nouns referring to written material such as *document, novel, record, research, romance*; portions of time such as *epoch, era, period, stage, time*; happenings such as *episode, event, experience, incident, occurrence*; relevant information about preceding events such as *background, circumstances, environment, framework, surroundings*, etc.

(43) philosophic vs. philosophical
   a. He is an amazingly philosophic author.
   b. He is famous for philosophical essays.

The two adjectives are derived from the noun *philosophy*, 'the study of the nature of existence and reality', but they are disparate. What explicates the disparity is construal. In (43a), the adjective *philosophic* means 'pertaining to the typical feature of philosophy'. A philosophic author is one who is calm or unflinching in the face of trouble. *Philosophic* collocates with nouns referring to people such as *author, columnist, historian, ideologist, thinker*; viewpoints such as *attitude, outlook, perspective, position, stance*, etc. In (43b), the adjective *philosophical* means 'pertaining to the area of philosophy'. A philosophical essay is one that deals with the study of philosophy. *Philosophical* collocates with nouns referring to literary works such as *article, essay, poem, story, writing*; contention in argument such as *argument, brawl, debate, discussion, dispute*, etc.

(44) politic vs. political

a. It would not be politic for a minister to ignore the reporters.

b. They are caught between two opposing political ideologies.

The two adjectives are derived from the noun *politics*, 'the ideas and activities that are connected with the gaining and using of power', but they are disparate. What explicates the disparity is construal. In (44a), the adjective *politic* means 'pertaining to the typical feature of politics'. Of persons, it means prudent or shrewd. Of actions, it means judicious or expedient. *Politic* is used almost exclusively in *it*-constructions. In (44b), the adjective *political* means 'pertaining to the area of politics'. A political ideology is one that belongs to the science or art of politics, a set of principles on which a political party is based. *Political* collocates with nouns referring to people such as *correspondent, leader, prisoner, reporter, scientist*; connection of interests such as *alliance, bloc, coalition, party, union*; a system of principles such as *belief, creed, doctrine, ideology, philosophy*; issues such as *crisis, development, security, settlement, sovereignty*, etc.

(45) tragic vs. tragical

a. The hospital authorities admitted that a tragic error had taken place.

b. During his acting career, he played all Shakespeare's tragical plays.

The two adjectives are derived from the noun *tragedy*, 'a sad event especially involving death or suffering', but they are disparate. What explicates the disparity is construal. In (45a), the adjective *tragic* means 'pertaining to the typical feature of tragedy'. A tragic error is one that is serious or unpleasant, often involving loss and pain. *Tragic* collocates with nouns referring to people such as *boxer, figure, hero, inmate, pilot*; imperfection such as *blemish, defect, error, flaw, mistake*; destructive events such as *accident, calamity, disaster, mishap, misfortune*; unfavourable results such as *death, end, loss, murder, ruin*; other things such as *circumstances, scene, site, situation, time*, etc. In (45b), the adjective *tragical* means 'pertaining to the area of tragedy'. A tragical play is one that relates to literature about death or suffering. *Tragical* collocates with nouns referring to literary works such as *myth, novel, play, story, tale*, etc.

4.5 The domain of resemblance

Resemblance or similarity refers to an area of knowledge in which one thing is likened to another in such a way as to make it easier to understand or enhance its value. It involves correspondence in either essence or appearance. In *There is a clear resemblance between Susan and her sister*, the speaker wants to show a similarity between the two persons especially in the way they look.

4.5.1 Morphological exponents

In morphology, the domain of *resemblance* is expressed by rival suffixes, but with differences in meaning. *Resemblance* is expressed in two ways: *essence* or *appearance*. In essence, the resemblance is either in substance or feature. Morphologically, essence is represented by the suffixes *–en* and *–y*, but with a difference in meaning. The suffix *–en* denotes the material or substance, expressed by the combining root, which the noun modified is made of. The suffix *–y* denotes a quality or feature, expressed by the combining root, which is a natural part of the noun modified (Section 4.5.2.1). In appearance, the resemblance is either in category or pattern. Morphologically, appearance is represented by the suffixes *–type* and *–style*, but with a difference in meaning. The suffix *–type* signals the category or the form, expressed by the combining root, which distinguishes the noun modified. The suffix *–style* signals the pattern or the manner, expressed by the combining root, of carrying out the noun modified (Section 4.5.2.2).

4.5.2 Semantic distinctions

A pair of adjectives can be derived from the same root by means of suffixes belonging to the domain of *resemblance*. Although such adjectives are similar-looking, their meanings are markedly separate. Each adjective has its distinctive meaning in the lexicon. To apply these adjectives correctly, one needs to look at their definitions to determine how different they are in use. The key to using these adjectives rests on the types of perspective imposed on their conceptual content, which are lexically realised by different suffixes. The suffixes make a difference in how two words that look alike are defined, as such pairs of adjectives certainly demonstrate. A closer look at the adjectives shows that it is the suffix that accounts for the difference in meaning between the two. Below are details of the semantic distinctions within the domain of *resemblance* and the rival suffixes that represent them.

4.5.2.1 The substance-feature distinction –en vs. –y

These suffixes are members of the domain of *resemblance*, but they are quite distinct. The distinction rests on such parameters as substance vs. feature. *Substance* is the material which a thing can be made of, whereas *feature* is its typical quality. *Substance* is conveyed by the suffix *–en*, which means 'resembling the thing designated by the nominal root in make'. *Feature* is conveyed by the suffix *–y*, which means 'resembling the thing designated by the nominal root in quality' A thorough search of the concordance listings in the corpus unearths some new information. Nouns that come next to adjectives in *–en* include objects or the material of which they are made. Nouns that come next to adjectives in *–y* refer to smell and taste, vocal utterance or conception. As for colligation, adjectives ending in *–en* are usually used before nouns, whereas adjectives ending in *–y* are used either before or after nouns. This contrast can be illuminated by adjective pairs such as the following:

(46) earthen vs. earthy
a. The hut had an earthen floor and a thatched roof.
b. The old cellar was damp and had an earthy smell.

The two adjectives are derived from the noun *earth*, 'the land surface of the world as opposed to the sky or sea'. Though similar in root, the adjectives are distinguishable in use. In (46a), the adjective *earthen* means 'resembling earth in make'. An earthen floor is floor that is made of soil or composed of baked clay. *Earthen* collocates with nouns referring to crockery such as *bowl, cup, pan, plate, saucer*; a barrier such as *barricade, dam, floor, rampart, wall*, etc. In (46b), the adjective *earthy* means 'resembling earth in quality'. An earthy cellar is a cellar that resembles earth in smell. *Earthy* collocates with nouns referring to smell and taste such as *flavour, odour, scent, smell, taste*; degree of luminosity of a colour such as *colour, hue, shade, tinge, tone*; quality of an entity such as *bitterness, glamour, realism, sweetness, wisdom*, etc[34].

(47) silken vs. silky
a. The film star wore a silken nightdress.
b. His silky voice bowled the crowd over.

The two adjectives are derived from the noun *silk*, 'a delicate and soft cloth made from a thread produced by a silkworm'. Though similar in root, the adjectives are distinguishable in use. In (47a), the adjective *silken* means 'resembling silk in make'. A silken dress is a dress that is made of silk. *Silken* collocates with nouns referring to pieces of clothing such as *cloak, nightdress, nightgown, shirt, underwear*; bedroom objects such as *bedspreads, cushion, curtains, drapes, sheets*; material for making clothes such as *cord, cotton, fibre, ribbon, thread*, etc. In (47b), the adjective *silky* means 'resembling silk in quality'. A silky voice is a voice that resembles silk in being soft or smooth. *Silky* collocates with nouns referring to vocal utterance such as *accent, sound, tone, utterance, voice*, and the word *hair.*

(48) waxen vs. waxy
a. The man sells waxen effigies of prominent people.
b. The apples on the table have a slightly waxy skin.

The two adjectives are derived from the noun *wax*, 'a solid substance made out of fats or oils used to make candles, which softens and melts at a low temperature'. Though similar in root, the adjectives are distinguishable in use. In (48a), the adjective *waxen* means 'resembling wax in make'. A waxen effigy is an effigy that is made of wax. *Waxen* collocates with nouns referring to objects such as *blooms, effigies, flowers, fruits, leaves*, etc. In (48b), the adjective *waxy* means 'resembling wax in quality'. A waxy skin is skin that is like wax in being shiny or oily. *Waxy* collocates with nouns referring to a covering such as *coating, husk, mantle, rind, skin*; appearance such as *complexion, face, flesh, look, make-up*, etc.

(49) wooden vs. woody
 a. Their house was surrounded by a tall wooden fence.
 b. At the party, the guests had wine with a woody scent.

The two adjectives are derived from the noun *wood*, 'the hard substance which trees are made of'. Though similar in root, the adjectives are distinguishable in use. In (49a), the adjective *wooden* means 'resembling wood in make'. A wooden fence is a fence that is made of wood. *Wooden* collocates with nouns referring to pieces of furniture such as *beds, cabinets, chairs, cupboards, tables*; houses and their parts such as *cottage, fence, house, hut, porch*, etc. In (49b), the adjective *woody* means 'resembling wood in quality'. Woody wine is wine that has been aged in oak barrels, which gives it a smell of wood. *Woody* collocates with nouns referring to smell and taste such as *aroma, flavour, odour, scent, taste*; vocal utterance such as *accent, sound, tone, utterance, voice*, etc.

(50) woollen vs. woolly
 a. The girl is wearing a blue woollen jumper.
 b. The idea is woolly, not presented carefully.

The two adjectives are derived from the noun *wool*, 'the soft thick hair that sheep and goats have on their body, or the thread made from this'. Though similar in root, the adjectives are distinguishable in use. In (50a), the adjective *woollen* means 'resembling wool in make'. A woollen jumper is a jumper that is manufactured from wool. *Woollen* collocates with nouns referring to garments such as *cardigan, jumper, suit, sweater, tights*, etc. In (50b), the adjective *woolly* means 'resembling wool in quality'. A woolly idea is an idea that resembles wool in lacking in clearness or definition. *Woolly* collocates with nouns referring to a conception such as *concept, idea, picture, terminology, thought*, etc.

4.5.2.2 The category-pattern distinction –type vs. –style

These suffixes are representatives of the domain of *resemblance*, but they have different functions. The difference is based on such criteria as category vs. pattern. *Category* is a type or a group of things having some features that are the same, whereas *pattern* is a way in which something is done, organised or happens. *Category* is revealed by the suffix *–type*, which means 'resembling the thing designated by the nominal root in specimen'. It is used when reference is made to the form, model or genre of something which makes it a typical example of a class. *Pattern* is revealed by the suffix *–style*, which means 'resembling the thing designated by the nominal root in mode'. It is used when reference is made to the manner of behaving or the mechanisms of executing a thing. An exhaustive search of the concordance listings in the corpus turns up some interesting facts. The point where the two suffixes converge is when they describe concrete objects or places. The point where they diverge is when the suffix *–style* is used to describe processes such as showing traits, designing buildings, producing objects or performing tasks. This contrast can be illustrated by adjective pairs such as the following:

(51) family-type vs. family-style
a. They were in a family-type hotel, with a fair proportion of guests.
b. In small firms, workers are expected to show family-style loyalty.

The two suffixes are attached to the noun *family*, 'a social group of people consisting of a parent, or parents, and their children'. The adjectives, though similar in root, are distinguishable in use. In (51a), the adjective *family-type* means 'resembling a family in specimen'. A family-type hotel has the size that is typical of a family, which distinguishes it from other ones. *Family-type* collocates with nouns referring to types of residence such as *guest house, home, hostel, hotel, pension*; their prevailing mood such as *ambience, atmosphere, aura, character, vibes*, etc. In (51b), the adjective *family-style* means 'resembling a family in mode'. Family-style loyalty is a trait that is characteristic of family members. *Family-style* collocates with nouns referring to the act or manner of showing something such as *adherence, allegiance, dedication, devotion, loyalty*; a relationship such as *affinity, bond, closeness, intimacy, rapport*, etc.

(52) aircraft-type vs. aircraft-style
a. They installed aircraft-type data recorders on new trains.
b. The hovercraft is fitted with aircraft-style passenger seats.

The two suffixes are attached to the noun *aircraft*, 'any vehicle with or without an engine, which can fly such as a plane or helicopter'. The adjectives, though similar in root, are distinguishable in use. In (52a), the adjective *aircraft-type* means 'resembling aircraft in specimen'. An aircraft-type recorder has a form that serves as a representative instance of aircraft production. *Aircraft-type* collocates with nouns referring to objects such as *designator, engine, kit, recorder, tank*, etc. In (52b), the adjective *aircraft-style* means 'resembling aircraft in mode'. An aircraft-style seat is made in such a way as to provide comfort, which is characteristic of aircraft seats. *Aircraft-style* collocates with nouns referring to modes of producing objects such as *gas caps, interior lights, lock nuts, on/off switches, passenger seats*, etc.

(53) military-type vs. military-style
a. Boys are more likely to receive toys for military-type games.
b. They drew up a military-style plan to carry out the operation.

The two suffixes are attached to the noun *military*, 'the armed forces of a country'. The adjectives, though similar in root, are distinguishable in use. In (53a), the adjective *military-type* means 'resembling the military in specimen'. A military-type game has the form, structure or character, which serves as an imitative example of a military. *Military-type* collocates with nouns referring to objects such as *bags, cables, games, helmet, wrist watch*; clothing such as *flight suit, jackets, trench coat, trousers, uniform*, etc. In (53b), the adjective *military-style* means 'resembling the military in mode'. A military-style plan employs a particular mechanism in executing a task or performing an operation, which is characteristic of a military. *Military-style* collocates with nouns referring to acts of planning such as *device, plan, scenario, scheme, strategy*; acts of attacking such as *ambush, assault, offensive, raid, strike*, etc.

(54) village-type vs. village-style
a. A village-type apartment is often sold at a high price.
b. The dwelling has charming village-style architecture.

The two suffixes are attached to the noun *village*, 'a group of houses which is smaller than a town, usually in the countryside'. The adjectives, though similar in root, are distinguishable in use. In (54a), the adjective *village-type* means 'resembling a village in specimen'. A village-type apartment has the ideal qualities, which is a perfect representation of a village. *Village-type* collocates with nouns referring to places such as *apartment, flat, hotel, house, pub*, etc. In (54b), the adjective *village-style* means 'resembling a village in mode'. Village-type architecture is a definite pattern in which a building is made, distinguished by special characteristics of structure or ornamentation, often found in villages. *Village-style* collocates with nouns referring to the act of designing buildings such as *architecture, composition, construction, design, structure*, etc.

(55) Hollywood-type vs. Hollywood-style
a. They keep trying to make a Hollywood-type film.
b. A Hollywood-style marketing campaign is costly.

The two suffixes are attached to the noun *Hollywood*, 'the centre of the US film industry'. The adjectives, though similar in root, are distinguishable in use. In (55a), the adjective *Hollywood-type* means 'resembling Hollywood in specimen'. A Hollywood-type film has a general form or structure, which is an imitation of Hollywood. *Hollywood-type* collocates with nouns referring to moving pictures such as *cinema, film, movie, production, show*; clothing such as *bra, costume, dresses, outfit, tops*, etc. In (55b), the adjective *Hollywood-style* means 'resembling Hollywood in mode'. A Hollywood-style campaign is a connected series of operations designed to bring about a result in a way characteristic of Hollywood. *Hollywood-style* collocates with nouns referring to processes such as *assessment, campaign, propaganda, review, transformation*, etc.

4.6 The domain of motion

Motion is an area of knowledge which refers to the process of moving someone or something from one place to another, or the way someone or something changes position or direction. In *The rocking motion of the boat made Sylvia feel sick*, the speaker wants to show that the movement of the boat from one side to another had affected Sylvia.

4.6.1 Morphological exponents

In morphology, the domain of *motion* is expressed by rival suffixes, but with differences in meaning. *Motion* involves three oppositions: *location* vs. *motion*, *direction* vs. *destination*, and *mobility* vs. *restriction*. For each opposition, the speaker uses a different suffix. For *location*, the speaker uses the suffix *–ern*, which specifies the region where something is situated. For *motion*, the speaker uses the suffix *–ly*, which denotes going to or coming from the region designated by the combining noun (Section 4.6.2.1). To express *direction*, the speaker uses the suffix *–ward*, which implies facing the region designated by the combining noun. To express *destination*, the speaker uses the suffix *–bound*, which implies travelling towards a particular place designated by the combining noun (Section 4.6.2.2). Concerning *mobility*, the speaker uses the suffix *–based*, which implies moving around. Concerning *restriction*, the speaker uses the suffix *–bound*, which implies getting stuck in a particular place (Section 4.6.2.3).

4.6.2 Semantic distinctions

A pair of adjectives can be derived from the same root by means of suffixes belonging to the domain of *motion*. Because the adjectives look alike, some speakers tend to substitute one for the other. In spite of such frequent misuses, the adjectives are distinguishable in meaning. The way to keep them separate in application is to know the types of perspective that the speaker imposes on their conceptual content and the types of suffixes that are compatible with the perspectives. To know the meanings of the suffixes is to know the differences in their application. These adjectives serve as good examples of how words take on new connotations once they end in different suffixes. Observing the distinction in the connotations of these adjectives helps the speaker to avoid getting into a bind by interchanging them indiscriminately. Below are details of the semantic distinctions within the domain of *motion* and the rival suffixes that represent them.

4.6.2.1 The location-motion distinction –ern vs. –ly

These suffixes imply the domain of *motion*, but they specify different parts of it, which deal with location vs. motion. *Location* refers to the site where something is situated, whereas *motion* refers to the movement of the thing involved. The first meaning is expressed by the suffix *–ern*, which means 'situated in the region expressed by the nominal root'. Precisely, it focuses on position, the place where a thing is located. The second meaning is expressed by the suffix *–ly*, which means 'moving towards or coming from the region expressed by the nominal root'. Precisely, it focuses on shifting, moving towards or coming from the point designated by the root. A review of the collocations in the corpus supports the argument. The suffix *–ern* is compatible with nouns denoting immobile objects represented by countries, provinces or regions, whereas the suffix *–ly* is compatible with nouns denoting mobile objects represented by types of wind such as *breeze, current, gale, storm, wind*, or nouns denoting direction or movement. This contrast is suggested by the adjective pairs below:

(56) eastern vs. easterly
a. The eastern part of the country is very mountainous.
b. The wind in the Atlantic is almost always easterly.

The two adjectives are derived from the noun *east*, 'the direction from which the sun rises in the morning'. Due to the discrete ways of construing the root, the adjectives diverge in usage. In (56a), the adjective *eastern* means 'situated in the East'. An eastern part is a region that is situated in the East. *Eastern* collocates with nouns referring to countries and/or location such as *flank, front, part, suburb, territory*, etc. In (56b), the adjective *easterly* means 'coming from the East'. An easterly wind is a wind that comes or blows from the East. *Easterly* collocates with nouns referring to winds and/or direction.

(57) northern vs. northerly
  a. Severe floods hit northern Europe last summer.
  b. He stumbled slowly along in a northerly direction.

The two adjectives are derived from the noun *north*, 'the direction which is above the Equator'. Due to the discrete ways of construing the root, the adjectives diverge in usage. In (57a), the adjective *northern* means 'situated in the North'. Northern Europe is a region that is situated in the North of the continent. *Northern* collocates with nouns referring to countries and/or continents. In (57b), the adjective *northerly* means 'moving towards the North'. A northerly direction is a direction that moves towards the North. *Northerly* collocates with nouns referring to winds and/or direction.

(58) southern vs. southerly
  a. There will be rain in southern England.
  b. The ship sailed in a southerly direction.

The two adjectives are derived from the noun *south*, 'the direction which is below the Equator'. Due to the discrete ways of construing the root, the adjectives diverge in usage. In (58a), the adjective *southern* means 'situated in the South'. Southern England is a region that is situated in the South of the country. *Southern* collocates with nouns referring to countries or location such as *beach, border, coast, entrance, shore*, etc. In (58b), the adjective *southerly* means 'moving towards the South'. Southerly direction is a direction that moves towards the South. *Southerly* collocates with nouns referring to winds and/or direction.

(59) western vs. westerly
  a. Their cousins live in the western outskirts of the town.
  b. The building faces west to catch the westerly breezes.

The two adjectives are derived from the noun *west*, 'the direction in which the sun goes down in the evening'. Due to the discrete ways of construing the root, the adjectives diverge in usage. In (59a), the adjective *western* means 'situated in the West'. A western outskirt is a region that is situated in the West of a town. *Western* collocates with nouns referring to location such as *edge, fringe, outskirts, periphery, slope*, etc. In (59b), the adjective *westerly* means 'coming from the West'. A westerly breeze is a breeze that comes or blows from the West. *Westerly* collocates with nouns referring to winds and/or direction.

4.6.2.2 *The direction-destination distinction –ward vs. –bound*

These suffixes pertain to the domain of *motion*, but each has a distinctiveness in meaning, which centres around *direction* vs. *destination*. *Direction* refers to the position towards which someone or something moves or faces, whereas *destination* refers to the place to which a person is going or to which a thing is being sent or taken. *Direction* is demonstrated by the suffix *–ward*, which means 'looking towards the point expressed by the nominal root'. *Destination* is demonstrated by the suffix *–bound*, which means 'leading towards the point expressed by the nominal root'. A scan through the collocations in the corpus underlines the statement. The suffix *–ward* co-occurs with nouns implying movement, whereas its rival suffix *–bound* co-occurs with nouns denoting location. This contrast is manifested in the adjective pairs below:

(60) homeward vs. home-bound
a. He covered the homeward journey at full pelt.
b. The home-bound train leaves at 22.00 hours.

The two adjectives are derived from the noun *home*, 'the house, apartment or the place where a person lives'. Owing to the alternate ways of construing the root, the adjectives go in different directions in usage. In (60a), the adjective *homeward* means 'looking towards home'. A homeward journey is a journey that faces or looks towards home. *Homeward* collocates with nouns meaning travel such as *cruise, flight, journey, trip, voyage*; movement such as *ride, run, rush, sail, walk*, etc. In (60b), the adjective *home-bound* means 'leading towards home'. A home-bound train is a train that leads towards home or whose destination is home. It means that *home* is the terminus or the final destination of the train. *Home-bound* collocates with nouns indicating a location such as *highway, lane, path, platform, track*; vehicles such as *bus, car, plane, ship, train*, etc.

(61) northward vs. north-bound
a. They try to control the northward rush of the traffic.
b. The north-bound carriageway is still closed to traffic.

The two adjectives are derived from the noun *north*, 'the direction which is above the Equator'. Owing to the alternate ways of construing the root, the adjectives go in different directions in usage. In (61a), the adjective *northward* means 'looking towards the north'. A northward rush is a rush that looks towards the north. *Northward* collocates with nouns meaning movement such as *ride, run, rush, sail, walk*, etc. In (61b), the adjective *north-bound* means 'leading towards the north'. A north-bound carriageway is a carriageway that leads towards the north. It means that north is the ultimate destination of the traffic. *North-bound* collocates with nouns meaning location such as *avenue, carriageway, lane, track, trail*, etc. The same distinction applies to the other points of direction.

(62) seaward vs. sea-bound
a. Pine wood shielded the seaward side of the field.
b. The visitors are on the sea-bound railway route.

The two adjectives are derived from the noun *sea*, 'the salty water that covers much of the earth's surface'. Owing to the alternate ways of construing the root, the adjectives go in different directions in usage. In (62a), the adjective *seaward* means 'looking towards the sea'. A seaward side is a side that looks towards the sea, or faces the sea. *Seaward* collocates with nouns meaning parts of a place that faces something else such as *edge, end, side, slope, throng*, etc. In (62b), the adjective *sea-bound* means 'leading towards the sea'. A sea-bound route is a route that leads towards the sea. It means that the *sea* is the last stop or the station at the end of the railway route. *Sea-bound* collocates with nouns meaning location such as *bend, circuit, curve, route, track*, etc.

4.6.2.3 The mobility-restriction distinction –based vs. –bound

These suffixes involve the domain of *motion*, but each has taken on a particular meaning, which revolves around *mobility* vs. *restriction*. *Mobility* refers to the condition where the movements or actions of someone or something are not limited, whereas *restriction* refers to the condition where the movements or actions of someone or something are limited. *Mobility* is shown by the suffix *–based*, which means 'positioned in but moving around the place expressed by the nominal root'. With this suffix, the subject is positioned in a certain place, but has the freedom to move elsewhere. *Restriction* is shown by the suffix *–bound*, which means 'restricted or confined to the place expressed by the nominal root'. With this suffix, the subject is stuck in a certain place with no choice of movement. Precisely, it implies preventing one from leaving a place because of an unwanted condition. A study of the collocations in the corpus confirms the premise. The suffix *–based* tends to collocate with nouns referring to people who perform activities or offer services, whereas the suffix *–bound* tends to collocate with nouns referring to people who are in dire need of services. This contrast is borne out by the adjective pairs below:

(63) college-based vs. college-bound
a. In 2005, Christine did a college-based course in Linguistics at Newcastle.
b. The programme is for college-bound students who desire to play baseball.

The two adjectives are derived from the noun *college*, 'a place for advanced education in a particular subject or skill'. Because of the various ways of construing the root, the adjectives separate in usage. In (63a), the adjective *college-based* means 'positioned in but moving around a college'. A college-based course is a course that is centred in a college but its scientific activities extend beyond it. *College-based* collocates with nouns referring to people; a plan of study such as *course, education, module, practice, study*, etc. In (63b), the adjective *college-bound* means 'restricted or confined to a college'. A college-bound student is a student who is confined to a college where he studies, or his activities are restricted to the college. *College-bound* collocates with nouns referring to people and the services, training or tuition they receive.

(64) house-based vs. house-bound
 a. She established a house-based engineering consultancy.
 b. During his long illness, he was completely house-bound.

The two adjectives are derived from the noun *house*, 'a place where people, usually one family, live'. Because of the various ways of construing the root, the adjectives separate in usage. In (64a), the adjective *house-based* means 'positioned in but moving around a house'. A house-based consultancy is a consultancy that is established at home, but its activities extend beyond it. *House-based* collocates with nouns referring to people such as *freelancer, lawyer, midwife, physician, tutor*; services such as *advocacy service, consulting company, engineering consultancy, marriage agency, pastoral care*, etc. In (64b), the adjective *house-bound* means 'restricted or confined to a house'. A house-bound person is a person who is confined to a house, and so could not leave it for a reason beyond his control. *House-bound* collocates with words preceded by *the* to describe people such as *cripple, disabled, elderly, infirm, invalid*, etc.

(65) hospital-based vs. hospital-bound
 a. The patient looked up a directory of hospital-based therapists.
 b. Bronchoscopy is a time-consuming, hospital-bound procedure.

The two adjectives are derived from the noun *hospital*, 'a place where people who are ill or injured are treated'. Because of the various ways of construing the root, the adjectives separate in usage. In (65a), the adjective *hospital-based* means 'positioned in but moving around a hospital'. Hospital-based services are services that are stationed in a hospital, but can be offered elsewhere at request. *Hospital-based* collocates with nouns referring to people such as *diabetologist, psychiatrist, rheumatologist, specialist, therapist*, etc. In (65b), the adjective *hospital-bound* means 'restricted or confined to a hospital'. A hospital-bound procedure is a procedure that is positioned and operated in a hospital only. *Hospital-bound* collocates with nouns referring to medical services such as *procedure, programme, remedy, therapy, treatment*, etc.

4.7 The domain of trouble

Trouble is an area of knowledge referring to the state in which problems make things difficult, spoil plans, cause worry, etc. In *They are having a lot of trouble with the new baby*, the speaker wants to show that the parents are facing a problem with the baby, which is a constant source of worry to them.

4.7.1 Morphological exponents

In morphology, the domain of *trouble* is expressed by rival suffixes, but with a distinction in meaning. *Trouble* is shown in two ways: *affliction* on the one hand and *privation* on the other. *Affliction* means making someone suffer or experience serious problems. Affliction could be either *sudden* or *chronic*. Morphologically, *affliction* is represented by the suffixes *–stricken* and *–ridden*, but with a difference in meaning. With the use of the suffix *–stricken*, an element of suddenness or surprise is emphasised, while with the use of the suffix *–ridden* an element of entrenchment is emphasised (Section 4.7.2.1). *Privation* means lacking something that is good to own, or lacking something that is good to disown. *Privation* could be either *permanent* or *temporary*. Morphologically, *privation* is represented by the suffixes *–less*, and *–free*, but with a difference in meaning. The suffix *–less* indicates that the absence of the thing is of permanent nature, while the suffix *–free* indicates that it is of temporary nature, (Section 4.7.2.2).

4.7.2 Semantic distinctions

A pair of adjectives can be derived from the same root by means of suffixes belonging to the domain of *trouble*. On the surface, these adjectives seem similar, but in actual fact they are dissimilar. One can set one's mind at ease over them by ascertaining their individual meanings and thus resist using them as synonyms. A shade of meaning exists between them that is worth noting and applying whenever they are used. The shade of meaning is reflected by the particular suffix that ends the adjective. In each case, the suffix contributes a special dimension of meaning to the adjective, which is compatible with the particular perspective the speaker takes on the content. Below are details of the semantic distinctions within the domain of *trouble* and the rival suffixes that represent them.

4.7.2.1 The sudden-chronic distinction –stricken vs. –ridden

These suffixes are components of the domain of *trouble*, but they play different roles. The difference is influenced by the benchmark of *sudden* vs. *chronic affliction*. *Sudden* means happening or done quickly and without warning, whereas *chronic* means continuing for a long time. *Sudden affliction* is asserted by the suffix *–stricken*, which means 'hit by the thing imparted by the nominal root'. *Chronic affliction* is asserted by the suffix *–ridden*, which means 'plagued by the thing imparted by the nominal root'. With both suffixes, an element of suffering is present. They differ, I hypothesise, in two ways. First, with the use of *–stricken* an element of suddenness or surprise is emphasised, whereas with the use of *–ridden* no such element is emphasised. As evidence, a sentence with *–stricken* accepts expressions like *suddenly*, whereas a sentence with *–ridden* accepts expressions like *habitually* or *consistently*. Second, with the use of *–stricken* the thing referred to in the root is at its early stages or coming into existence, while with the use of *–ridden* it is already in existence. Taking a look at the collocational occurrences in the corpus validates the hypothesis. The suffix *–stricken* prefers to collocate with nouns referring to people or parts of their body which reflect feelings. The suffix *–ridden* prefers to collocate with nouns referring to types of locations, people or their mental actions, or animals.

Let us now examine some adjective pairs. The first two pairs express emotion, while the rest express non-emotion.

(66) grief-stricken vs. grief-ridden
a. When her husband died, Mrs Williams was grief-stricken.
b. Since the death of her husband, she has been grief-ridden.

The two adjectives are derived from the noun *grief*, 'extreme sadness, especially at the death of someone'. The adjectives differ, although they share the same root. In (66a), the adjective *grief-stricken* means 'hit by grief. A grief-stricken woman is a woman who is hit by and overcome with grief. Her husband's death came as a great shock; it was so immediate or unexpected. *Grief-stricken* collocates with nouns referring to people such as *figure, husband, mistress, parent, wife*; body parts reflecting feelings such as *complexion, face, look, tone, voice*, etc. In (66b), the adjective *grief-ridden* means 'plagued by grief'. A grief-ridden woman is a woman who is plagued, oppressed or obsessed by grief. She is unable to stop thinking about her husband, and so her sadness continues unabated, without weakening in strength or force. *Grief-ridden* collocates with nouns referring to people such as *father, mother, sufferer, survivor, widow*; resulting actions such as *default, failure, flop, loss, mistake*, etc.

(67) guilt-stricken vs. guilt-ridden
   a. He was guilt-stricken when his business collapsed.
   b. He was guilt-ridden at the way he had treated her.

The two adjectives are derived from the noun *guilt*, 'a strong feeling of shame and sadness because you have done something wrong'. The adjectives differ, although they share the same root. In (67a), the adjective *guilt-stricken* means 'hit by guilt'. A guilt-stricken man is a man who is hit by guilt and affected by its influence. Guilt hit him instantly, leaving him in a period of deep anxiety. *Guilt-stricken* collocates with nouns referring to people such as *boss, entrepreneur, financier, investor, worker*, etc. In (67b), the adjective *guilt-ridden* means 'plagued by guilt'. A guilt-ridden man is a man who is plagued by or full of guilt. Guilt has been his main preoccupation, which of course causes him a ceaseless feeling of nervousness or worry. *Guilt-ridden* collocates with nouns referring to people such as creature, *consumer, driver, person, widower*; images passing through their minds such as *dream, fancy, fantasy, imagination, speculation*, etc.

(68) disease-stricken vs. disease-ridden
   a. They provided medicine for the disease-stricken areas following the recent floods.
   b. He contemplated the disease-ridden camps when doctors did more harm than good.

The two adjectives are derived from the noun *disease*, 'an illness, especially one caused by infection rather than by accident'. The adjectives differ, although they share the same root. In (68a), the adjective *disease-stricken* means 'hit by disease'. A disease-stricken area is an area which is hit by a disease abruptly or rapidly, as a result of which the people are in dire need of help. *Disease-stricken* collocates with nouns referring to countries; parts within them such as *area, belt, outpost, province, region*, etc. In (68b), the adjective *disease-ridden* means 'plagued by disease'. A disease-ridden camp is a camp which is plagued by disease. The disease is entrenched or deep-rooted, and so exacts a heavy death toll. *Disease-ridden* collocates with nouns referring to cities; buildings within them such as *camp, garrison, jail, prison, school*; people such as *patient, migrant, nation, population, society*; animals such as *cow, fish, insect, pest, sheep*; dead bodies such as *cadaver, carcass, corpse, remains, skeleton*, etc.

(69) drought-stricken vs. drought-ridden
   a. There was an immediate response to the appeals of the drought-stricken country.
   b. There has been a massive influx of refugees from the drought-ridden territories.

The two adjectives are derived from the noun *drought*, 'a long period of dry weather when there is little or no rain'. The adjectives differ, although they share the same root. In (69a), the adjective *drought-stricken* means 'hit by drought'. A drought-stricken country is a country which is hit by the unforeseen catastrophe of drought, which damaged the harvest and so aroused the need for a swift importation of grain. *Drought-stricken* collocates with nouns referring to countries; land such as *bush, landscape, plain, square*, *veld*, etc. In (69b), the adjective *drought-ridden* means 'plagued by drought'. A drought-ridden territory is a territory which has been plagued by or suffering from the long-standing disaster of drought, causing great harm, damage or destruction. *Drought-ridden* collocates with nouns referring to countries; areas within them such as *area, coast, region, river*, *territory*, etc.

(70) poverty-stricken vs. poverty-ridden
a. Cities should provide work for the poverty-stricken farmers.
b. Many agencies raise money to help poverty-ridden districts.

The two adjectives are derived from the noun *poverty*, 'the condition of being extremely poor'. The adjectives differ, although they share the same root. In (70a) the adjective *poverty-stricken* means 'hit by poverty'. A poverty-stricken farmer is a farmer who is hit by poverty, and so suffers from the effects of being extremely poor. It describes a situation where the countryside is suddenly hit by the unexpected problem of poverty, consequently forcing many peasants to search for work in the cities. *Poverty-stricken* collocates with nouns referring to countries; people such as *beggars, children, farmers, peasants, students*, etc. In (70b), the adjective *poverty-ridden* means 'plagued by poverty'. A poverty-ridden district is a district that is plagued by or excessively full of poverty. It describes a situation where some districts suffer from the long-lasting problem of poverty, making people more or less hopeless. *Poverty-ridden* collocates with nouns referring to countries; parts of a city such as *district, ghetto, municipality, precinct, slum*; people such as *community, inhabitants, masses, nation, society*, etc[35].

4.7.2.2 The permanent-temporary distinction[36] –less vs. –free

These suffixes are segments of the domain of *trouble*, but they serve distinct purposes. The distinction is controlled by the yardstick of *permanent* vs. *temporary privation*. *Permanent* means lasting for a long time or forever, whereas *temporary* means not lasting or needed for very long. *Permanent privation* is represented by the suffix *–less*, which means 'devoid of the thing imparted by the nominal root perpetually'. *Temporary privation* is represented by the suffix *–free*, which means 'lacking the thing imparted by the nominal root momentarily'. A concomitant difference resides in the maximality represented by *–less* compared with the minimality represented by *–free*. Doing something to the maximum means doing it to the greatest possible degree, whereas doing something to the minimum means doing it to the least possible level. As evidence, a sentence with *–less* accepts adverbs indicating high frequency such as *always*, *often*, etc., whereas a sentence with *–free* accepts adverbs indicating low frequency such as *occasionally*, *rarely*, etc. Besides, a sentence with *–less* accepts expressions like *entirely*, whereas a sentence with *–free* accepts expressions like *partially*. Casting a glance at the collocational occurrences in the corpus substantiates the theory. The suffix *–less* collocates with nouns referring to people, assignments, achievements or baked foods. By contrast, the suffix *–free* collocates with nouns referring to people, activities, countries, raw materials or events.

Let us examine some adjective pairs. The pairs in (71), (72) and (75) express something that is good to own, while the pairs in (73) and (74) express something that is bad to own.

(71) careless vs. carefree
a. He was charged with causing death by careless driving.
b. She went on a carefree excursion to the nearby island.

The two adjectives are derived from the noun *care*, 'serious attention paid, especially to the details of something'. The adjectives differ, although they have a common root. In (71a), the adjective *careless* means 'devoid of care perpetually'. Careless driving refers to driving that is habitually heedless, negligent and thoughtless. It means the driver is completely without care in doing his assignments to an absolute level. *Careless* collocates with nouns referring to people such as *camper, customer, driver, officer, singer*; their activities such as *camping, driving, singing, talking, wasting*, etc. In (71b), the adjective *care-free* means 'lacking care momentarily'. A care-free excursion is an excursion that is free of care in an admirable or at least an enviable way. It means that the tourist is temporarily without care and enjoying the holiday. *Carefree* collocates with nouns referring to people such as *bachelor, couple, opponent, tourist, youth*; travel such as *cruise, excursion, journey, trip, voyage*; way of living such as *attitude, life, nature, spirit, style*; time such as *days, hours, periods, spans, years*, etc.

(72) childless vs. child-free
a. He gives medical advice to childless couples after marriage.
b. Before giving birth, Beatrice took a final child-free holiday.

The two adjectives are derived from the noun *child*, 'a boy or girl from the time of birth until he or she is an adult'. The adjectives differ, although they have a common root. In (72a), the adjective *childless* means 'devoid of children perpetually'. A childless couple is a couple that has no children. Such a state is perpetual, continuing forever in the same way. *Childless* collocates with nouns referring to people such as *couple, family, man, woman, widow*, etc. In (72b), the adjective *childfree* means 'lacking children momentarily'. A childfree holiday is a holiday at the time of which the person is without a child, but s/he may later have one. Such a state is momentary, continuing a very short period of time. *Child-free* collocates with nouns referring to people such as *adults, employees, friends, people, singles*; events such as *ceremony, holiday, leave, party, wedding*, etc. A strong argument in favour of the explanation is that one can say the couple are childfree by choice, but not childless by choice.

(73) effortless vs. effort-free

a. The sprinter showed no joy at his effortless victory.

b. Johnson's rise in politics appears to be effort-free.

The two adjectives are derived from the noun *effort*, 'great physical or mental activity needed to achieve something'. The adjectives differ, although they have a common root. In (73a), the adjective *effortless* means 'devoid of effort perpetually'. An effortless victory is a victory that is done easily, without using much energy. It means that the victor exerts or appears to exert no effort in achieving his goal. *Effortless* collocates with nouns referring to people; a piece of work such as *assignment, duty, mission, task, work*; their achievements such as *mastery, success, triumph, victory, win*, etc. In (73b), the adjective *effort-free* means 'lacking effort momentarily'. An effort-free rise is a rise that is comfortable or calm. It means that the politician exerted only little effort in achieving his goal. *Effort-free* collocates with nouns referring to actions such as *advance, climb, ride, rise, strike*; qualities such as *delight, enjoyment, happiness, recreation, relaxation,* etc.

(74) fearless vs. fear-free

a. The fearless hunter spent two weeks on his own in the jungle.

b. In his annual speech, the activist called for a fear-free world.

The two adjectives are derived from the noun *fear*, 'an unpleasant feeling of being frightened or worried that something bad might happen'. The adjectives differ, although they have a common root. In (74a), the adjective *fearless* means 'devoid of fear perpetually'. A fearless hunter is a hunter who shows no sign of fear. It means he is unaffected by fear, i.e. bold or intrepid. *Fearless* collocates with nouns referring to people such as *hunter, player, soldier, trainer, warrior*; quality such as *ambition, creativity, determination, prowess, strength*; way of acting such as *behaviour, conduct, demeanour, deportment, manner*, etc. In (74b), the adjective *fear-free* means 'lacking fear momentarily'. A fear-free world is a world that is free of fear to a minimum. It means the world contains the smallest possible level or amount of fear. *Fear-free* collocates mainly with the word *world*, nouns referring to countries and activities such as *campaign, live, sell, speak, vote*, etc.

(75) sugarless vs. sugar-free
a. Chewing sugarless gum stimulates the flow of saliva.
b. To be healthy, it is important to have a sugar-free diet.

The two adjectives are derived from the noun *sugar*, 'a sweet substance which is obtained from the plants and used to sweeten food and drinks'. The adjectives differ, although they have a common root. In (75a), the adjective *sugarless* means 'devoid of sugar perpetually'. Sugarless gum is gum that is used as a device to enable saliva, a watery liquid, to keep the mouth wet and prepare food for digestion. Such a state is constant, staying the same, not getting less or more. *Sugarless* collocates mainly with the word *gum*, and other nouns referring to baked foods such as *biscuits, cake, candy, pastry, pie*, etc. In (75b), the adjective *sugar-free* means 'lacking sugar momentarily'. A sugar-free diet is a diet that contains a limited amount of sugar, which one takes when one wants to be healthy. Such a state is provisional, continuing for the present time but likely to change. *Sugar-free* collocates mainly with the word *diet*, and other nouns used within the categories of cereals, dairy products, drinks, fruits, etc.

4.8 The domain of disposition

Disposition is an area of knowledge which refers to the tendency of someone or something to act or react in characteristic ways in certain situations. In *Neither side shows the slightest disposition to compromise*, the speaker wants to show that the people involved in an argument have no tendency to reach an agreement.

4.8.1 Morphological exponents

In morphology, the domain of *disposition* is expressed by rival suffixes, but with a distinction in meaning. *Disposition* can be expressed in two ways: *awareness* and *inclination*. *Awareness* refers to the ability to notice things using one's senses, or realise the existence of things. Morphologically, it is represented by the suffix *–conscious*. *Inclination* refers to the tendency to act in a certain way under certain circumstances. The tendency could be either to something desirable or something undesirable. Morphologically, desirable inclination is represented by the suffix *–minded* (Section 4.8.2.1). Undesirable inclination is represented by the suffix *–prone* (Section 4.8.2.2). The difference between awareness and inclination resides, I argue, in terms of passive knowledge vs. active performance. When the speaker wants to express awareness of a situation with no intention to embark on any action, s/he opts for the suffix *–conscious*. The speaker has cognisance of the situation, or s/he is inwardly aware of it. On the other hand, when the speaker wants to express willingness to embark on the action, s/he opts for *–minded* or *–prone*. The speaker has a mind to do something, or s/he is intending, disposed or inclined to do it.

4.8.2 Semantic distinction

A pair of adjectives can be derived from the same root by means of suffixes belonging to the domain of *disposition*. Although the adjectives relate to the same root, they are quite different in meaning. The difference in meaning is sufficient to call for one's using each adjective in its precise context. Any indecision one may have over the use of these adjectives disappears once one recognises the difference in their definitions. The nicety of difference in their definitions is the function of the perspective taken on their content, which is reflected by the particular suffix tacked onto them. Each suffix makes a specific contribution that seasons the adjective with a peculiar shade of meaning. Understanding this paves the way for the proper use of each adjective. Below are details of the semantic distinctions within the domain of *disposition* and the rival suffixes that represent them.

4.8.2.1 The awareness-desirable inclination distinction –conscious vs. –minded

These suffixes are ingredients of the domain of *disposition*, but they suit different situations. The difference stems from the *awareness* vs. *desirable inclination*. *Awareness* means knowing that something exists, whereas *desirable inclination* means tending to do something good. *Awareness* is carried by the suffix *–conscious*, which means 'aware of the thing conveyed by the nominal root'. It implies focusing one's attention on something or being even preoccupied by it. It implies vigilance in observation or alertness in drawing inferences from what one experiences. *Desirable inclination* is carried by the suffix *–minded*, which means 'inclined towards the thing conveyed by the nominal root'. It implies regarding something with attention, considering it important and having it in mind as a purpose or goal. To have a purpose is to be in a state of mind that is favourably directed towards bringing about some state of affairs. Analysing concordances in the corpus and surfing pages in the internet bears out the assumption. Nouns following adjectives ending in *–conscious* refer to people who consider doing something, their trend of mind or business concerns. Nouns following adjectives ending in *–minded* refer to people who like something and are willingly involved in it, or to their approaches. A discussion of some adjective pairs will clarify the contrast:

(76) calorie-conscious vs. calorie-minded
a. This recipe is highly recommended to calorie-conscious consumers.
b. For calorie-minded slimmers, try microwaving an apple after coring it.

The two adjectives are derived from the noun *calorie*, 'a unit for measuring the amount of energy that food produces'. The adjectives are not equal in usage, which is caused by construal. In (76a), the adjective *calorie-conscious* means 'aware of calories'. A calorie-conscious consumer is a consumer who is aware of or alert to calories, i.e. thinks about it. *Calorie-conscious* collocates with nouns referring to people such as *buyer, consumer, customer, purchaser, shopper*; food such as *collation, meal, menu, recipe, repast*, etc. In (76b), the adjective *calorie-minded* means 'inclined towards calories'. A calorie-minded slimmer is a slimmer who is inclined towards or believes in calories and is anxious to follow the stipulations so as to lose weight. *Calorie-minded* collocates with nouns referring to people such as *devotee, fiend, follower, freak, slimmer*, etc.

(77) career-conscious vs. career-minded
a. In this career-conscious world, many couples put off raising a family.
b. Her daughter is career-minded; she has no intention to start a family.

The two adjectives are derived from the noun *career*, 'a job that you have been trained for and intend to do for several years'. The adjectives are not equal in usage, which is caused by construal. In (77a), the adjective *career-conscious* means 'aware of one's career'. A career-conscious world is a world in which people are aware of or give attention to a particular subject such as career at the expense of another. *Career-conscious* collocates with nouns referring to people such as *man, person, student, undergraduate, woman*, and the word *world*. In (77b), the adjective *career-minded* means 'inclined towards one's career'. A career-minded person is a person who is inclined towards a career and thinks that a career is more important than anything else, and even gives up something valuable to be successful in it. *Career-minded* collocates with nouns referring to people such as *chief, daughter, director, executive, manager*, etc.

(78) fashion-conscious vs. fashion-minded
a. Nancy appreciates elegant clothes; she's very fashion-conscious.
b. She spends a lot of money on clothes; she's very fashion-minded.

The two adjectives are derived from the noun *fashion*, 'a style that is popular at a particular time, especially in clothes, hair or behaviour'. The adjectives are not equal in usage, which is caused by construal. In (78a), the adjective *fashion-conscious* means 'aware of fashion'. A fashion-conscious person is a person who is aware of and thinks a lot about fashion. She is aware of what clothes are considered stylish. *Fashion-conscious* collocates with nouns referring to people such as *female, girl, lass, teenager, youngster*; businesses such as *automobile industry, costume store, merchandising service, record company, teenage magazine*, etc. In (78b), the adjective *fashion-minded* means 'inclined towards fashion'. A fashion-minded person is a person who is inclined towards and interested in fashion to the extent of getting involved in it wholeheartedly. *Fashion-minded* collocates with nouns referring to people such as *adherent, admirer, buff, fanatic, lover*, etc.

(79) profit-conscious vs. profit-minded
a. In such conditions, profit-conscious companies should alter mode of operations.
b. Besides his academic career, John is a profit-minded promoter of social events.

The two adjectives are derived from the noun *profit*, 'money that is gained by selling things or doing business'. The adjectives are not equal in usage, which is caused by construal. In (79a), the adjective *profit-conscious* means 'aware of profit'. A profit-conscious company is a company that is aware of and thinks a lot about profit and is ready to take any necessary step towards realising it. *Profit-conscious* collocates with nouns referring to people such as *farmer, grocer, manufacturer, merchant, professional*; business concerns such as *company, enterprise, firm, industry, organisation*, etc. In (79b), the adjective *profit-minded* means 'inclined towards profit'. A profit-minded promoter is one who is inclined towards or attaches importance to profit, and is actually engaged in realising it. *Profit-conscious* collocates with nouns referring to people such as *employer, entrepreneur, marketer, producer, promoter*, and their approaches, etc.

(80) safety-conscious vs. safety-minded
a. By being safety-conscious, Martin narrows the odds of a nasty accident.
b. Due to safety-minded drivers, there is a decline in the number of deaths.

The two adjectives are derived from the noun *safety*, 'the state of being safe from danger or harm'. The adjectives are not equal in usage, which is caused by construal. In (80a), the adjective *safety-conscious* means 'aware of safety'. A safety-conscious person is a person who is aware of and well-informed about safety, i.e. has a lot of knowledge or information and passes his thoughts on to the others. *Safety-conscious* collocates with nouns referring to countries; people; a trend of mind such as *character, disposition, habit, nature, temper*, etc. In (80b), the adjective *safety-minded* means 'inclined towards safety'. A safety-minded driver is a driver who is inclined towards and confers importance on safety by observing its rules to avoid accidents. *Safety-minded* collocates with nouns referring to people such as *driver, electrician, employee, pilot, technician*; manner of doing things such as *approach, mode, style, technique, treatment*, etc.

4.8.2.2 The awareness-undesirable inclination distinction –conscious vs. –prone

These suffixes are constituents of the domain of *disposition*, but they fit different requirements. The difference is judged by the principle of *awareness* vs. *undesirable inclination. Awareness* means knowing that something exists, whereas *undesirable inclination* means tending to do, or being affected by, something bad. *Awareness* is carried by the suffix *–conscious*, which means 'aware of the thing conveyed by the nominal root'. It implies focusing attention on something to avoid its occurrence. *Undesirable inclination* is carried by the suffix *–prone*, which is the opposite of *–minded*, and means 'susceptible to the thing conveyed by the nominal root'. It implies either being easily influenced by something undesirable or having a fancy for it. Analysing concordances in the corpus and surfing pages on the internet backs up the assumption. Nouns following adjectives ending in *–conscious* refer to people or companies and their strategies. Nouns following adjectives ending in *–prone* refer to people who are either reckless or powerless. A discussion of some adjective pairs will clarify the contrast:

(81) accident-conscious vs. accident-prone
a. Accident-conscious mechanisms must be put in place.
b. The girl is always falling over, she is accident-prone.

The two adjectives are derived from the noun *accident*, 'a happening that damages something or injures someone'. The adjectives are far from being equal, and this distinction is triggered by construal. In (81a), the adjective *accident-conscious* means 'aware of accident'. An accident-conscious mechanism is a way of doing something in which someone is aware of what is happening around him. *Accident-conscious* collocates with nouns referring to people; companies; a plan aimed at achieving a goal such as *blueprint, design, mechanism, policy, strategy*, etc. In (81b), the adjective *accident-prone* means 'susceptible to accident'. An accident-prone person is a person who is susceptible to accidents, or has a greater than average number of accidents, either because she is awkward or clumsy or because she has personality traits that predispose her to accidents. *Accident-prone* collocates with nouns referring to people.

(82) injury-conscious vs. injury-prone
a. Injury-conscious motor racing requires wearing helmets.
b. The rider doing a lap on the circuit is rather injury-prone.

The two adjectives are derived from the noun *injury*, 'physical harm or damage to part of someone's body caused by an accident'. The adjectives are far from being equal, and this distinction is triggered by construal. In (82a), the adjective *injury-conscious* means 'aware of injury'. Injury-conscious motor racing is an event in which someone is aware of the dangers involved in an event, and so takes the necessary steps to avoid damage. *Injury-conscious* collocates with nouns referring to people, especially those who take part in sporting events. In (82b), the adjective *injury-prone* means 'susceptible to injury'. An injury-prone rider is a rider who is susceptible to injury, and so gets injuries; a rider who is aware of the dangers that lie ahead but is disposed to taking risks. *Injury-prone* collocates with nouns referring to people, especially those who do something dangerous and not care about the risks and the possible results.

5 Domain interaction

This chapter investigates the role of multiple domains in the semantic interpretation of composite expressions. It attempts to substantiate the CS principle that the meanings of expressions can evoke different domains for their interpretation. Applying this principle to morphology, I argue that the meanings of an adjective pair can be identified through the domains they activate. Each meaning is realised by means of a specific suffix, which evokes an appropriate domain. Each suffix represents a particular construal imposed by the speaker on the content of the root with which it combines. To that end, the chapter is structured as follows. Section 1 introduces the notions of *conceptual content* and *construal*. Section 2 presents the notion of multiple domains, with emphasis laid on its implications and relevance to suffixation. Section 3 explains interaction between suffixes belonging to different de-verbal domains. Section 4 probes interaction between suffixes belonging to different de-nominal domains. Section 5 investigates interaction between suffixes belonging to both de-verbal and de-nominal domains.

5.1 Introduction

One of the fundamental principles of CS, which the present study confirms, is that the meaning of an expression can be described in terms of two important aspects: *conceptual content* and *construal*. As Langacker (1988a:7) claims, the meaning of an expression involves not only the properties inherent to the scene conceptualised, but also the way the speaker chooses to construe its conceptual content. *Conceptual content* includes the properties of the expression's components, with its character being influenced by the *cognitive domain* which the determinant component evokes. Taylor (2002:439) defines it as 'any knowledge configuration which provides the context for the conceptualisation of a semantic unit'. *Construal* is the way in which the speaker conceives and expresses the conceptual content. Langacker (1987:487–488) defines it as 'the relationship between a speaker (or hearer) and a situation that he conceptualises and portrays'. Two expressions may invoke the same conceptual content, yet differ semantically by virtue of the construals they impose on that content. By analogy, alternative morphological expressions represent different construals imposed on a conceptual content.

5.2 Multiple domains

One striking characteristic of CS, as Taylor (2002:197) stresses, is its emphasis on the idea that a semantic unit can be conceptualised against more than one domain. Domains do not constitute strictly separated configurations of knowledge. Typically, they overlap and interact in numerous and complex ways. In describing the concept *father*, for instance, the domain of a kinship network has to be evoked. Although this domain captures an important facet of its meaning, other domains are involved as well. In the domain of physical objects, *father* is a physical being with weight and dimensions. In the domain of living things, *father* is a creature who has a beginning and an end. In the domain of family relations, *father* has a significant role to play. Each of these constitutes a domain against which the word *father* is conceptualised. Each is connected with the other domains, in one way or another. The set of domains which provide the context for the full understanding of a semantic unit is referred to by Langacker (1991a:147) as *matrix*.

Langacker (1987:154) illustrates the notion of domain matrix on the example of *banana*. The concept *banana* includes in its matrix many specifications: shape in the spatial domain, colour in the colour domain, and taste/smell in the sense domain. In addition to such concrete domains, the concept *banana* evokes some abstract domains, e.g. the knowledge that bananas are eaten, that they grow in bunches on trees, that they come from tropical areas, and so on. As is seen, each use of the word activates a certain domain. In other words, different uses of the word highlight different domains against which it is understood. This is in line with the assumption that different uses of a word activate different facets of its semantic structure. For most concepts, it is necessary to make reference to multiple domains for their full characterisation. Domains are not equal in status, however. Some are more central, more intrinsic to the concept than others. Moreover, not every domain is invoked on every occasion on which the word is used.

5.2.1 Pivotal implications

The evocation of multiple domains in the interpretation process has important implications for the nature of word meanings.

The first implication pertains to semantic flexibility. Word meanings cannot be considered constant, stable or invariable entities. Rather, they are flexible in that they are capable of adapting to new, different or changing requirements. The meanings associated with a word tend to vary according to the context in which the word is used. From every context, a new domain emerges. Consider some examples involving the word *banana*. In *A banana is a long curved fruit*, the word evokes the domain of shape. In *A banana has a yellow skin*, the word focuses on the domain of colour. In *A banana contains sweet white flesh*, the word highlights the domain of taste. In *He orders a banana milkshake*, the word brings in the domain of nutrition. The examples point to the salience of the different domains against which the word is described. Each domain serves as an effective cue for the recall of the relevant example. Whatever is predicated of a nominal is predicated of the nominal's profile. In *A banana is a long curved fruit*, curved fruit is predicated of *banana* as having shape, not of *banana* as having colour, and so on.

The second implication concerns domain interaction. The domains evoked by the word do not exist as separate patterns of knowledge. Rather, they interact with and react to each other. In the preceding paragraph, I mentioned that in *A banana is a long curved fruit* curved fruit is predicated of *banana* as having shape, not of *banana* as having colour. Nevertheless, it is easy to combine both conceptualisations without any sense of anomaly, as in *A banana is a long curved fruit with a yellow skin*. This is so because the background knowledge necessary to understand the concept of *banana* is distributed over several domains, which may be selectively activated according to context. This suggests that the concept of *banana* is not a rigid or fixed entity; rather it is dynamic in that its various meanings emerge in different contexts of use. In specific contexts, the concept is constructed out of elements which reside in a rich network of domain-based knowledge. What is involved in comprehension then is one's store of knowledge about a word and the analysis of the context in which the word is used.

The third implication relates to encyclopaedic knowledge. Word meanings are neither restricted in use nor constricted in application. Rather, they are comprehensive in nature in the sense that they cover a large range of knowledge and are supported by a vast network of interrelated knowledge. The *encyclopaedic* approach implies the presence of all relevant knowledge in linguistic meaning. It postulates reference to all the domains relevant to the word and incorporates them into its meaning. However, the approach does not entail that everything that a person knows about a word is linguistically relevant. Not every facet of what a person knows is equally central to a word. Some facets are intrinsic; others are peripheral, while some others are irrelevant. The shape, colour and nutritional value of bananas are probably central to the word and would need to be included in an account of its meaning. The fact that people can slip on banana skins is probably peripheral. The reason for adopting an *encyclopaedic* approach is that we need to appeal to domain-based knowledge in order to account for how words are used.

That these implications have relevance to adjectival suffixation is beyond doubt. The task of the next section is to demonstrate this.

5.2.2 Suffixal interactions

In the light of the previous discussion, I argue that a composite adjective ties together a range of knowledge in a single package, thus facilitating certain communicative tasks. This is so because in forming adjectives some roots are flexible in character, and so incorporate different meanings. The meaning of a composite adjective can be characterised in terms of the multi-faceted content it has as well as the different construals imposed on that content. To accentuate each facet of meaning, the root takes on a different suffix. For its part, each suffix activates a certain domain. The form of a derived adjective is thus motivated by its cognitive organisation, and morphological differences between various derivatives reflect meaning differences. This means that in representing the meaning of a composite adjective more than one domain is involved. However, as we have seen, these domains do not form independent patterns of knowledge. Rather, they are related to each other and interact in many ways, although they vary in degree of centrality. To show how this works, let us discuss some examples representing different types of interaction.

In some cases, different de-verbal domains are invoked for the full characterisation of adjective pairs derived from a common root. That is to say in such cases we need to make reference to more than one domain to characterise the adjective pairs fully. For example, in describing the meaning difference between *verified* vs. *verifiable* we need to resort to different de-verbal domains. The two adjectives are derived from the verb *verify*, which means 'to prove the truth of something', but they are distinct in use. In *The verified results of the study have been published*, the de-verbal suffix *–ed* evokes the domain of *aspect*, and means 'being in the state signified by the verbal root'. A verified result is a result that has been verified, i.e. proved true. In *Throughout the trial, he didn't produce a verifiable fact*, the de-verbal suffix *–able* evokes the domain of *voice*, and means 'capable of undergoing the action referred to in the verbal root'. A verifiable fact is a fact that is capable of being verified, i.e. not yet proved true.

In other cases, different de-nominal domains are enforced to account for the patterning of adjective pairs derived from the same root. For example, in characterising the meaning difference between *fateful* vs. *fatal* we need to resort to different de-nominal domains. The two adjectives are derived from the noun *fate*, which means 'the things that will happen to someone, especially unpleasant events'. In *The president made a fateful announcement*, the de-nominal suffix *–ful* evokes the domain of *possession*, and means 'full of the thing denoted by the nominal root'. A fateful announcement is an announcement that is extremely important, leading to either good or bad ends. In *Meningitis is a fatal disease is some cases*, the de-nominal suffix *–al* evokes the domain of *relation*, and means 'relating closely to the thing named by the nominal root'. A fatal disease is a disease that is extremely dangerous, resulting in death or disaster.

In further cases, different de-verbal and de-nominal domains are implemented to provide explanations for the adjectives under discussion. For example, to tell the difference between a pair such as *respectable* vs. *respectful*, we need to solicit different domains. In *She is a respectable woman from a good family*, the adjective *respectable* is derived from the verb *respect*, which means 'to show admiration for someone or something that has good qualities'. The de-verbal suffix *–able* evokes the domain of *voice*, and means 'capable of undergoing the action referred to in the verbal root'. A respectable woman deserves respect by reason of good qualities. In *He taught his son to be respectful of other people*, the adjective *respectful* is derived from the noun *respect*, which means 'admiration shown for someone or something that has good qualities'. The de-nominal suffix *–ful* evokes the domain of *possession*, and means 'full of the thing denoted by the nominal root'. A respectful son has deference for other people and their beliefs[37].

In what follows, I present evidence for the important roles played by different domains in the understanding of adjective pairs.

5.3 Interaction between de-verbal domains

In some cases, an adjective pair is derived from a verbal root. Even though the adjectives are related in derivation, they are not interchangeable. Each adjective has meaning of its own, which is conceptually triggered by the particular construal imposed on its content and linguistically expressed by the particular suffix it ends with. The suffixes, which are used to derive the adjectives, belong to different domains. In what follows, I explain the role of multiple domains in the interaction between and interpretation of suffixes belonging to de-verbal domains.

5.3.1 The patientive-stative distinction *able* vs. *–ed*

The suffixes *–able* and *–ed* are de-verbal. Yet, they call to mind different domains. The suffix *–able* calls to mind the domain of *voice* and means 'capable of undergoing the action referred to in the verbal root'. By contrast, the suffix *–ed* calls to mind the domain of *aspect* and means 'having been in the state signified by the verbal root'. From the collocational examples provided by the corpus, one can identify different patterns. With common nouns, *–able* implies a future perspective, whereas *–ed* implies a past perspective. That is, with *–able* the state of affairs is potential in nature, whereas with *–ed* it is actual in nature. With other nouns, *–able* tends to collocate with materials that can be manipulated or physical objects, whereas *–ed* tends to collocate with information and its containers or educational institutions. This distinction is identified by such adjective pairs as:

(1) distributable vs. distributed
  a. The shareholders would be paid dividends out of distributable profits.
  b. Distributed systems are considered to be the next wave of computing.

The two adjectives are derived from the verb *distribute*, which means 'to give something out to several people, or spread something over a large area'. Despite this, construal draws a line of demarcation between them. In (1a), the adjective *distributable* means 'capable of being distributed'. A distributable profit is one that is capable of being sent to people who own shares in a company. The semantic preference associated with *distributable* is economy and administration such as *assets, earnings, profits, reserves, shares*, etc. In (1b), the adjective *distributed* means 'having been distributed'. A distributed system is one in which the software has been shared between a server and a client. A client sends requests to a server, according to some protocol, asking for information or action, and the server responds. The semantic preference associated with *distributed* is computing such as *applications, database, format, network, system*; containers of information such as *booklets, brochures, handouts, leaflets, pamphlets*, etc.

(2) electable vs. elected
  a. George's personality makes him an extremely electable candidate.
  b. The elected leader is widely respected even among the opposition.

The two adjectives are derived from the verb *elect*, which means 'to choose someone for an official position by voting'. Despite this, construal draws a line of demarcation between them. In (2a), the adjective *electable* means 'capable of being elected'. An electable candidate is one who is capable of being elected, i.e. an attractive prospect for election. *Electable* chooses names of political parties or their candidates for collocation such as *Conservative, Democrat, Labour, Liberal, Republican*, etc. In (2b), the adjective *elected* means 'having been elected'. An elected leader is one who has been chosen by vote for office, as distinguished from other modes of election. *Elected* chooses names of individual nominees such as *executive, leader, official, president, representative*; names of assemblies such as *committee, council, government, leadership, parliament*, etc.

(3) recognisable vs. recognised
a. The Eiffel Tower is an instantly recognisable landmark.
b. Lucy goes to a recognised school of music in her town.

The two adjectives are derived from the verb *recognise*, which means 'to know someone or something because one has seen, heard or experienced them in the past'. Despite this, construal draws a line of demarcation between them. In (3a), the adjective *recognisable* means 'capable of being recognised'. A recognisable landmark is one that is capable of being identified. The contextual preference of *recognisable* is nouns denoting indication such as *feature, sign, symbol, symptom, syndrome*; prominent objects on land such as *effigy, landmark, monument, shrine, statue*; human body parts such as *eye, face, mouth, smell, voice*, etc. In (3b), the adjective *recognised* means 'having been recognised'. A recognised school is one that has been acknowledged for its quality. The contextual preference of *recognised* is accredited institutions such as *college, faculty, institute, school, university*; nouns referring to individuals such as *expert, first aider, teacher, therapist, volunteer*; a collection of people such as *body, guild, league, party, union*; sports events such as *championship, competition, contest, match, tournament*, etc.

(4) recyclable vs. recycled
a. Most of the steel on this site is recyclable.
b. The restaurant sells Coke in recycled cans.

The two adjectives are derived from the verb *recycle*, which means 'to treat used objects so that they can be used again'. Despite this, construal draws a line of demarcation between them. In (4a), the adjective *recyclable* means 'capable of being recycled'. Recyclable steel is steel that is capable of being recovered through a series of treatments. *Recyclable* prefers to collocate with nouns denoting materials such as *glass, paper, plastic, steel, wood*, etc. In (4b), the adjective *recycled* means 'having been recycled'. A recycled can is one that has been processed and restored for human use. *Recycled* prefers to collocate with nouns denoting products such as *bottles, cans, cars, plates, shoes*, etc. Whereas the adjective *recyclable* refers to the phase before treating the substance, the adjective *recycled* refers to the phase after treatment.

(5) usable vs. used
a. The software he has written is old but it is still usable.
b. She went into the business of dealing in used furniture.

The two adjectives are derived from the verb *use*, which means 'to put something such as an object, a tool, skill or building to a particular purpose'. Despite this, construal draws a line of demarcation between them. In (5a), the adjective *usable* means 'capable of being used'. A usable software is one that is capable of being used because it still works well. *Usable* is preferable in the contexts of computing such as *design, software, web menu, web page, website*; location such as *area, path, road, tennis court, storage space*, etc. In (5b), the adjective *used* means 'having been used'. Used furniture is furniture that has been made use of by someone else before. *Used* is preferable in the context of products such as *artefacts, books, electrodes, furniture, vehicles*, etc.

5.3.2 The patientive-terminative distinction *–able vs. –ant*

The suffixes *–able* and *–ant* are de-verbal. Yet, they bring to mind different domains. The suffix *–able* brings to mind the domain of *voice* and means 'capable of undergoing the action referred to in the verbal root'. By contrast, the suffix *–ant* brings to mind the domain of *aspect* and means 'apt to do the action signified by the verbal root'. From the collocational examples provided by the corpus, one can identify different patterns. The pattern of collocation of *–able* consists of nouns referring to objects that can be processed, actions and consequences, or places and qualities. The pattern of *–ant* consists of nouns referring to human beings, whether individuals or groups. The difference between the two is that with the first the influence comes from the outside, whereas with the second it comes from the inside. This distinction is reflected in such adjective pairs as:

(6) observable vs. observant
a. After the speech, a change in public sentiment is clearly observable.
b. A highly observant lifeguard stops risky situations before they start.

The two adjectives are derived from the verb *observe*, which means 'to see or notice the way something happens or someone does something'. In spite of this, construal draws a line of separation between them. In (6a), the adjective *observable* means 'capable of being observed'. An observable sentiment is capable of being noticed, i.e. visible. Often, *observable* co-occurs with nouns denoting alteration such as *change, contrast, difference, divergence, variation*;

testimony such as *data, evidence, fact, proof, token*; processes such as *decline, decrease, development, increase, rise*; peculiar features such as *attribute, characteristic, property, quality, trait*; repercussion such as *consequences, effects, outcomes, results, upshots*, etc. In (6b), the adjective *observant* means 'apt to observe'. An observant person is a person who is apt to notice things. Often, *observant* co-occurs with nouns referring to people such as *man, lifeguard, teacher, traveller, walker*, etc.

(7) pliable vs. pliant

a. He wanted a sweet, pliable, obedient wife, and that wasn't for me!

b. After the strike, the manager became more pliant in his position.

The two adjectives are derived from the verb *ply*, which, when applied to people, means 'to bend in will or disposition'. In spite of this, construal draws a line of separation between them. In (7a), the adjective *pliable* means 'capable of being plied'. A pliable wife is one who is capable of being controlled by her husband, i.e. flexible in character. *Pliable* co-occurs with nouns referring to people such as *boy, child, girl, man, wife*; their body parts such as *limb, lip, mouth, muscles, wrist*, etc. When applied to objects such as *clay, leather, plastics, rope, soles*, it means easy to bend without breaking. In (7b), the adjective *pliant* means 'apt to ply'. A pliant manager is one who is willing to accept change, welcome new ideas, adjust policy, position, or the like. *Pliant* co-occurs with nouns referring to people such as *authority, judge, manager, minister, landlady*, etc.

(8) reliable vs. reliant

a. He has shown himself to be charming, sincere and very reliable.

b. Well, she is heavily reliant on her parents for financial support.

The two adjectives are derived from the verb *rely*, which means 'to trust someone or something to do what one expects them to do'. In spite of this, construal draws a line of separation between them. In (8a), the adjective *reliable* means 'capable of being relied on'. Someone who is reliable is capable of being counted on because they always behave well and in the way one expects. *Reliable* co-occurs with nouns referring to people such as *driver, guide, manufacturer, safeguard, watchman*; knowledge such as *data, facts, figures, information, records;* investigation such as *check, criterion, probe, test, trial*, etc. Only *reliable* is used with pieces of apparatus such as *aircraft, gauge, printer, scales, stove*, etc. In (8b), the adjective *reliant* means 'apt to rely on'. Someone who is reliant counts on someone else for something that is badly needed. *Reliant* co-occurs with nouns referring to people such as *child, friend, farmer, journalist, patient*; business organisations such as *company, concern, corporation, firm, syndicate*, etc. In a predicative position, the adjective is followed by the preposition *(up)on.*

(9) tolerable vs. tolerant
a. The weather was just about tolerable, but the mood was amiable.
b. The staff are very tolerant of all extremes of consumer behaviour.

The two adjectives are derived from the verb *tolerate*, which means 'to accept something unpleasant or difficult, even though one does not like it'. In spite of this, construal draws a line of separation between them. In (9a), the adjective *tolerable* means 'capable of being tolerated'. Tolerable weather is weather that is capable of being endured although it is not nice. *Tolerable* co-occurs with nouns implying restriction such as *bound, brink, edge, limit, point*; measurement such as *amount, degree, level, rate, volume*; places for someone to live in such as *accommodation, apartment, flat, hotel, hostel*; states of atmosphere such as *climate, heat, rainfall, temperature, weather*; things such as *behaviour, drug, food, job, pain*, etc. In (9b), the adjective *tolerant* means 'apt to tolerate'. Tolerant staff are workers who endure what other people say or do even if they do not agree with it. *Tolerant* co-occurs with nouns referring to people such as *audience, partner, people, staff, writer*, etc. In most cases, the adjective is followed by the preposition *of*[38].

(10) expectable vs. expectant
a. The radiation leak has an expectable effect on the environment.
b. The expectant audience waited in silence for the show to begin.

The two adjectives are derived from the verb *expect*, which means 'to think that something will happen because it has been planned'. In spite of this, construal draws a line of separation between them. In (10a), the adjective *expectable* means 'capable of being expected'. An expectable effect is an effect that is capable of being anticipated, i.e. considered probable or certain to occur. *Expectable* co-occurs with nouns implying a condition traceable to a cause such as *consequence, development, effect, outcome, result*, etc. In (10b), the adjective *expectant* means 'apt to expect'. An expectant audience is an audience that looks forward to the beginning of a show. *Expectant* co-occurs with nouns referring to people such as *audience, crowd, onlookers, spectators, viewers*; their body parts such as *eye, face, gaze, look, smile*, etc[39].

5.4 Interaction between de-nominal domains

In the preceding section, I dealt with interaction between suffixes belonging to de-verbal domains. In what follows, I extend the impact of multiple domains to the description of suffixes belonging to de-nominal domains. In this respect, an adjective pair can be derived from a noun by means of two different suffixes. Each adjective has its own definition, which is contributed by the construal of the speaker and encoded by the use of the appropriate suffix. Each suffix focuses on a particular facet of the content and adds a special meaning to the host root.

5.4.1 The characteristic-essential distinction *–ous* vs. *–al*

The suffixes *–ous* and *–al* are de-nominal. Yet, they belong to different domains. The suffix *–ous* belongs to the domain of *possession* and means 'characterised by the thing denoted by the nominal root'. By contrast, the suffix *–al* belongs to the domain of *relation* and means 'relating closely to the thing named by the nominal root'. As the examples in the corpus show, adjectives ending in *–ous* tend to collocate with nouns referring to people, their actions or behaviour, whereas adjectives ending in *–al* tend to collocate with nouns referring to events or things covering names of places, items of clothing, or positions held. This distinction is manifested in adjective pairs such as the following:

(11) ceremonious vs. ceremonial

a. He bid her an unusually ceremonious farewell.

b. They took part in every ceremonial occasion.

The two adjectives are derived from the noun *ceremony*, 'a formal or traditional set of actions used at an important social or religious event'. Nonetheless, construal reveals a difference between them in use. In (11a), the adjective *ceremonious* means 'characterised by ceremony'. A ceremonious farewell is one that is too formal or polite, in which the person exercises observance of formalities. *Ceremonious* collocates with nouns referring to people or their behaviour such as *farewell, greeting, leave-taking, salutation, welcome*, etc. In (11b), the adjective *ceremonial* means 'relating closely to ceremony'. A ceremonial occasion is one that relates to or consists of a ceremony or rite, i.e. stresses careful attention to form and detail. *Ceremonial* collocates with nouns denoting events such as *bonfire, meeting, occasion, parade, procession*; appointment such as *duty, job, position, post, role*; clothes such as *costume, dress, outfit, robe, suit*, etc.

(12) imperious vs. imperial

a. She sent away the guests with an imperious wave of the hand.

b. The office is dubbed by some observers as an imperial palace.

The two adjectives are related to the noun *empire*, 'a group of countries ruled by the ruler or government of one country'. Nonetheless, construal reveals a difference between them in use. In (12a), the adjective *imperious* means 'characterised by empire'. An imperious wave is one that is overbearing, tyrannical and dictatorial, in which the person exercises a commanding influence and expects obedience. *Imperious* collocates with nouns referring to people or their behaviour such as *gaze, gesture, stare, tap, wave*, etc. In (12b), the adjective *imperial* means 'relating closely to empire'. An imperial palace is a palace which relates to an empire or the person who rules it. *Imperial* collocates with nouns referring to countries; places such as *capital, college, court, house, palace*; military formations such as *forces, guards, navy, troops, warships*, etc.

(13) industrious vs. industrial

a. He is a very industrious worker.

b. She lives in an industrial town.

The two adjectives are derived from the noun *industry*, 'the people and companies involved in the production of goods in factories'. Nonetheless, construal reveals a difference between them in use. In (13a), the adjective *industrious* means 'characterised by industry'. An industrious worker is a worker who is diligent and hard-working. *Industrious* collocates with nouns referring to people such as *immigrant, player, student, trader, worker*, etc. In (13b), the adjective *industrial* means 'relating closely to industry'. An industrial town is a town which relates to industry or productive labour. *Industrial* collocates with nouns referring to towns such as *borough, city, metropolis, municipality, town*; localities within them such as *building, complex, district, quarter, site*; business concerns such as *company, enterprise, establishment, firm, organisation*, etc.

(14) judicious vs. judicial

a. Frank offered some judicious thoughts on the question.

b. They started judicial proceedings against the offenders.

The two adjectives are derived from the noun *judgement*, 'an official decision given by a judge or a court of law'. Nonetheless, construal reveals a difference between them in use. In (14a), the adjective *judicious* means 'characterised by judgement'. A judicious thought is one that is discreet, sensible and wise, in which the person makes a sound judgement. *Judicious* collocates with nouns referring to people or their actions such as *analysis, choice, decision, thought, use*, etc. In (14b), the adjective *judicial* means 'relating closely to judgement'. Judicial proceedings are proceedings that relate to a court of law or a judge in the process. *Judicial* collocates with nouns referring to legal events such as *hearing, enquiry, proceedings, process, review*, etc.

(15) officious vs. official

a. She sounded strict, domineering, almost officious.

b. The Queen is on an official visit to the Bahamas.

The two adjectives are derived from the noun *office*, 'a position of responsibility in a government or other organisation'. Nonetheless, construal reveals a difference between them in use. In (15a), the adjective *officious* means 'characterised by office'. An officious person is a person who is bossy, telling people what to do or using the power to give orders. *Officious* collocates with nouns referring to people or their actions such as *meddling, interference, intervention, refereeing, tampering*, etc. In (15b), the adjective *official* means 'relating closely to office'. An official visit is a visit which relates to the tenure of office and discharge of duties, done not for a private purpose. *Official* collocates with nouns referring to events such as *ceremony, inauguration, opening, tour, visit*; an account of events such as *description, message, record, report, statement*, etc[40].

5.4.2 The characteristic-peripheral distinction *–ous vs. –ary*

The suffixes *–ous* and *–ary* are de-nominal. Yet, they join different domains. The suffix *–ous* joins the domain of *possession* and means 'characterised by the thing denoted by the nominal root'. It evokes an extra attribute that can be extracted from the root. It applies more to events than to people. By contrast, the suffix *–ary* joins the domain of *relation* and means 'relating closely to the thing named by the nominal root'. It evokes a normal attribute that is suggested by the root. It applies more to things than to events. As the examples in the corpus show, adjectives ending in *–ous* tend to collocate with nouns referring to people's actions, whereas adjectives ending in *–ary* tend to collocate with nouns referring to things and states. This distinction is shown in adjective pairs such as the following:

(16) extemporaneous vs. extemporary

a. He gave an extemporaneous speech on human rights.

b. The publisher is an enthusiast of extemporary poetry.

The two adjectives are derived from the Latin expression *extempore*, 'the act of doing something without any previous preparation or the state of existing at the moment'. Nevertheless, construal exposes a difference between them in use. In (16a), the adjective *extemporaneous* means 'characterised by extempore'. An extemporaneous speech is one that is done or said without any preparation or thought in advance. *Extemporaneous* collocates with nouns referring to people's vocal actions such as *address, oration, recital, sermon, speech*, etc. In (16b), the adjective *extemporary* means 'relating closely to extempore'.

Extemporary poetry is poetry that relates to the time being or made for the occasion. *Extemporary* collocates with nouns referring to people's literary or artistic performances such as *composition, essay, painting, poetry, verse*, etc.

(17) contemporaneous vs. contemporary
a. This work is contemporaneous with his active period.
b. The students like contemporary, not classical, music.

The two adjectives are derived from the Latin expression *contemporane*, 'the state of existing at the same time or belonging to the present time'. Nevertheless, construal exposes a difference between them in use. In (17a), the adjective *contemporaneous* means 'characterised by contemporane'. A contemporaneous work is one that exists or occurs at the same time as another. *Contemporaneous* collocates with nouns referring to people's actions such as *development, interaction, investment, study, work*, etc. In (17b), the adjective *contemporary* means 'relating closely to contemporane'. Contemporary music is music that exists or happens now or is up-to-date. *Contemporary* collocates with nouns referring to works of art such as *architecture, film, movie, music, painting*, etc.

(18) momentous vs. momentary
a. No one knows the motives behind his momentous decision.
b. His visits gave his grandparents some momentary pleasure.

The two adjectives are derived from the noun *moment*, 'a very short period of time'. Nevertheless, construal exposes a difference between them in use. In (18a), the adjective *momentous* means 'characterised by moment'. A momentous decision is one that is important or serious because of its effects on future events. *Momentous* collocates with nouns referring to people's actions such as *announcement, claim, decision, declaration, deliberation*, etc. In (18b), the adjective *momentary* means 'relating closely to moment'. A momentary pleasure is one that lasts for only a moment, or has a brief life. *Momentary* collocates with nouns referring to feelings such as *disappointment, excitement, impatience, pleasure, satisfaction*; breaks such as *halt, hiatus, interlude, lapse, pause*, etc.

5.5 Interaction between de-verbal and de-nominal domains

In the preceding sections, I explained interaction between suffixes belonging to the same domains. In this section, I shed light on interaction between suffixes belonging to separate domains, i.e. de-verbal and de-nominal ones. Recall from Chapter 1 that prototypically an adjective pair shares the same word class and displays a contrast in the suffixes only. The majority of the adjective pairs that have been analysed so far fit this requirement. In what follows, some of the adjective pairs are marginal. By marginal, I mean the adjectives contrast in both the suffixes and the word class of the root. I take such pairs because they still compete and may be confused by most speakers. In order to avoid repetition, I will define the root once, relying on the function that is widely used.

5.5.1 The agentive- exhibitive distinction *–ive vs. –ful*

The suffixes *–ive* and *–ful* represent different categories and domains. The suffix *–ive* is de-verbal and belongs to the domain of *voice*. It means 'performing or tending to perform the action referred to in the verbal root'. The suffix *–ful* is de-nominal and belongs to the domain of *possession*. It means 'full of the thing denoted by the nominal root'. A full investigation of the concordances in the corpus shows that adjectives ending in *–ive* prefer nouns referring to people's actions or approaches. By contrast, adjectives ending in *–ful* prefer nouns referring to people and their character, or places and their mood. To comprehend the distinction, let us discuss some adjective pairs:

(19) deceptive vs. deceitful
a. The language was misleading and deceptive.
b. Alice was a crafty and deceitful old woman.

The two adjectives are derived from word classes of the same root, but the construal represented by each adjective is quite specific. In (19a), the adjective *deceptive* is derived from the verb *deceive*, which means 'to persuade someone that something false is true'. It means 'tending to deceive'. A deceptive language is one that tends to make a mistaken impression, which is not intentional. *Deceptive* collocates with nouns referring to communication such as *discourse, expression, language, speech, statement*; customary action such as *action, method, mode, practice, way*; quality such as *depth, immediacy, mildness, physicality, simplicity*, etc. In (19b), the adjective *deceitful* is derived from the noun *deceit*, which means 'an act of keeping the truth hidden, especially to get an advantage'. It means 'full of deceit'. A deceitful person is a person who is full of tricks, intending to mislead to gain an advantage, which is intentional. *Deceitful* collocates with nouns referring to people and their nature.

(20) purposive vs. purposeful
a. Teaching is a purposive policy.
b. She looks quiet and purposeful.

The two adjectives are derived from the noun *purpose*, 'an intention or aim', but the construal represented by each adjective is quite specific. In (20a), the adjective *purposive* means 'tending to serve'. A purposive policy is a policy that tends to fulfil a design or adapt something to some end. *Purposive* collocates with nouns referring to ways of dealing with something such as *approach, method, policy, strategy, style*, etc. As is seen, in this example the suffix *–ive* is attached to a nominal root, not a verbal one as it prototypically does. In (20b), the adjective *purposeful* means 'full of purpose'. A purposeful person is a person who is goal-directed and knows what she wants to do. *Purposeful* collocates with nouns referring to people or their actions.

(21) restive vs. restful
 a. He has been growing restive under their close supervision.
 b. It was a modern hotel with a quiet and restful atmosphere.

The two adjectives are derived from word classes of the same root, but the construal represented by each adjective is quite specific. In (21a), the adjective *restive* is derived from the verb *rest*, which means 'to stop doing a particular activity either to show discontent or to relax'. It means 'tending to rest'. A restive person is a person who tends to resist control because he is bored or not satisfied with the way something is being done. *Restive* collocates with nouns referring to people such as *audience, crowds, mourners, population, working class*, etc. Generally, *restive* is used with the word *horse* to mean 'resisting control', as in *The horse became restive and attempted to throw its rider*. In (21b), the adjective *restful* is derived from the noun *rest*, which means 'a period of time in which one stops doing a particular activity'. It means 'full of rest'. A restful hotel is a hotel that is full of repose, free from strife or disturbance. *Restful* collocates with nouns referring to places such as *hotel, inn, lounge, pub, room*; their mood or tone such as *atmosphere, background, environment, milieu*, etc.

The two adjectives are, but the construal represented by each adjective is quite specific.

5.5.2 The agentive-characteristic distinction *–ive vs. –ous*

The suffixes *–ive* and *–ous* represent different categories and domains. The suffix *–ive* is de-verbal and activates the domain of *voice*. It means 'performing or tending to perform the action referred to in the verbal root'. The suffix *–ous* is de-nominal and activates the domain of *possession*. It means 'characterised by the thing denoted by the nominal root'. A thorough investigation of the concordances in the corpus shows that adjectives ending in *–ive* collocate with nouns referring to the actions people take, whereas adjectives ending in *–ous* collocate with nouns referring to the people themselves. To appreciate the distinction, let us consider some adjective pairs:

(22) illustrative vs. illustrious

a. The new book contains a lot of illustrative examples.

b. Their special guest comes from an illustrious family.

The two adjectives are derived from the Latin expression *illustrare*, which means 'to embellish or make clear, or distinguish or make famous', but construal keeps them separate in use. In (22a), the adjective *illustrative* means 'tending to illustrate'. An illustrative example is an example that tends to make something clear. *Illustrative* collocates with nouns referring to exemplification such as *cases, examples, patterns, samples, specimens;* drawings such as *charts, diagrams, figures, graphs, pictures*, etc. In a predicative position, it is followed by the preposition *of.* In (22b), the adjective *illustrious* means 'characterised by illustration'. An illustrious person is a person who is characterised by fame by reason of high birth or rank. *Illustrious* collocates with nouns referring to people such as *ancestor, circle, family, forebear, predecessor*; their activities as in *He enjoyed a long and illustrious career as a radio producer.*

(23) presumptive vs. presumptuous

a. The doctor has made a presumptive diagnosis of the disease.

b. It would be presumptuous of him to comment on the matter.

The two adjectives are derived from the verb *presume*, which means 'to think that something is likely to be true although there is no proof', but construal keeps them separate in use. In (23a), the adjective *presumptive* means 'tending to presume'. A presumptive diagnosis is a diagnosis that tends to base judgement on probability rather than certainty. *Presumptive* collocates with nouns referring to close examinations such as *analysis, conclusion, diagnosis, interpretation, result*, etc. In (23b), the adjective *presumptuous* means 'characterised by presumption'. A person who is presumptuous is characterised by impertinence in opinion or conduct, by doing things he has no right or authority to do. *Presumptuous* collocates with nouns referring to people. As the example shows, the adjective occurs mostly in *it*-constructions.

(24) infective vs. infectious

a. The illness is caused by victuals with infective bacteria.

b. Patients who are infectious are usually kept in isolation.

The two adjectives are derived from the verb *infect*, which means 'to pass a disease to a person, animal or plant', but construal keeps them separate in use. In (24a), the adjective *infective* means 'tending to infect'. An infective bacterium is a bacterium that tends to transmit or cause a disease. *Infective* collocates with nouns referring to micro-organisms such as *agent, bacterium, egg, germ, microbe*, etc. In (24b), the adjective *infectious* means 'characterised by infection'. A patient who is infectious has a disease and could pass it to others through contact. *Infectious* collocates with nouns referring to people or the diseases that they carry.

5.5.3 The patientive-exhibitive distinction *–able vs. –ful*

The suffixes *–able* and *–ful* represent different categories and domains. The suffix *–able* is de-verbal and elicits the domain of *voice*. It means 'capable of undergoing the action referred to in the verbal root'. By contrast, the suffix *–ful* is de-nominal and elicits the domain of *possession*. It means 'likely to do the action denoted by the verbal root'. A look at the concordance examples in the corpus indicates that adjectives ending in *–able* accept nouns referring to things, events or processes, whereas adjectives ending in *–ful* accept nouns referring to people, their body parts or reactions, as the adjective pairs below elucidate:

(25) forgettable vs. forgetful
a. He played small roles in a number of forgettable movies.
b. She worries because her mother is getting very forgetful.

The two adjectives are derived from the verb *forget*, which means 'to be unable to remember something that happened in the past', but construal keeps them apart in use. In (25a), the adjective *forgettable* means 'capable of being forgotten'. A forgettable movie is a movie that is capable of being forgotten because it is not important or interesting. *Forgettable* collocates with nouns referring to types of entertainment such as *drama, movie, musical, show, thriller*; events such as *birthday, comeback, game, journey, match*, etc. In (25b), the adjective *forgetful* means 'likely to forget'. A forgetful person is a person who is likely to forget, one who does not remember things, for example owing to old age. *Forgetful* collocates with nouns referring to people such as *child, man, person, pupil, worker*, etc. In most cases, the adjective is followed by the preposition *of*. In *He has become very forgetful of his duties*, the adjective *forgetful* means he pays no attention to his duties.

(26) regrettable vs. regretful
a. The dropout of boys remains regrettable in schools.
b. She cast a last regretful glance towards the entrance.

The two adjectives are derived from the verb *regret*, which means 'to feel sad about something one has done and wish one had not done it', but construal keeps them apart in use. In (26a), the adjective *regrettable* means 'capable of being regretted'. A regrettable dropout is a dropout that may be regretted, one that makes people feel sad. *Regrettable* collocates with nouns referring to processes such as *absence, dropout, manifestation, tendency, transition*; things such as *error, joke, incident, mistake, trouble*, etc. In some cases, the adjective occurs in the pattern *it+be+adj+that*. In (26b), the adjective *regretful* means 'likely to regret'. A regretful glance is a glance that is likely to show remorse because of what is lost, gone or done. *Regretful* collocates with nouns referring to people or their reactions such *glance, look, shrug, sigh, smile*[41], etc.

(27) watchable vs. watchful

a. It's not the most profound film I've ever seen, but it's very watchable.

b. The boys played on the shore under the watchful eye of their mother.

The two adjectives are derived from the verb *watch*, which means 'to look at something that is happening', but construal keeps them apart in use. In (27a), the adjective *watchable* means 'capable of being watched'. A watchable film is a film that is capable of being watched, one that is worthy of observation. It is not a great film or particularly well made but it tells a good story and is lightly entertaining. *Watchable* collocates with nouns referring to types of entertainment such as *drama, film, movie, performance, thriller*, etc. In (27b), the adjective *watchful* means 'likely to watch'. A watchful eye is an eye that is observant or attentive. *Watchful* collocates with nouns referring to people or their body parts[42].

5.5.4 The patientive-abundant distinction *–able vs. –ous*

The suffixes *–able* and *–ous* represent different categories and domains. The suffix *–ive* is de-verbal and belongs to the domain of *voice*. It means 'capable of undergoing the action referred to in the verbal root'. The suffix *–ous* is de-nominal and belongs to the domain of *possession*. It means 'abounding in the thing denoted by the nominal root'. A glance at the concordance examples in the corpus demonstrates that adjectives ending in *–able* co-occur with nouns describing things or processes, whereas adjectives ending in *–ous* co-occur with nouns describing people, their actions or behaviour, as the adjective pairs below illuminate:

(28) desirable vs. desirous

a. Reducing the size of classes in schools is a desirable aim.

b. The Smith family was desirous of a truly elegant abode.

The two adjectives are derived from the verb *desire*, which means 'to want something strongly', but they go separate ways in usage. In (28a), the adjective *desirable* means 'capable of being desired'. A desirable aim is an aim that is capable of being achieved because of its pleasing properties. *Desirable* collocates with nouns referring to a purpose such as *aim, end, goal, plan, target*; objects such as *car, goods, house, product, property*; processes such as *change, development, increase, progress, speed*, etc. In (28b), the adjective *desirous* means 'abounding in desire'. A family that is desirous of an abode abounds in eagerness to have an elegant place for living. *Desirous* collocates with nouns referring to people, and is mostly followed by the prepositions *of* or *to*.

(29) enviable vs. envious
a. Germany has notched up an enviable record in sports.
b. Catherine is very envious of her neighbour's new car.

The two adjectives are derived from the verb *envy*, which means 'to wish that one had something that another person has', but they go separate ways in usage. In (29a), the adjective *enviable* means 'capable of being envied'. An enviable record is a record that is capable of being envied. It is often used as a term of praise. *Enviable* collocates with nouns implying esteem such as *position, record, renown, reputation, status*, etc. In (29b), the adjective *envious* means 'abounding in envy'. A person who is envious abounds in wishes that she had what another person has. It is often used in an unpleasant way. *Envious* collocates with nouns denoting people. It is mostly followed by the preposition *of*. As evidence, *envious* can only combine with negative adjectives as in *Ralph watched them, envious and resentful*.

(30) pitiable vs. piteous
a. The refugees were in a pitiable state.
b. She heard her daughter's piteous sob.

The two adjectives are derived from the verb *pity*, which means 'to feel sympathy for someone', but they go separate ways in usage. In (30a), the adjective *pitiable* means 'capable of being pitied'. A pitiable state is a state that is capable of being sympathised. *Pitiable* collocates mostly with nouns referring to a state of affairs or a set of circumstances such as *circumstance, condition, shape, situation, state*, etc. In (30b), the adjective *piteous* means 'abounding in pity'. A piteous sob is a cry that abounds in suffering and inspires sympathy. *Piteous* collocates with nouns referring to acts of suffering such as *cry, moan, sigh, sob, wail*, etc. In *Don't expect anybody to believe such a pitiful excuse*, the adjective *pitiful* means shameful, i.e. not good enough to deserve a serious consideration.

5.5.5 The patientive-abundant distinction *–ible* vs. *–ous*

The suffixes *–ible* and *–ous* represent different categories and domains. The suffix *–ible* is de-verbal and evokes the domain of *voice*. It means 'capable of undergoing the action referred to in the verbal root'. The suffix *–ous* is de-nominal and evokes the domain of *possession*. It means 'abounding in the thing denoted by the nominal root'. Casting a look in the concordances in the corpus reveals that adjectives ending in both suffixes are said of persons and their deeds. However, with adjectives ending in *–ible* the subject is either judged by other people or ushered to take a certain course of action. By contrast, with adjectives ending in *–ous* the subject judges other people or takes a certain course of action, as the adjective pairs below depict:

(31) contemptible vs. contemptuous
 a. What the rector has done is contemptible.
 b. The boss was contemptuous of her efforts.

The two adjectives are derived from the noun *contempt*, 'a feeling of disrespect for someone or something'. However, they show a difference in use, which is ascribed to construal. In (31a), the adjective *contemptible* means 'capable of being looked on with contempt'. A contemptible deed is a deed that is capable of being despised. *Contemptible* collocates with nouns referring to people or their deeds such as *argument, dispute, row, squabble, wrangle*; ways of thinking such as *attitude, opinion, outlook, perspective, viewpoint*, etc. In (31b), the adjective *contemptuous* means 'abounding in contempt'. A contemptuous view is a view that abounds in scorn or disdain. *Contemptuous* collocates with nouns referring to people or their deeds such as *expression, phrase, remark, statement, word*, etc. The adjective is mostly followed by the preposition *of*.

(32) sensible vs. sensuous
 a. It would be sensible to take an umbrella.
 b. She plays the role of a sensuous woman.

The two adjectives are derived from the noun *sense*, 'the ability to judge or react to something'. However, they show a difference in use, which is ascribed to construal. In (32a), the adjective *sensible* means 'capable of being sensed'. A sensible action is an action that is based on reason rather than emotion. *Sensible* collocates with nouns referring to people or their modes of procedure such as *approach, method, mode, plan, policy*, etc. The adjective mostly occurs in *it*-constructions. In (32b), the adjective *sensuous* means 'abounding in sense'. A sensuous woman is a woman who abounds in pleasure and exhibits it through the physical senses. *Sensuous* collocates with nouns referring to people or their body parts such as *eye, face, hair, lip, mouth*, etc.

5.5.6 The patientive-manner distinction *–able* vs. *–ly*

The suffixes *–able* and *–ly* represent different categories and domains. The suffix *–ible* is de-verbal and demands the domain of *voice*. It means 'capable of undergoing the action referred to in the verbal root'. The root implies a quality that describes character and personality. The suffix *–ly* is de-nominal and demands the domain of *evaluation*. It means 'having the manner of the thing specified by the nominal root'. The root implies a quality that describes appearance and behaviour. Casting a glance in the concordances in the corpus shows a difference in the behaviour of the two suffixes. Adjectives ending in *–able* are prototypically used with nouns referring to objects, things or places, whereas adjectives ending in *–ly* are prototypically used with nouns referring to people or their actions, as we see from the adjective pairs below:

(33) cleanable vs. cleanly
 a. It is only a hearth of cleanable brick.
 b. The girl is a plain but cleanly maid.

The two adjectives are derived from the verb *clean*, which means 'to remove dirt from something by rubbing or washing'. However, they display a difference in use, which is related to construal. In (33a), the adjective *cleanable* means 'capable of being cleaned'. A cleanable brick is a brick that is capable of being cleaned. *Cleanable* often collocates with nouns referring to objects. In (33b), the adjective *cleanly* means 'having a clean manner'. A cleanly person is a person who is habitually clean or carefully neat. *Cleanly* often collocates with nouns referring to people or their actions.

(34) likeable vs. likely
 a. He had a long career in likeable films.
 b. Her flatmate is a likely young woman.

The two adjectives are derived from the verb *like*, which means 'to enjoy or approve of something or someone'. However, they display a difference in use, which is related to construal. In (34a), the adjective *likeable* means 'capable of being liked'. A likeable film is a film that is capable of being liked because it has attractive or interesting qualities. *Likeable* collocates with nouns referring to types of entertainment such as *film, musical, programme, show, thriller*, etc[43]. In (34b), the adjective *likely* means 'having a likely manner'. A likely woman is a woman who is pleasant and attractive. *Likely* collocates with nouns referring to people or their actions.

(35) liveable vs. lively
 a. The apartment is liveable although it's far from perfect.
 b. They are looking for some energetic and lively people.

The two adjectives are derived from the verb *live*, which means 'to continue to be alive or have life'. However, they display a difference in use, which is related to construal. In (35a), the adjective *liveable* means 'capable of being lived in'. A liveable apartment is an apartment that is suitable to live in. *Liveable* collocates with nouns referring to accommodation such as *apartment, flat, house, lodgings, penthouse*, etc. In (35b), the adjective *lively* means 'having a lively manner'[44]. A lively person is a person who has a lot of energy or shows exciting thought. *Lively* collocates with nouns referring to people or their actions[45].

5.5.7 The patientive-essential distinction *–able* vs. *–al*

The suffixes *–able* and *–al* represent different categories and domains. The suffix *–able* is de-verbal and belongs to the domain of *voice*. It means 'capable of undergoing the action referred to in the verbal root'. In this function, the suffix evokes either positive or negative qualities. The suffix *–al* is de-nominal and belongs to the domain of *relation*. It means 'relating closely to the thing named by the nominal root'. A consideration of the concordance lines produced sheds light on a difference in the use of the two suffixes. Adjectives ending in *–able* are used with nouns referring to things that cause suffering, blueprints or processes, whereas adjectives ending in *–al* are used with nouns referring to people's possessions, activities or things, as shown by the adjective pairs below:

(36) practicable vs. practical
 a. In brief, it is an interesting strategy, but it is just not practicable.
 b. Qualifications are important but practical experience is an asset.

The two adjectives are derived from word classes of the same root, but there is a boundary that separates them in use. In (36a), the adjective *practicable* is derived from the verb *practise*, which means 'to do something regularly to become skilled at it'. It means 'capable of being practised'. A practicable strategy is a strategy that is capable of being put into practice. *Practicable* collocates with nouns referring to blueprints such as *design, plan, project, scheme, strategy*; processes such as *advocacy, amalgamation, deployment, production, solution*, etc. In (36b), the adjective *practical* is derived from the noun *practice*, which means 'action rather than thought'. It means 'relating closely to practice'. Practical experience is experience that relates to reality rather than theory. *Practical* collocates with nouns referring to knowledge gained by observation or trial such as *experience, expertise, knowledge, observation, skill*; ways of achieving something such as *measure, move, procedure, proceeding, step*; counselling such as *advice, counsel, guidance, hints, tips*; pieces of work such as *assignment, duty, errand, task, work*; subjects of debate such as *affair, issue, matter, problem, question*, etc[46].

(37) remediable vs. remedial

a. The doctor assured him that the disease is remediable.

b. He took remedial exercises to improve his reading skill.

The two adjectives are derived from word classes of the same root, but there is a boundary that separates them in use. In (37a), the adjective *remediable* is derived from the verb *remedy*, which means 'to do something to correct or improve something that is wrong'. It means 'capable of being remedied'. A remediable disease is a disease that is capable of being cured. *Remediable* collocates with nouns referring to things that cause suffering such as *affliction, defect, deficiency, disease, harm*, etc. In (37b), the adjective *remedial* is derived from the noun *remedy*, which is 'a successful way of dealing with a problem or curing an illness'. It means 'relating closely to remedy'. Remedial exercises are exercises that relate to remedy, intended to improve one's faulty habits or raise one's general competence. *Remedial* collocates with nouns referring to assignments such as *drills, exercises, homework, lessons, practice*; actions to achieve a purpose such as *action, approach, course, measure, step*, etc.

(38) seasonable vs. seasonal

a. They sought a seasonable time for discussion with the union.

b. The stalls in the market were piled with seasonal vegetables.

The two adjectives are derived from the noun *season*, 'one of the four periods in a year; spring, summer, autumn or winter', but there is a boundary that separates them in use. In (38a), the adjective *seasonable* means 'capable of being opportune'. A seasonable time is a time that is capable of being used to hold a discussion. *Seasonable* collocates with nouns referring to the time when something happens; weather conditions such as *frost, heat, shower, snow, temperatures*, etc. In (38b), the adjective *seasonal* means 'relating closely to season', i.e. seasons of the year, or one of them. Seasonal vegetables are vegetables that grow and are sold during a particular period in the year. *Seasonal* collocates with nouns referring to fruits; vegetables; festivities; employment as a means of livelihood such as *employment, job, occupation, trade, work*, etc[47].

5.5.8 The patientive-qualitative distinction –*able* vs. –*y*

The suffixes –*able* and –*y* represent different categories and domains. The suffix –*able* is de-verbal and belongs to the domain of *voice*. It means 'capable of undergoing the action referred to in the verbal root'. The suffix –*y* is de-nominal and belongs to the domain of *resemblance*. It means 'resembling the thing designated by the nominal root in quality'. The suffix adds a special meaning to the root. Browsing through the concordances in the corpus shows that adjectives ending in *–able* collocate with nouns naming objects, while adjectives ending in *–y* collocate with nouns highlighting characteristics of things, as illustrated by the adjective pairs below:

(39) breathable vs. breathy
a. The air in the countryside is breathable. What about having a picnic?
b. 'I'll get a doctor,' he said, his voice was breathy and distorted with shock.

The two adjectives are derived from the noun *breath*, 'the air that you take into and let out of your lungs', but there is a line that divides them in use. In (39a), the adjective *breathable* means 'capable of being breathed'. Breathable air is air that is capable of being inhaled. *Breathable* collocates with nouns referring to objects such as *jacket, leggings, shoe, trousers, uppers*; cloth materials such as *fabric, fibre, leather, linen, nylon*; and the word *air*. With cloth materials, the suffix means 'able to breath', where metaphorically the material lets air in and out to keep the wearer cool or dry. In (39b), the adjective *breathy* means 'resembling breath in quality'. A breathy voice is a voice that resembles breath in being heard. *Breathy* collocates with nouns referring to vocal utterances such as *conversation, cry, talk, voice, whisper*, etc.

(40) fishable vs. fishy
a. The pond nearby is fishable.
b. This chicken has a fishy taste.

The two adjectives are derived from the noun *fish*, 'an animal that lives in water, and uses its fins and tail to swim', but there is a line that divides them in use. In (40a), the adjective *fishable* means 'capable of being fished in'. A fishable pond is a pond that is fit for fishing. *Fishable* collocates with nouns referring to water areas such as *lake, pond, river, water, waterway*, etc. In (40b), the adjective *fishy* means 'resembling fish in quality'. A fishy chicken is a chicken that resembles fish in taste or odour. *Fishy* collocates with nouns referring to characteristics of food such as *flavour, odour, scent, smell, taste*, etc. In *There is something fishy going on here*, the adjective means 'dishonest'.

(41) smokable vs. smoky
a. Are these cigars or cigarettes smokable?
b. This meat has a delicious smoky flavour.

The two adjectives are derived from the noun *smoke*, 'grey gas that is produced from something burnt', but there is a line that divides them in use. In (41a), the adjective *smokable* means 'capable of being smoked'. A smokable cigarette is a cigarette that is pleasant when smoked. *Smokable* collocates with nouns referring to smoking substances. In (41b), the adjective *smoky* means 'resembling smoke in quality'. Smoky flavour is flavour that resembles smoke in taste. *Smoky* collocates with nouns referring to characteristics of food such as *flavour, odour, scent, smell, taste*, etc. With names of places as in *This café is too smoky for me,* the adjective means filled with smoke.

5.5.9 The stative-inducive distinction *–ed* vs. *–some*

The suffixes *–ed* and *–some* represent different categories and domains. The suffix *–ed* is de-verbal and calls forth the domain of *aspect*. It means 'being in the state signified by the verbal root'. The suffix *–some* is de-nominal and calls forth the domain of *possession*. It means 'causing or inspiring the thing denoted by the nominal root'. Raking through the concordances in the corpus signals a difference in their use. Adjectives ending in *–ed* collocate with nouns referring to people, their body parts or things, whereas adjectives ending in *–some* collocate with nouns referring to people, their activities or afflictions. To illustrate the distinction, here are some adjective pairs:

(42) loathed vs. loathsome
a. He was the most loathed teacher in the school.
b. He was loathsome, unpredictable and violent.

The two adjectives are derived from the verb *loathe*, which means 'to hate someone or something very much'. Yet, construal marks a difference between them in usage. In (42a), the adjective *loathed* means 'being loathed'. A loathed teacher is a teacher who is hated by other people because he is strict. *Loathed* collocates with nouns referring to people, school curriculum or periods of time. In (42b), the adjective *loathsome* means 'causing or inspiring loathing'. A loathsome person is a person who inspires strong feelings of hate because he intends to harm or upset other people. *Loathsome* collocates with nouns referring to people; wrongdoings such as *crime, murder, offence, terror*, *transgression*; illnesses such as *ailment, disease, disorder, infirmity, malady*, etc.

(43) tired vs. tiresome
a. She spoke in a tired voice.
b. Weeding is a tiresome job.

The two adjectives are derived from the verb *tire*, which means 'to feel that you want to rest or sleep'. Yet, construal marks a difference between them in usage. In (43a), the adjective *tired* means 'being tired'. A tired voice is a voice that is drained of strength and energy by exertion. *Tired* collocates with nouns referring to people or their body parts such as *arms, eyes, feet, legs, voice*, etc. In (43b), the adjective *tiresome* means 'causing or inspiring tiredness'. A tiresome job is a job that causes annoyance by reasons of continuance, sameness or lack of interest. *Tiresome* collocates with nouns referring to people or their activities such as *business, commerce, dealings, trade, transactions*; pieces of work such as *duty, job, mission, task, undertaking*, etc.

(44) worried vs. worrisome

a. Worried people do not concentrate, hear or understand so well as usual.

b. The travelling burglars are worrisome because they are hard to catch.

The two adjectives are derived from the verb *worry*, which means 'to think about a problem which makes you feel anxious'. Yet, construal marks a difference between them in usage. In (44a), the adjective *worried* means 'being worried'. A worried person is a person who is affected, troubled or distressed by worry. *Worried* collocates with nouns referring to people. Very often, the adjective is used predicatively. In this case, it is followed by the preposition *about*. In (44b), the adjective *worrisome* means 'causing or inspiring worry'. A worrisome person is a person who causes worry or distress. *Worrisome* collocates with nouns referring to people, states of health such as *condition, harm, injury, state, wound*, etc.

5.5.10 The stative-trait distinction *–ed vs. –y*

The suffixes *–ed* and *–y* are attached to nouns referring to body parts to form adjectives, but with a difference in use. The suffix *–ed* is tacked on to a noun referring to a body part but used with a certain feature. The suffix is de-verbal and brings up the domain of *aspect*. It means 'having a particular kind of the thing specified by the nominal root'. The suffix *–y* is tacked on to a noun referring to a body part but used alone. The suffix is de-nominal and brings up the domain of *evaluation*. It means 'having the trait of the thing designated by the nominal root'. This use occurs mostly in colloquial English, or slang senses. Vetting the concordances in the corpus throws some light on the use of the suffixes. Both collocate with nouns referring to people, but there is a difference. Adjectives ending in *–ed* refer to appearance, whereas those ending in *–y* refer to character or personal attributes. Adjectives ending in *–y*, sometimes, collocate with nouns denoting unpleasant persons like *sod, swine*, and suchlike. As evidence, adjectives ending in *–y* usually combine with other adjectives implying negative qualities, as in *She is raucous, chesty and cynical.* To illuminate the distinction, here are some adjective pairs:

(45) cheeked vs. cheeky

a. He was rosy-cheeked after his jogging in the park.

b. 'Don't be so cheeky, Jack', complained the lady.

The two adjectives are derived from the noun *cheek*, 'the soft part of your face which is below your eye and between your mouth and ear'. Still, construal causes a difference between them in usage. In (45a), the adjective *cheeked* means 'having a particular kind of cheek'. Rosy-cheeked is cheek that is healthy. In (45b), the adjective *cheeky* means 'having the trait of rudeness'. A cheeky person is a person who is insolent.

(46) chested vs. chesty

a. She doesn't appeal to him. She is rather flat-chested.

b. They won the tournament, so they were pretty chesty.

The two adjectives are derived from the noun *chest*, 'the upper front part of the body of humans and some animals, between the stomach and the neck, enclosing the heart and lungs'. Still, construal causes a difference between them in usage. In (46a), the adjective *chested* means 'having a particular kind of chest'. Flat-chested is chest that is unattractive, i.e. she has small breasts. In (46b), the adjective *chesty* means 'having the trait of conceit'. A chesty person is a person who is boastful.

(47) lipped vs. lippy

a. He's been tight-lipped about what happened at the meeting.

b. On a few occasions, she can get a bit lippy with her parents.

The two adjectives are derived from the noun *lip*, which refers to 'one of the two narrow pieces of flesh which form the top and bottom edges of the mouth and are darker than the surrounding skin'. Still, construal causes a difference between them in usage. In (47a), the adjective *lipped* means 'having a particular kind of lip'. Tight-lipped is lip that is angry, i.e. he is pressing his lips together to avoid showing anger or to refuse to speak about something. In (47b), the adjective *lippy* means 'having the trait of disrespect'. A lippy person is a person who is discourteous[48].

6 Conclusions

This study has dealt with the semantics of adjective formation in English, namely the process of deriving an adjective by adding a suffix to the final position of a root. In adjective formation, three changes take place: phonological, categorial and semantic. Of the three changes, the present study has handled the last one because of the new contribution it makes to the topic of word formation. The main concern of the study has been to illustrate the fact that meaning is an emergent phenomenon. Meaning emerges as a result of the interaction between a given root and a given suffix, which make up a composite adjective. In other words, the meaning of a complex adjective consists of both conceptual content represented by the root and construal represented by the suffix. The specific concern of the study has been to testify to the fact that suffixes have meanings of their own which they contribute to the formations in which they appear. To establish their specificity, suffixes have been treated as rivals and exemplified in adjective pairs. The existence of adjective pairs has helped to identify the semantic information imparted by the rival suffixes and explore the nuances expressed by them.

To address the issue of rivalry between pairs of suffixes and the adjectives they derive and to ensure the best results, the study has integrated the insights of two linguistic methods: theoretical and empirical. This is so because the approach adopted here recognises no division between theoretical and empirical methods. The study has shown how the two methods can coexist to give a detailed description of the way language is used. The theoretical method makes the necessary assumptions, while the empirical method provides the tools to verify them. For the theoretical method, language is subjective knowledge stored in the mind of the speaker, whereas for the empirical method language is usage patterns produced by the speaker. The goal was to present a detailed corpus-based analysis of adjectival suffixation in English within the framework of CS. During the analysis, the study has invoked some of their key principles. Based on such principles, the study has put forward a number of hypotheses and attempted to check their validity through rigorous argumentation, extensive illustration and empirical evidence.

6.1 Theoretical findings

The theoretical method adopted in the present study is represented by CS, a theory that studies the relationship between the mind of the speaker and the language used to code his/her conceptualisations. CS holds a special stance on the nature of meaning, and its stance follows from its general principles. The first principle views language as part and parcel of cognition and describes linguistic structures with reference to cognitive processes. These processes are responsible for organising knowledge in the human mind and expressing it in linguistic form. The second principle concentrates on the correlation between form and meaning, and stipulates that the linguistic structure of an expression reflects its conceptual structure. This is called *empiricist* because it presupposes knowledge to be the product of embodied experience. The third principle attaches importance to the human being in providing the basic meanings coded in language, and recognises his/her capacity to construe a given situation in alternate ways.

Below are the specific principles of CS that the study has substantiated and the findings that the study has arrived at.

6.1.1 Suffixes form networks of interrelated senses

The first principle of CS, which the study has confirmed, is that there are no semantically empty forms in language. A form is always created to meet a requirement in language. This has two implications. One implication is that as forms all lexical items are attributed semantic values, which motivate their linguistic behaviour. Linguistic items are pairings of form and meaning, which are connected by conceptual considerations. In Chapter 2, the study has explored this principle with regard to the description of adjectival suffixes. A suffix was argued to be meaningful, and its presence adds semantic import to the construction in which it occurs. A suffix functions as the profile determinant of the host construction because it is responsible for its character and because it shares a semantic correspondence with it. The specific form of a suffix is motivated by its conceptual organisation, and thus inseparable from it. Every suffix is a vehicle of a certain meaning. This means that suffixal alternatives available to the speaker should not be treated on an equal footing.

Another implication is that a linguistic item, morphological or lexical, involves categorisation. A linguistic item is polysemous by nature, and its alternate senses compose a category. These senses form a network which is structured in terms of prototype and periphery. The prototype of a lexical item represents its central sense, from which other senses can somehow be extended. The prototype is usually the most frequent sense and the first sense which is learnt in acquiring a language. The periphery of a lexical item comprises its other senses, regular and irregular, which are linked to the prototype via extensions. The study has explored this principle in relation to the description of adjectival suffixes. A suffix was argued to be polysemous, and its categorisation requires specifying its prototypical as well as peripheral senses. The aim was to underpin the *prototype* approach, one stipulation of which is that the different senses of a lexical item can be analysed by referring to the typical example of the category they form.

For easy reference, the multiple senses of the adjectival suffixes presented in Chapter 2 are summarised in the following tables. The first table sums up de-verbal bound suffixes, the second sums up de-nominal bound suffixes, and the third sums up de-nominal free suffixes.

Note that ■ represents the prototype, ♦ represents direct extensions and ● represents indirect extensions.

Table 1: The multiple senses of de-verbal bound suffixes forming adjectives in English

suffix	prototype	periphery
-able	■ 'capable of undergoing the action referred to in the verbal root', as in *a washable shirt* ♦ 'capable of doing the action referred to in the verbal root', as in *perishable food* ♦ 'capable of doing or undergoing the action referred to in the verbal root', as in *an adaptable worker*	● 'worthy of or deserving the quality referred to in the nominal root', as in *a habitable area* ● 'having or showing the quality referred to in the nominal root', as in *a knowledgeable debater*
-ant	■ 'liable to do the action signified by the verbal root', as in *a defiant protester* ♦ 'apt to do the action signified by the verbal root', as in *a compliant child*	● 'being in the condition signified by the verbal root', as in *a radiant bride*
-ed	■ 'affected by the action referred to in the verbal root', as in *an excited crowd* ♦ 'having been in the state signified by the verbal root', as in *a retired officer*	● 'demonstrating the feature signified by the nominal root', as in *a bearded man* ● 'implying the feature signified by the nominal root', as in *a cultured woman*

-en	■ 'being in the state designated by the verbal root', as in *a forbidden subject*	• 'resembling the thing designated by the nominal root in make', as in *a wooden fence* • 'situated in the region expressed by the nominal root', as in *an eastern suburb*
-ible	■ 'capable of undergoing the action referred to in the verbal root', as in *a discernible difference* ♦ 'capable of doing the action referred to in the verbal root', as in *a collapsible chair* ♦ 'capable of doing or undergoing the action referred to in the verbal root', as in *a flexible sole*	• 'involving the quality referred to in the nominal root', as in *a forcible entry* • having or showing the quality referred to the nominal root', as in *a sensible person*
-ing	■ 'causing the action referred to in the verbal root', as in *an interesting programme* ♦ 'keep on the activity signified by the verbal root', as in *a recurring crisis*	
-ive	■ 'performing or tending to perform the action referred to in the verbal root', as in *a creative designer* ♦ 'apt to do the action signified by the verbal root', as in *a responsive engine* ♦ 'performing or apt to perform the action referred to in the verbal root', as in *protective clothing*	• 'marked by the quality named by the nominal root', as in *an abusive practice*
-ory	■ 'performing or tending to perform the action referred to in the verbal root', as in *an accusatory look* ♦ 'apt to do the action referred to in the verbal root', as in *a retaliatory measure* ♦ 'performing or apt to perform the action referred to in the verbal root', as in *an advisory board*	• 'associated with the quality described by the nominal root', as in *a respiratory disease* • 'containing the quality described by the nominal root', as in *a declamatory style*

Table 2: The multiple senses of de-nominal bound suffixes forming adjectives in English

suffix	prototype	periphery
-al	■ 'relating closely to the thing named by the nominal root', as in *an environmental issue* ♦ 'showing the location of the thing named by the nominal root', as in *a coastal town* ♦ 'showing the proportion of the thing named by the nominal root', as in *an occasional vacation*	• 'showing the character of the thing named by the nominal root', as in *a brutal dictator*
-ary	■ 'relating closely to the thing named by the nominal root', as in *a budgetary policy* ♦ 'serving to do the thing named by the nominal root', as in *a complementary service*	• 'embodying the characteristics of the entity referred to by the nominal root', as in *a legendary broadcaster*
-ful	■ 'full of the thing denoted by the nominal root', as in *an eventful period* ♦ 'giving rise to the quality denoted by the nominal root', as in *a painful memory* ♦ 'displaying the quality denoted by the nominal root', as in *a manful attempt*	• 'full of the quality denoted by the nominal root', as in *a powerful person* • 'featuring the quality denoted by the nominal root', as in *a delightful neighbour* • 'likely to do the action denoted by the verbal root', as in *a forgetful child*
-ic	■ 'pertaining to the thing named by the nominal root', as in *a telegraphic apparatus* ♦ 'pertaining to the place or the language named by the nominal root', as in *an Icelandic language* ♦ 'having the element named by the nominal root to a high degree', as in *chloric acid* ♦ 'pertaining to the typical feature of the thing named by the nominal root', as in *a philosophic stance*	• 'applying the typical feature of the thing named by the nominal root', as in *an optimistic person* • 'pertaining to the person named by the nominal root', as in *Byronic style*
-ical	■ 'pertaining to the thing named by the nominal root', as in *a philosophical essay*	

-ish	■ 'having the character of the thing specified by the nominal root', as in *a raffish appearance* ♦ 'given to or preoccupied with the thing specified by the nominal root', as in *a bookish reader* ♦ 'coming from or belonging to the thing specified by the nominal root', as in *a Finnish student* ♦ 'having the quality specified by the root to some degree', as in *a purplish birthmark*	• 'having the character of the thing specified by the nominal root', as in *a foolish person*
-ly	■ 'having the manner of the thing specified by the nominal root', as in *a leisurely action* ♦ 'moving towards or coming from the point specified by the nominal root', as in *an easterly wind* ♦ 'recurring with the regularity of the thing specified by the nominal root', as in *a daily shower* ♦ 'bearing the character of the thing specified by the nominal root', as in *a costly holiday* ♦ 'having the nature of the thing specified by the root', as in *a deadly conversation*	• 'befitting the thing specified by the nominal root', as in *a motherly treatment*
-ous	■ 'abounding in the thing denoted by the nominal root', as in *a dangerous mission* ♦ 'having the element denoted by the nominal root to a low degree', as in *chlorous acid* ♦ 'causing or inspiring the thing denoted by the nominal root', as in *a contentious subject*	• 'filled with the thing denoted by the nominal root', as in *an ambitious athlete* • 'characterised by the thing denoted by the nominal root', as in *a courteous man*
-some	■ 'having the thing denoted by the nominal root', as in *toilsome efforts* ♦ 'causing or inspiring the thing denoted by the joining root', as in *an awesome event* ♦ 'willing to do the thing denoted by the joining root', as in *a quarrelsome kid*	• 'retaining the thing denoted by the nominal root', as in *a mettlesome team*

-y	■ 'full of the thing specified by the nominal root', as in *a sandy beach* ♦ 'having the content of the thing specified by the nominal root', as in *a cottony pad* ♦ 'having the appearance of the thing specified by the nominal root', as in *baggy trousers* ♦ 'resembling the thing specified by the nominal root in quality', as in *an okay wine* ♦ 'producing or triggering the thing denoted by the verbal root', as in *a chilly pool* ♦ 'suggesting the quality denoted by the adjectival root', as in *greeny purple*	• 'having the trait of the thing designated by the nominal root', as in *a witty remark* • 'tending to do the action denoted by the root', as in *a sleepy baby*

Table 3: The multiple senses of de-nominal free suffixes forming adjectives in English

suffix	prototype	periphery
-based	■ 'the thing expressed by the nominal root forms the most important part of the noun it modifies, as in *an oil-based economy* ♦ 'positioned in but moving around the place expressed by the nominal root', as in *a land-based missile*	• 'the thing expressed by the nominal root forms the most important feature of the noun it modifies', as in *insurance-based health*
-bound	■ 'restricted or confined to the place or environment expressed by the nominal root', as in *a fog-bound ship* ♦ 'leading towards the point expressed by the nominal root', as in *an eastbound train* ♦ 'indicating the sort of covering expressed by the nominal root', as in *a leather-bound book*	• 'being held by or placed under the effect of the thing expressed by the nominal root', as in *a duty-bound official*

-conscious	■ 'aware of the thing (concrete) conveyed by the nominal root', as in *a dress-conscious teenager*	● 'aware of the (abstract) thing conveyed by the nominal root', as in *a budget-conscious businessman*
-free	■ 'lacking the undesirable thing imparted by the nominal root', as in *dust-free furniture* ♦ 'lacking the desirable thing imparted by the nominal root', as in *a child-free gathering*	● 'lacking the undesirable thing imparted by the nominal root', as in *a pain-free operation*
-less	■ 'devoid of the undesirable thing imparted by the nominal root', as in *a flawless performance* ♦ 'devoid of the desirable thing imparted by the nominal root', as in *a characterless room*	● 'devoid of the quality imparted by the nominal root', as in *harmless fun* ● 'unable to perform or have performed the action imparted by the verbal root', as in *countless stamps*
-like	■ 'having the character of the thing specified by the nominal root', as in *godlike power* ♦ 'having the peculiarity of the thing specified by nominal root', as in *a dagger-like claw*	● 'having the characteristic of the thing specified by the adjectival root', as in *a grim-like smile*
-minded	■ 'inclined towards the thing (appearance) conveyed by the nominal root', as in *a chic-minded person*	● 'inclined towards the thing (activity) conveyed by the nominal root', as in *a business-minded chef* ● 'having the tendency conveyed by the adjectival root', as in *broad-minded parents*
-prone	■ 'disposed to the thing conveyed by the nominal root', as in *a mischief-prone child* ♦ 'susceptible to the thing conveyed by the nominal root', as in *an accident-prone child*	● 'susceptible to the thing conveyed by the nominal root', as in *a confusion-prone person*

-related	■ 'relating remotely to the thing named by the nominal root', as in *a school-related enquiry* ♦ 'caused by the thing named by the nominal root', as in *a drink-related fine*	• 'relating remotely to the thing named by the nominal root', as in *a work-related regulation*
-ridden	■ 'plagued by the thing imparted by the nominal root', as in *cyclone-ridden terrain* ♦ 'afflicted by the thing imparted by the nominal root', as in *an acne-ridden face*	• 'cursed by the thing imparted by the nominal root', as in *a crime-ridden city* • 'oppressed by the thing imparted by the nominal root', as in *fear-ridden children*
-stricken	■ 'hit by the thing imparted by the nominal root', as in *a famine-stricken region*	• 'overcome by the thing imparted by the nominal root', as in *a grief-stricken mother*
-style	■ 'resembling the thing designated by the nominal root in mode', as in *a Beatles-style band* ♦ 'akin to the thing designated by the nominal root', as in *antique-style furniture*	• 'of the quality of the thing designated by the adjectival root', as in *an old-style suit*
-type	■ 'resembling the thing designated by the nominal root in specimen', as in *a Swedish-type house* ♦ 'representative of the thing designated by the nominal root', as in *a circus-type room*	• 'of the quality of the thing designated by the adjectival root', as in *domestic-type work*
-ward	■ 'looking towards the point expressed by the nominal root', as in *a northward facade* ♦ 'moving towards the region expressed by the nominal root', as in *ceiling-ward smoke*	• 'describing the inside or the outside of the thing expressed by the preposition', as in *inward interpretation*

6.1.2 Suffixes gather together in cognitive domains

The second principle of CS, which the study has confirmed, is that concepts do not occur as isolated units in the mind, but can only be understood in a context of background knowledge. The generic term for the background knowledge is *domain*, a knowledge configuration that functions as a context for the description of a concept. The ensuing argument is that in order to understand the meaning of a concept the speaker must first invoke knowledge of its conceptual structure, which is derived from experience and gained through practice. The knowledge invoked includes not only the concept in question but also other concepts. These concepts are related in such a way that to understand any one concept it is necessary to understand the entire domain. At the language level, these concepts are realised by different linguistic items. A domain spells out all the similarities and differences that exist among the linguistic items, and in doing so can be used to offer insight into the structure of their semantic values.

In Chapters 3–4, the study has explored this principle with reference to the description of adjective-forming suffixes. A *domain* has been defined as a semantic structure which subsumes a number of adjectival suffixes and provides the basis for their description. A suffix cannot be characterised independently of the domain in which it is embedded. Namely, the semantic value of a suffix can only be specified on the basis of the domain to which it belongs, and in which it contrasts with the other suffixes. To see how this works, the study has first classified adjectival suffixes into de-verbal and de-nominal. Second, the study has grouped the suffixes within each class into separate domains on the basis of semantic similarity. Third, the study has shown, through examples, the specifics of each suffix within the domain. The purpose behind this was to confirm the *domain* approach, one stipulation of which is that the meaning of a lexical item can be identified by comparing it with the other lexical items in the domain to which they belong.

To understand the meanings of the de-verbal suffixes *–ive* and *–ory*, the speaker has to think of the domain of *voice* which they evoke. Both share the general meaning of 'performing or tending to perform the action referred to in the verbal root', but they differ when one gets down to the specifics. The suffix *–ive* underlines an action that an agent initiates and receives, whereas the suffix *–ory* underscores an action that an agent initiates but others receive. Let us demonstrate this through a pair. The adjective pair *delusive* and *delusory* are derived from the verb *delude*, which means 'to make someone believe something that is not true', but they are not synonyms. In *My only guide to the future is delusive hope*, the adjective *delusive* means 'tending to delude'. Delusive hope is hope that tends to deceive its holder. By the evidence of the BNC, the adjective *delusive* collocates with nouns that an agent initiates and receives such as *belief, dream, expectation, faith, hope*, etc. In *They were beguiled by delusory pleasures*, the adjective *delusory* means 'tending to delude'. Delusory pleasure is pleasure that tends to deceive its receiver. By the evidence of the BNC, the adjective *delusory* collocates with nouns that an agent initiates but others receive such as *pleasure, reality, sources, statement, world*, etc.

To understand the meanings of the de-nominal suffixes *–ic* and *–ical*, the speaker has to think of the domain of *relation* which they evoke. Their general meaning is 'pertaining to the thing named by the nominal root', but they differ when one goes into the details. The suffix *–ic* underlines a core property of something, whereas the suffix *–ical* underscores a field of knowledge or scientific terminology. Let us show this through a pair. The adjectives *rhythmic* and *rhythmical* derive from the noun *rhythm*, 'a regular repeated pattern of sounds or movements', but they differ in use. In *Good breathing is rhythmic*, the adjective *rhythmic* means 'pertaining to rhythm'. Rhythmic breathing is breathing that is so repeated that it forms a regular beat. As the BNC testifies, the adjective *rhythmic* collocates with nouns which relate to things other than music, and hence imply no sound such as *breathing, change, energy, lift, movement*, etc. In *They played rhythmical music*, the adjective *rhythmical* means 'pertaining to rhythm'. Rhythmical music is music that involves rhythm. As the BNC verifies, the adjective *rhythmical* collocates with nouns which relate to music, and hence imply sound such as *bass, buzz, dance, hiss, music*, etc.

For easy reference, the (sub)domains presented in Chapters 3 and 4 that adjectival suffixes in English evoke are summarised in the following tables. The first table summarises the (sub)domains evoked by de-verbal suffixes, whereas the second summarises the (sub)domains evoked by de-nominal ones.

Table 4: The (sub)domains evoked by de-verbal adjectival suffixes in English

domains	subdomains	exponents	meaning differences
voice	agentivity	*-ive*	describes an action which an agent initiates and imposes on the self, as in *compulsive gambling*
		-ory	describes an action which an agent initiates and imposes on others, as in *compulsory schooling*
	patientivity	*-able*	describes an action, of specific nature, which a patient undergoes, as in *an accessable file*
		-ible	describes an action, of general nature, which a patient undergoes, as in *an accessible town*

	cause	*-ing*	describes an action which an agent causes, as in *an amusing story*
	effect	*-ed*	describes an effect which a patient receives, as in *an amused child*
aspect	activity	*-ing*	profiles a process which goes on indefinitely, as in *increasing demand*
	state	*-ed*	profiles a condition which occurred in the past and stays the same for some time, an in *increased expenditure*
	accomplishment	*-ive*	profiles a process, in ordinary contexts, which comes to an end, as in *a depressive atmosphere*
		-ant	profiles a process, in technical contexts, which comes to an end, as in *a depressant drug*
	achievement	*-ive*	profiles a whole act, in ordinary contexts, which occurs at a point in time, as in *an acceptive answer*
		-ant	profiles a whole act, in technical contexts, which occurs at a point in time, as in *an acceptant signal*

Table 5: The (sub)domains evoked by de-nominal adjectival suffixes in English

domains	subdomains	exponents	meaning differences
evaluation	favourable	*-like*	evaluates character in a positive sense, as in *a childlike figure*
	unfavourable	*-ish*	evaluates character in a negative sense, as in *a childish figure*
	neutral	*-ly*	evaluates manner in a positive way, as in *a statesmanly reflection*, or a negative way, as in *a beastly attitude*
		-y	evaluates the appearance of an animal negatively, as in *a doggy voice*, or a thing positively, as in *a flowery blouse*

possession	exhibitive	*-ful*	possesses a quality that is natural, as in *an artful arrangement*
		-y	possesses a quality that is artificial, as in *arty furniture*
	inducive	*-ous*	possesses a quality that induces a proper action, as in *an adventurous consultant*
		-some	possesses a quality that induces an improper action, as in *an adventuresome hunter*
relation	internal	*-al*	relates to the principal characteristics of a thing, as in *elemental diet*
		-ary	relates to the secondary characteristics of a thing, as in *elementary knowledge*
		-ic	relates to the core property of a thing, as in *a historic monument*
	external	*-related*	relates to the outer characteristics of a thing, *a tradition-related question*
		-ical	relates to the area of knowledge or subject of study, as in *a historical novel*
resemblance	essence	*-en*	denotes the substance of which a thing is made, as in *a waxen effigy*
		-y	denotes the feature that a thing has, as in *a waxy skin*
	appearance	*-type*	denotes the category or form that a thing has, as in *a military-type bag*
		-style	denotes the pattern or manner in which a thing is done, as in *a military-style plan*
motion	location	*-en*	means situated in the region designated, as in *a western outskirt*
	motion	*-ly*	means moving towards or coming from the region designated, as in *a westerly breeze*
	direction	*-ward*	means looking towards the point designated, as in *a homeward journey*
	destination	*-bound*	means leading towards the point designated, as in *a home-bound train*

	mobility	*-based*	means positioned in but moving around the place designated, as in *a hospital-based therapist*
	restriction	*-bound*	means restricted or confined to the place designated, as in *a hospital-bound therapy*
trouble	affliction	*-stricken*	indicates that the thing experienced is sudden, as in *a poverty-stricken farmer*
		-ridden	indicates that the thing experienced is chronic, as in *a poverty-stricken district*
	privation	*-less*	indicates that the thing lacked is of permanent nature, as in *a childless couple*
		-free	indicates that the thing lacked is of temporary nature, as in *a child-free holiday*
disposition	awareness	*-conscious*	aware of a thing, desirable or undesirable, with no intention to embark on action, as in *a fashion-conscious magazine* and *an accident-conscious mechanism*
	inclination	*-minded*	aware of a desirable thing with intention to embark on action, as in *a fashion-minded fanatic*
		-prone	aware of an undesirable thing with intention to embark on action, as in *an accident-prone driver*

6.1.3 Suffixes embody alternative construals of a content

The third principle of CS, which the study has confirmed, is that there is no synonymy in language. No two linguistic items are interchangeable without a reason. In a context where two linguistic items compete in a context, each correlates with a different meaning. The difference between the two linguistic items is a function of *construal*, the cognitive ability to conceive a situation in alternate ways and express them in language by using different linguistic structures. Construal is a relationship between semantic representation in the mind and the world which the speaker experiences. The mind is an active participant in the creation of meaning and construes the experiences of the speaker in the world in different ways. The ensuing argument is that the meaning of a linguistic item can be characterised relative to the particular construal imposed on its conceptual content. Linguistic items differ in meaning depending on not only the entities they designate but also the construals employed to structure their contents.

The study has explored this principle with regard to the description of adjectival suffixes. One aspect of the meaning of an adjective is the function of construal in the sense that the form of an adjective is partially motivated by the construal imposed on its scene. Morphological properties of an adjective can largely be predicted from its conceptual description. That is, the semantics of an adjective diagrams its morphological form. Each chapter was entrusted with the task of investigating in greater depth and breadth one dimension of construal with a view to establishing its correlation with the morphological structure of the adjective it triggers. The aim was to support the *construal* approach, where meaning represents the specific way in which a given expression structures a conceptual content. Precisely, the aim was to show that there is no exact equivalence in meaning between two adjectives. Each adjective has an individual meaning, which is associated with a distinct morphological shape and used in a particular context.

Chapter 3 has tackled the construal of *prominence* in the interpretation of adjectives belonging to de-verbal domains. Prominence is the quality of eminence given to the substructures of a conception relative to their importance. When two expressions evoke the same content, they differ by virtue of the *subject status* they confer on a participant or the *profile* they attach to it. The choice of either type of prominence was found to be the outcome of the way the speaker construes a situation.

First, let us examine an adjective pair to show how the construal of *subject status* works. Both *detective* and *detectable* include the verbal root *detect*, yet they are not equivalent in meaning. The speaker uses the adjective *detective* when s/he describes something as performing the action expressed by the root. For example, *detective work* is work that detects hidden information. This is reflected by the suffix *–ive*, which means 'performing or tending to perform the action referred to in the verbal root'. As validated by the BNC, the adjective *detective* collocates with nouns referring to literature such as *fiction, novel, story, work*, etc. By contrast, the speaker uses the adjective *detectable* when s/he describes something as undergoing the action expressed by the root. For example, *detectable change* is change that can be detected. This is reflected by the suffix *–able* which means 'capable of undergoing the action referred to in the verbal root'. As corroborated by the BNC, the adjective *detectable* collocates with abstract nouns such as *benefit, change, discontent, expertise, source*, or names of gases or illnesses.

Second, let us analyse an adjective pair to show how the construal of *profile* works. Both *haunting* and *haunted* relate to the root *haunt*, but they are not interchangeable. The speaker uses the adjective *haunting* when s/he profiles something as interesting. *A haunting melody* is so pleasant that it remains in the listener's mind. This is reflected by the suffix *–ing* which means 'keep on the activity signified by the verbal root'. As the BNC supports, the adjective *haunting* combines with nouns denoting music such as *ballad, lyrics, melody, song, tune*; literary products such as *epic, fiction, legend, story, tale*; practical enterprise such as *adventure, encounter, experience, incident, occurrence*, etc. By contrast, the speaker uses the adjective *haunted* when s/he profiles something as frightening. *A haunted house* is uncomfortable because it has repeatedly been visited by a ghost. This is reflected by the suffix *–ed* which means 'having been in the state signified by the verbal root'. As the BNC proves, the adjective *haunted* combines with nouns referring to places such as *forest, house, palace, path, villa*; people such as *creature, lady, man, ogre, person*; ways of showing feelings such as *expression, face, glare, look, stare*, etc.

Chapter 4 has handled the construal of *perspective* to the interpretation of adjectives belonging to de-nominal domains. Perspective is a particular way of viewing a situation, which is influenced by one's experiences. The selection of a given form of adjective was found to be the outcome of the viewpoint from which its content is conceptualised. Let us demonstrate this by an adjective pair. Both *wolfish* and *wolf-like* contain the nominal root *wolf*, but they are not substitutable. When the speaker evaluates someone or something in a negative way, s/he opts for *wolfish*. *A wolfish appetite* is an appetite that is ferocious and uncivilised. This is reflected by the suffix *–ish*, which means 'having the character of the thing specified by the nominal root', with focus on an unfavourable feature. On the evidence of the BNC, the adjective *wolfish* collocates with nouns referring to body parts of human beings or their actions. When the speaker evaluates someone or something in a positive or neutral way, s/he chooses *wolf-like*. *A wolf-like person* is a person who is clever at grabbing opportunities. This is reflected by the suffix *–like*, which means 'having the character of the thing specified by the nominal root', with focus on a favourable feature. On the evidence of the BNC, the adjective *wolf-like* collocates with nouns referring to animate entities.

Chapter 5 has dealt with the role of interaction in the interpretation of adjectives belonging to different domains, viz. de-verbal and de-nominal domains. The chapter has shown that domains do not exist separately but interact in numerous ways. So, the meaning of an adjective pair can be conceptualised against multiple domains. For illustration, let us examine the adjective pair *peaceable* vs. *peaceful*. The meanings of the two adjectives overlap, but they should be kept separate. On the one hand, the speaker uses the adjective *peaceable* when s/he describes someone as showing peace. *A peaceable man* is one who shows peace. This is reflected by the de-verbal suffix *–able*, which, when attached to nominal roots, means 'showing the quality of the thing referred to in the nominal root'. As the BNC attests, the adjective *peaceable* collocates with nouns referring to animate entities. On the other hand, the speaker uses the adjective *peaceful* when s/he describes something as abounding in peace. *A peaceful village* is one that is full of quietness. This is reflected by the de-nominal suffix *–ful*, which in this case means 'full of the thing denoted by the nominal root'. As the BNC affirms, the adjective *peaceful* collocates with nouns referring to inanimate entities.

6.2 Empirical findings

The empirical method adopted in the present study is represented by Corpus Linguistics, a methodology that deals with the practice of using corpora in language study. A *corpus* is a collection of linguistic data used to verify an assumption about language. It is characterised by the following main features. The first is authenticity, which means that the material included in a corpus is taken from genuine communication between people. In this way, the corpus serves as a reliable basis for generalisations about language. The second is sampling, which means that the material constructed in a corpus is representative of the whole language variety under examination, not individual texts or authors. In this way, the corpus provides an accurate picture of the tendencies of that variety. The third is machine-readability, which means that the material stored in the form of texts is processed by a computer. In this way, the data can be searched, selected, sorted and counted by means of software. In short, the corpus serves as a reservoir of data, but it is the linguist who conducts the analysis and unravels the semantic distinctions.

Below are the specific precepts of Corpus Linguistics which the study has substantiated and the findings that the study has arrived at.

6.2.1 Suffixes are instances of actual use

The first precept of Corpus Linguistics, which the study has confirmed, is that language should be studied in terms of authentic data, which are realised in texts. By *text*, it is meant an instance of language, either spoken or written, which speakers actually use. The study has explored this precept with regard to the description of adjectival suffixes. The study has found that the suffixes are used in real-life communication among participants in discourse. Each suffix has been found to impart one or more messages. To attest to their authenticity, the study has extracted data from the BNC. The extraction of the data was made possible by the WordSmith Tools concordancer. This is a software programme devised to produce listings of words in contexts. The programme was meant to perform two tasks. One was to search the occurrences of the suffixes within their contexts in the corpus. The second was to present the results of the search in an appropriate format. Each occurrence of a suffix was shown in the centre of a line which is 80 characters long.

By way of example, let us consider a pair of adjectival suffixes. As linguistic items, the suffixes *–ful* and *–y* have been found to be instances of actual use. To assess their distinct behaviour, the study has looked at the concordance lines in which they occur. The reason for choosing factual data is to make an indubitable assessment. In *The décor is tasteful*, the suffix *–ful* means 'displaying the quality denoted by the nominal root'. Tasteful décor is décor that exhibits good taste in the sense of aesthetic discrimination. That is to say the décor is very attractive in appearance. The adjective *tasteful* collocates with nouns denoting objects such as *bar, décor, gloves, handbag, room*, etc. In *The soup is tasty*, the suffix *–y* means 'full of the thing specified by the nominal root in quality'. Tasty soup is soup that is full of taste. That is to say the soup is very pleasant in content. The adjective *tasty* collocates with nouns denoting food such as *food, lamb, meal, sauce, soup*, etc.

6.2.2 Suffixes are pairings of meaning and form

The second precept of Corpus Linguistics, which the study has confirmed, is that language consists of communication acts and is manifested in linguistic items which can be observed, recorded and analysed. A linguistic item has both meaning and form. The specific form of a linguistic item is inseparable from its semantic organisation. The study has explored this precept through a description of adjectival suffixes. The study has found that a suffix is meaningful and its form reflects a particular kind of construal imposed on it. Since suffixes convey distinct meanings, the alternatives available to the speaker are dissimilar. All morphological choices are motivated by conceptual considerations. From this, one notices that each suffix represents a particular construal. To determine the meanings of the suffixes, the linguist needs to look at their occurrences in the corpus. In the course of the investigation, the study has opted for a qualitative analysis. This is in line with the main goal, which is to describe aspects of actual usage.

By way of example, let us consider a pair of suffixes. The relationship between *master* and *masterful* or *masterly* is not arbitrary. Rather, there is a strong correspondence between the contents of *–ful* and *–ly* and the modes of expression they take. The mode of expression can be seen as a result of the construal imposed on the content. In *She established herself as a masterful lawyer*, the suffix *–ful* evokes the domain of *possession*, and means 'full of the thing denoted by the nominal root'. A masterful lawyer is a lawyer who has the skills of a master in being competent and qualified. The adjective *masterful* collocates with nouns denoting people. In *He was rewarded for his masterly handling of the problem*, the suffix *–ly* evokes the domain of *evaluation*, and means 'having the manner of the thing specified by the nominal root'. Masterly handling is a way of doing things extremely well, as if it is done by a master. The adjective *masterly* collocates with nouns denoting ways of doing things such as *approach, fashion, manner, style, way*, or ways of dealing with things such as *handling, management, manipulation, supervision, treatment*, etc.

6.2.3 Suffixes exhibit association patterns

The third precept of Corpus Linguistics, which the study has confirmed, is that linguistic items exhibit, as part of their meanings, patterns of different nature. The study has explored this precept through its description of adjectival suffixes. To discover such patterns, the study has used two techniques of text analysis. One technique has revealed semantic differences between rival adjectives and is called *collocation*. The other technique has revealed syntactic differences between them and is called *colligation*. The techniques proved valuable in removing confusion surrounding the adjectives and in making generalisations concerning their behaviour. In the present analysis, they have been shown to be of great significance. In deriving two adjectives from a single root, they end in different suffixes and occur in different patterns. What the techniques have shown is that each adjective collocates with different types of lexical or grammatical patterns. From this, one comes to the conclusion that semantics and syntax are interdependent.

6.2.3.1 Lexical association

As an indication of their individuality, adjective pairs have been found to associate with different collocations. *Collocation* refers to the occurrence of two or more words in the immediate vicinity of each other in a text. It provides the researcher with information about a word's normal environment as well as its semantic features. Let us explain this through the adjective pair *luxurious* vs. *luxuriant*, which relate to *luxury* and *luxuriate*, respectively. When something is described as being characterised by luxury, *luxurious* is used. *A luxurious house* is a house that is comfortable and expensive. This is reflected by the suffix *–ous*, which in this case means 'characterised by the thing denoted by the nominal root'. As evidence of this meaning, the adjective *luxurious* collocates with things that are stable such as *hotel, house, palace, suite*, *villa,* etc. When something is described as producing abundantly, *luxuriant* is used. *Luxuriant hair* is hair that grows profusely. This is reflected by the suffix *–ant*, which in this case means 'apt to do the action signified by the verbal root'. As evidence of this meaning, the adjective *luxuriant* collocates with things that grow such as *bush, garden, hair, plant, whiskers*, etc.

6.2.3.2 Grammatical association

As an indication of their individuality, adjective pairs have been found to associate with different colligations. *Colligation* refers to patterns based on syntactic groups rather than individual words. It provides information with respect to the syntactic surroundings of a word as well as its syntactic properties. Let us explain this through the adjective pair *wooden* and *woody*. Both adjectives relate to the root *wood*, 'a hard substance which forms the branches and trunks of trees and which can be used for making things, or as a fuel', but they are different in use. *Wooden* means 'resembling the thing designated by the nominal root in make', whereas *woody* means 'resembling the thing designated by the nominal root in quality'. In addition to the semantic difference which they exhibit, a survey of their occurrences in the corpus has given hints about a syntactic difference between them. The adjective *wooden* has been shown to occur in attributive positions, as in *the wooden fence*. By contrast, the adjective *woody* has been shown to occur in attributive as well as predicative positions, as in *the woody fence* and *the fence is woody*.

In conclusion, I would like to say that the cognitive framework, within which the present analysis has been rooted, has proved to be a rewarding approach to morphological description because it has provided new insights into such a thorny issue in suffixation as rivalry, which has not received enough attention in the literature. Specifically, the framework helped to offer a revelatory account of two phenomena in morphology. One phenomenon is the existence of a correspondence between the content of a suffix and the mode of expression it takes. The study has found that each suffix imparts a particular meaning which is distinguishable from the other. Another phenomenon is the existence of rivalry between morphologically admissible but semantically divergent pairs of suffixes. The study has found that it is not rules that govern their distribution, but cognitive processes such as *participant choice*, *profiling* and *perspective*. It is hoped that this new way of describing language will take its place in future studies.

Notes

Chapter 1

1 A *root* is a word portion that cannot be analysed further into meaningful elements, as in *touch*. A *base* is analysable. It consists of a root and a derivational affix to which a further derivational affix can be added. The word *touchable* functions as a base for a prefix like *un-* to give *untouchable*. A *stem* is reserved for inflection. It consists of a root and a derivational affix to which an inflectional affix can be added. The word *untouchable* functions as a stem for an inflectional affix like *-s* to give *untouchables*.

2 The adjective *triumphal* collocates with events such as *march, parade, pomp, procession, show*, etc. The adjective *triumphant* collocates, by contrast, with people or a collection of people such as *army, forces, marcher, team, troops*; body reactions such as *expression, feeling, grin, look, smile*; acts such as *acceptance, conclusion, exhibition, reception, success*, etc.

3 The difference in interpretation between the adjectives *repetitive* and *repetitious* hinges on the type of collocation. *Repetitive* collocates with nouns referring to what people are supposed to do such as *business, chore, job, routine, task*; or what people are exposed to such as *drills, games, injury, probe, treatment*, etc. *Repetitious* collocates with nouns referring to forms of language, oral or written, such as *conversation, speech, sermon, utterance, wording*, etc.

4 The adjective *sensual* collocates with nouns that arouse physical appetite or sexual desire like *drink, food, love, massage, sex*, etc. The adjective *sensuous* collocates with nouns that are aesthetically pleasing or spiritually uplifting like *music, painting, poetry, sculpture, tapestry*, etc. Other adjectives having the same root are *sensory* and *sensitive*. *Sensory* means 'associated with the senses'. It means related to the five physical senses, as in *Sensory input is relayed to the brain*. *Sensitive* means 'marked by sense'. It means either showing awareness of other people's problems as in *The government must be sensitive to people's needs*, or easily hurt or offended as in *The drug may cause irritation to a sensitive skin*.

5 According to Taylor (2002:454–455), predicative uses of adjectives have a more limited range of meanings than the attributive ones. An attributive adjective tends to denote an inherent property of a noun because it specifies a type. *A handy tool* means 'a tool that is inherently easy to manipulate'. *My old friend* means 'the relationship is old'. A predicative adjective tends to denote a temporary property of a noun because it specifies a designated instance. *A tool that is handy* means 'a tool that is momentarily within easy reach'. *My friend is old* means 'the friend is old'.

Chapter 2

6 The other approach to the analysis of suffixes traces their development over time. This approach is called *grammaticalisation*, defined by Hopper & Traugott (1993:XV) as 'the process whereby lexical items and constructions come in certain linguistic contexts to serve grammatical functions, and, once grammaticalised, continue to develop new grammatical functions' *Grammaticalisation* is viewed as a historical process of obtaining a grammatical element or a new meaning from lexical items. Concerning suffixes, the major source is full words or free morphemes, which have gradually evolved into bound morphemes. For example, in tracing the source of the suffix *-ful* we find that it originates from the adjective *full*. As a suffix, it has gradually acquired the more abstract meaning of possessing some value to a high degree. This explains why derivatives ending in *-ful* tend to be restricted to abstract roots, as in *beautiful*.

7 Etymology of de-verbal bound suffixes: The suffix *-able* goes back to Middle English, from Old French, from Latin *-abil(is)*. The suffix *-ant* goes back to Middle English, from Old French, from Latin *-ant* and *-ans*. The suffix *-ed* goes back to Middle English, from Old English *-ede, -ode* and *-ade*. The suffix *-en* goes back to Middle English, from Old English *-en*. The suffix *-ible* goes back to Middle English, from Old French, from Latin *-ibil(is)*. The suffix *-ing* goes back to Middle English, from Old English *-ende*. The suffix *-ive* goes back to Middle English, from Middle French, from Latin *-iv(us)*, *-iv(a)* and *-iv(um)*. The suffix *-ory* goes back to Middle English, from Latin *-ori(us)*, *-ori(a)* and *ori(um)*.

8 The suffixes *-able* and *-ible* are graphically different but phonetically similar. In the literature, it is claimed that they do not have any semantic difference. In the present analysis, I treat them separately because they form pairs that display contextual preferences. This is shown by the different collocations that accompany them. For example, *accessable* is reserved for computer contexts, whereas *accessible* is used in all other contexts. For details, see 3.3.2.3.

9 Etymology of de-nominal bound suffixes: The suffix *-al* is derived through Middle English, from Latin *-al(is)*. The suffix *-ary* is derived through Middle English and Middle French, from Latin *-ari(us)*. The suffix *-ful* is derived through Middle English, from Old English *-ful*. The suffix *-ic* is derived through Middle English, from Old French, from Latin *-ic(us)*, and from Greek *-ik(os)*. The suffix *-ical* is derived through Middle English, from Latin *-ical(is)*. The suffix *-ish* is derived through Middle English, from Old English *-isc*. The suffix *-ly* is derived through Middle English, from Old English *-lic*. The suffix *-ous* is derived through Middle English, from Old French, from Latin *-os(us)*, *-os(a)* and *-os(um)*. The suffix *-some* is derived through Middle English, from Old English *-sum*. The suffix *-y* is derived through Middle English, from Old English *-ig*.

10 Etymology of de-nominal free suffixes: The suffix *-based* originates in Middle English, Middle French, Latin *-basis*, Greek *-bainein*. The suffix *-bound* originates in Middle English, Old English *-binden*. The suffix *-conscious* originates in Latin *-conscius*. The suffix *-free* originates in Middle English, Old English *-fréo*. The suffix *-less* originates in Middle English, Old English *-léas*. The suffix

-like originates in Middle English, Old English *-gelic.* The suffix *-minded* originates in Middle English, Old English *-gemynd.* The suffix *-related* originates in Latin *-relatus.* The suffix *-stricken* originates in Middle English *-striken.* The suffix *-style* originates in Greek *-styl(os).* The suffix *-type* originates in Middle English, Latin *-typ(us)*, Greek *-typ(os).* The suffix *-ward* originates in Middle English, Old English *-weard.*

Chapter 3

11 Likewise, the adjective *imaginative* can be compared with the adjective *imaginary.* When the speaker wants to describe a situation as having or showing a creative imagination, he chooses *imaginative*. By comparison, when the speaker wants to describe a situation as not real, something that exists only in fancy, he opts for *imaginary. An imaginative man* is one who imagines much, one who is rich in fancy. *An imaginary man* is one who is non-existent, one who is being conceived of in one's imagination.

12 In the sentence *In thinking, we tend to move from perceptual images to concepts*, the adjective *perceptual* means 'pertaining to perception', which is due to the presence of the suffix *-al.*

13 In modern use, the adjective *permissive* implies reference to sexual matters and means tolerant or liberal, as in *a permissive society.*

14 Some adjectives end in *-able* and *-ible*. They look like pairs, but they are not because they come from different roots.

In *Some girls are conversable, while others are reserved*, the adjective *conversable* is derived from *converse*, which means 'to talk to other people about thoughts, feelings, or ideas'. In *To be carnal and to be weak are conversible terms*, the adjective *conversible* is derived from *convert*, which means 'to cause to change in form, character or opinion'.

In *His secret thoughts are not impartable*, the adjective *impartable* is derived from *impart*, which means 'to give or make known information to someone else'. In *The soul is an impartible substance*, the adjective *impartible* is derived from *part*, which means 'to cause to separate', and the negative prefix *im-*.

In *This mint is infusable in tea*, the adjective *infusable* is derived from *infuse*, which means 'to leave tea leaves or herbs in hot water so that its flavour goes into the liquid'. In *Iron ore is infusible at a low temperature*, the adjective *infusible* is derived from *fuse*, which means 'to cause something to melt', and the negative prefix *in-*.

In *The roads were passable only with care*, the adjective *passable* is derived from *pass*, which means 'to go past something or someone'. In *He remained passible to pressure*, the adjective *passible* is derived from *pati*, which means 'to suffer'. The same distinction applies to the negative forms of the adjectives, which begin with *im-*.

15 The same distinction applies to other descriptive pairs of adjectives like *alarming/alarmed, amazing/amazed, appalling/appalled, astonishing/astonished,*

astounding/astounded, bewildering/bewildered, boring/bored, challenging/challenged, charming/charmed, compelling/compelled, confusing/confused, convincing/convinced, depressing/depressed, devastating/devastated, disgusting/disgusted, distracting/distracted, distressing/distressed, disturbing/disturbed, embarrassing/embarrassing, enchanting/enchanted, encouraging/encouraged, exhausting/exhausted, frightening/frightened, frustrating/frustrated, harassing/harassed, humiliating/humiliated, infuriating/infuriated, inspiring/inspired, insulting/insulted, intimidating/intimidated, intriguing/intrigued, menacing/menaced, mocking/mocked, overwhelming/overwhelmed, pleasing/pleased, puzzling/puzzled, relaxing/relaxed, rewarding/rewarded, satisfying/satisfied, sickening/sickened, shocking/shocked, startling/startled, stimulating/stimulated, surprising/surprised, tempting/tempted, terrifying/terrified, thrilling/thrilled, threatening/threatened, tiring/tired, touching/touched, worrying/worried, etc.

16 To see the difference between situation types, Huddleston & Pullum (2002:121–123) provide linguistic tests. *Activity* expressions occur as complement to aspectual verbs as in *He began to work*, occur with progressive aspect as in *He was working*, accept *for*-phrases denoting duration as in *He worked for an hour*, but do not occur with *it*-phrases denoting time measurement as in **It took him an hour to work*. *Accomplishment* expressions occur as complement to aspectual verbs as in *He finished walking a mile*, occur with progressive aspect as in *He was walking a mile*, do not accept *for*-phrases denoting duration as in **He walked a mile for an hour*, but occur with *it*-phrases denoting time measurement as in *It took him an hour to walk a mile*. *Achievement* expressions do not occur as complement to aspectual verbs as in **She stopped finding the key*, do not occur with progressive aspect as in **She is finding the key*, do not accept *for*-phrases as in **She found the key for an hour*, accept *it*-phrases as in *It took her an hour to find the key*. *State* expressions occur with simple present as in *She likes him*, do not occur with progressive aspect as in **She is liking him*, and unlike occurrences do not accept pseudo-clefts as in **What she did next was know her*. For more extensive study on *aspect*, see Vendler (1967).

17 The pair can also be applied to people. *A decided person* means ‘a person who is resolute or firm’, which is due to the presence of the suffix *-ed*. *A decisive person* means ‘a person who is liable to make decisions’, which is due to the presence of the suffix *-ive*.

18 In *She has a dominating influence over the family*, the adjective *dominating* means ‘keep on dominating’, i.e. the person described has a very strong personality and controls people around her.

19 In *The events being held highlight the varying lifestyles of people*, the adjective *varying* means ‘keep on varying’. A varying lifestyle is one that keeps on varying, i.e. does not remain uniform. In *Consumer preferences are so variable that planning is almost impossible*, the adjective *variable* means ‘capable of being varied’. A variable preference is one that is capable of being varied, i.e. subject to change.

20 The same distinction applies to other classifying pairs of adjectives like *decreasing/decreased, dwindling/dwindled, existing/existed, recurring/recurred, reigning/reigned, remaining/remained, ruling/ruled*, etc.

In exceptional cases, the verbal root can be transitive, as in *occupy*. In *The occupying force consisted of a single unit*, the adjective *occupying* means 'keep on occupying'. An occupying force is a force that keeps on invading a place and taking control of it. Collocates that are frequently used with *occupying* include nouns that refer to names of occupying countries; their fighting forces such as *army, force, military, troop, unit*; a group of people governing such places such as *administration, authority, command, government, regime*; individuals such as *marines, officers, paratroopers, servicemen, soldiers*, etc. In *The killing has set off widespread rioting in the occupied territory*, the adjective *occupied* means 'being occupied'. An occupied territory is a territory that is being occupied by a foreign force. Collocates that are frequently used with *occupied* include nouns that refer to names of countries, cities or territories such as *belt, land, region, territory, zone*, etc.

21 In *I was in love with her, 'was' being the operative word*, the adjective *operative* means that the word 'was' is the most important one in the sentence. In *There will be a delay before the modified machines are operable*, the adjective *operable* means 'capable of being operated', i.e. practised. The same distinction applies to the words in the negative. The adjective *inoperative* means 'not apt to operate'. With a machine as in *an inoperative clock*, it means 'not apt to work as usual'. With a law as in *an inoperative regulation*, it means 'not apt to have effect'. *Inoperable* means 'incapable of being operated', i.e. cannot be made to work as in *an inoperable system*.

22 In *I find mountain air much more stimulating*, the adjective *stimulating* means 'causing stimulation', i.e. making one feel more active and healthy.

Chapter 4

23 In *After days of manful defence, they surrendered upon discretion*, the adjective *manful* means 'having or showing courage', i.e. resolution. *Manful* collocates with nouns denoting tasks such as *attempt, defence, effort, performance, resistance*, etc.

24 In connection with adjectival suffixation, Malkiel (1977:341–364) argues that there are some devices placed at the disposal of the speakers for deriving adjectives from animal names, at the forefront of which come the two rival suffixes *-ish* and *-y*. Before expatiating on the relation between them, Malkiel examines their range of general uses with a view to finding out their semantic cores. Both suffixes seem to be productive, which can be demonstrated by the large number of resulting coinages. In the process of extracting adjectives from designations of animals, Malkiel comes across some doublets that end in the two suffixes *-ish* and *-y*, as in *rammish/rammy*. In fact, there are on record a very small number of triplets, as in *doggish/doggy/dogged*. Such derivatives are not free from a certain overlap since they exhibit only partial differentiation of meaning. The

adjectival form *rammish* means 'like a ram in having a disagreeable taste or smell', whereas the adjectival form *rammy* means 'resembling a ram'. The adjective *doggish* means 'like a dog in temper', the adjective *doggy* means 'resembling a dog in smell', and the adjective *dogged* means 'obstinate'.

25 In describing colours, both suffixes *-ish* and *-y* can be used. Both suffixes refer to a shade of the colour, but there is a difference in use. The suffix *-ish* describes something as having a small amount of the colour, whereas the suffix *-y* describes something as being similar to the colour. In *The flame is greenish*, the adjective *greenish* means 'having the colour green to a small degree'. A greenish flame is somewhat green or has a tinge of green. In *The flame is greeny*, the adjective *greeny* means 'suggesting the colour green'. A greeny flame has a shade of colour that is quite similar to green. The same applies to the other colours, except *white* or *black* which are not used with *-y*.

26 Nominal roots of various denotations other than animals can also take the suffixes *-ish* and *-y*. Such roots include *snob, snap* and *stock*.

Both *snobbish* and *snobby* are derived from *snob*, but they are separate in use. In *John wouldn't go to a football match; he is too snobbish*, the adjective *snobbish* means 'having the character of a snob'. A snobbish person is one who dislikes being with people from a lower social class or doing the things they do. *Snobbish* collocates predominantly with nouns denoting people or things related to them such as *concern, habit, policy, reason, view*, etc. In *He quickly got rid of the snobby atmosphere which prevails in most jewellery stores*, the adjective *snobby* means 'having the show of a snob'. A snobby atmosphere is one that is socially exclusive. S*nobby* collocates predominantly with names of places such as *bureau, office, school, shop, street*, or things related to them such as *atmosphere*, etc.

Both *snappish* and *snappy* are derived from *snap*, but they are separate in use. In *Children are often spiteful and snappish*, the adjective *snappish* means 'having the character of something which snaps'. Snappish children are children who are easily annoyed or bad-tempered. *Snappish* collocates with nouns denoting people. In *The layout of the picture is snappy*, the adjective *snappy* means 'having the appearance of something which snaps'. A snappy layout is one that is modern in style or effective in getting attention. *Snappy* collocates with nouns denoting objects such as *clothes, dress, leaflet, picture, suit*, or things related to them such as *design, headlines, layout, script, title*, etc.

Both *stockish* and *stocky* are derived from *stock*, but they are separate in use. In *Stop fooling around, you are so stockish*, the adjective *stockish* means 'having the character of a stock'. A stockish person is one who is dull or stupid like a block of wood. *Stockish* collocates with nouns denoting people. In *The man is short and stocky in figure*, the adjective *stocky* means 'having the appearance of a stock'. A stocky person is one who has wide shoulders and chest, and is often short in height. *Stocky* collocates with nouns denoting human shapes such as *body, build, figure, stature*, etc.

27 There are other roots which accept the suffixes *-like* and *-y*.

In some cases, the roots denote animals as in *fox*. Both *fox-like* and *foxy* are derived from *fox*, but they differ in use. In *The negotiator is very crafty, just fox-like*, the adjective *fox-like* means 'having the character of a fox'. A fox-like negotiator is one who is clever, tricky and politic. *Fox-like* collocates with nouns referring to people or their actions. In *He was a tall, thin man with a narrow foxy face*, the adjective *foxy* means 'having the appearance of a fox'. A foxy face is one that is pointed. *Foxy* collocates mainly with the word *face*.

In other cases, the roots denote events as in *dream*. Both *dream-like* and *dreamy* are derived from *dream*, but they differ in use. In *There is a dream-like quality to the final stages of the film*, the adjective *dream-like* means 'having the character of a dream'. A dream-like quality is one that is unsubstantial, vague or shadowy as a dream. *Dream-like* collocates with nouns referring to a property of something such as *aspect, facet, feature, quality, state*; location such as *house, lake, landscape, paradise, tunnel*, etc. In *When she talks about food, she gets a dreamy face*, the adjective *dreamy* means 'having the appearance of a dream'. A dreamy face is one that is filled with thoughts. *Dreamy* collocates with nouns referring to people's body parts such as *eyes, face, gaze, smile, voice*, or implying tunefulness such as *euphony, harmony, melody, music, song*, etc.

28 Another root taking the suffixes *-ful* and *-ous* is *plenty*. Both *plentiful* and *plenteous* are derived from *plenty*, but they are not interchangeable. In *The diet is plentiful*, the adjective *plentiful* means 'full of something'. A plentiful diet is one that contains a rich supply of food and drink. *Plentiful* collocates with nouns denoting necessities such as *coal, diet, food, fuel, water*; things such *as birds, buildings, examples, species, towels*, etc. In *The harvest is plenteous*, the adjective *plenteous* means 'causing or inspiring something'. A plenteous harvest is one that yields something greatly or inspires its productivity. *Plenteous* collocates with nouns denoting the time of the year when land produce is gathered or the act of gathering the produce such as *crop, fruitage, harvest, reaping, season*, etc.

29 In *I have got an awful lot of work to do*, the adjective *awful* is used to add force and means very great. In this use, *awful* has a negative semantic prosody. *Awesome* can also collocate with expressions such as *display of tantrums, spectre of crime, symbol of power, task of reconstruction, tingle of fear*, etc.

30 Another root taking the suffixes *-ful* and *-y* is *lust*. Both *lustful* and *lusty* are derived from *lust*, but they are not interchangeable. In *Max is having lustful thoughts about her*, the adjective *lustful* means 'full of lust'. Lustful thoughts are thoughts that are full of sexual desires. *Lustful* collocates with nouns denoting physical pleasure such as *embrace, fantasy, look, thought, touch*, etc. In *The lasses are pretty; the lads are lusty*, the adjective *lusty* means 'full of lust'. Lusty lads are lads who are full of energy, strength and power. *Lusty* collocates with nouns denoting people or their actions such as *bellowing, crying, posing, singing, yelling*, etc.

31 In *They had a troubled relationship*, the adjective *troubled* is derived from the verb *trouble*, which means 'to cause someone to have a problem or a difficulty'. The suffix *-ed* evokes the domain of aspect, and means 'being in the state signi-

fied by the verbal root'. A troubled relationship is a relationship that is being disturbed, agitated or disquieted.

32 Another root demonstrating rivalry between *-al* and *-related* is *environment*. In *The environmental damage caused by the chemical industry is getting sufficient attention in the campaign*, the adjective *environmental* means 'related closely to the environment'. Environmental damage is damage that is related practically to the environment, i.e. damage that affects the air, land and water on Earth. *Environmental* collocates with nouns such as *damage, disaster, harm, hazard, pollution*, etc. In *The company's expenditure on environment-related projects reached £ 300 million in 2000*, the adjective *environment-related* means 'relating remotely to environment'. An environment-related project is a project that is related theoretically to the environment. *Environment-related* collocates with nouns such as *issue, plan, project, research, study*, etc.

33 In an article, Kaunisto (1999:343–370) examines the distinction between the pairs *electric/electrical* and *classic/classical*. To do so, he reviews the previous studies attempting to account for the factors involved in the differentiation between *-ic* and *-ical* adjectives, but he does not find them attractive or illuminating. In his opinion, the choice of one adjective over the other is determined by prefixation. If an adjective is preceded by a prefix, the *-ic* suffix should be chosen so as to keep its form shorter. The prevalence of *prehistoric* over *prehistorical*, for instance, suggests that languages favour economy. In his opinion, the preference of an adjective over the other can also be determined by tracing the history of the adjectives in various types of texts from different periods. However, for the purposes of the present study, this analysis is of little use for two reasons. One is that it is restricted to two pairs, and so is unable to make any definite conclusion on the topic. Another is that it is not morphologically based, for one of the two pairs, namely *electric/electrical*, does not undergo any derivational process, for example *electric* cannot be divided into a root and a suffix. Moreover, the survey is based on newspaper articles, so the occurrences of the adjectives are not numerous enough to provide sufficient evidence.

34 In *She abandoned earthly concerns and entered a convent*, the adjective *earthly* means 'bearing the character of earth'. Earthly concerns are worries that bear on the material world of life on earth as opposed to spiritual life or life after death.

35 Another root bearing witness to rivalry between *stricken* and *ridden* is *fear*. In *When she entered, she talked in a fear-stricken voice*, the adjective *fear-stricken* means 'hit by fear. A fear-stricken person is one who is overcome by fear. *Fear-stricken* collocates with nouns referring to people, their body parts or reactions. In *Undeniably, they live in an alienated and fear-ridden society*, the adjective *fear-ridden* means 'plagued by fear'. A fear-ridden society is one that is oppressed by fear. *Fear-ridden* collocates with nouns referring to life and its atmosphere, people and their actions.

36 In two articles, Górska (1994:413–435, 2001:189–202) analyses, within a cognitive framework, privative adjectives ending in *-less* and *-free*. Even though the two suffixes share the common meaning 'without the thing named by the nomi-

nal base', there is far more to the semantics of the derivatives. In her opinion, the difference is generalised in terms of control and intention. With derivatives in *-less*, the speaker has neither control over the course of events nor the intention to change it, as in *moonless night*. That is why it is not possible to say *moon-free night* in English. By contrast, with derivatives in *-free* the speaker has both control over the course of events and the intention to change it to fulfil a desire, as in *smoke-free city*. That is why it is not possible to say *smokeless city* in English. With some bases, two derivatives exist as in *sugarless/sugar-free tea*, but they are used in different contexts. *Sugarless tea* is tea without sugar although we want sugar in it, while *sugar-free tea* is tea without sugar because we do not want sugar in it. From the viewpoint of the present study, this distinction seems ineffective for it works only in some examples. In such examples as *a stainless watch, a cordless telephone, a collarless shirt, spiceless salad, a flawless performance* and many others, the speaker has both control and intention over the course of the action or the event.

Chapter 5

37 *Respectable* collocates with nouns referring to people such as *caste, folk, populace, society, workers*; what they do such as *career, job, occupation, position, status*; things such as *journal, newspaper, picture, publication, suit*, etc. *Respectful* collocates with nouns referring to people such as *audience, government, members, men, youth*; their reactions such as *attitude, greeting, mood, opinion, tone*; the word *distance*, as in *He kept a respectful distance behind his team leader.*

38 Similar distinctions apply to the antonyms of these words. In *The heat in the little room is intolerable*, the adjective *intolerable* means 'incapable of being tolerated', i.e. too annoying for one to bear. In *He is intolerant of other people's political beliefs*, the adjective *intolerant* means 'not apt to tolerate', i.e. not willing to accept different opinions.

39 The adjective *expectant* co-occurs with nouns referring to women expecting a baby. In *She is an expectant mother*, the adjective *expectant* means 'apt to expect', e.g. the birth of a baby soon. In *The expected counter-attack never happened*, the adjective *expected* means 'being expected', i.e. believed to happen.

40 Both *continuous* and *continual* are derived from *continue*, but they have different connotations. The difference can be seen as one between continuity and continuation. In *The brain needs a continuous supply of blood*, the adjective *continuous* describes one action that goes on without interruption. It carries less of the idea that the repeated action is annoying. *Continuous* is used before and after a noun. In *These continual interruptions are driving me mad*, the adjective *continual* describes separate actions of the same sort which go on with interruption. It carries the idea that the repeated action is annoying. *Continual* is used only before a noun.

41 Both *usable* and *useful* are derived from *use*, but they are not interchangeable. In *The electrode is usable for three months*, the adjective *usable* means 'capable of

being used'. A usable electrode is one that can be used because it is convenient and practicable. *Usable* collocates with concrete nouns such as *ammunition, electrode, film, machine, tool*; abstract nouns such as *code, information, knowledge, law, software*, etc. In *Are the exercises useful?*, the adjective *useful* means 'full of use'. A useful exercise is one that is full of use because it is valuable and profitable. *Useful* collocates with nouns referring to activity such as *analysis, choice, evaluation, exercise, revision*; abstract nouns such as, *attribute, idea, property, suggestion, theme*, etc. *Useful* also occurs in *it*-construction.

42 Another pair where language users seldom make a distinction in meaning is *peaceable* vs. *peaceful*, as shown in *He is such a peaceable person*, and *It is such a peaceful city*. *Peaceable* collocates with nouns referring to people such as *community, follower, friend, legend, people*; their disposition such as *character, mood, nature, state*; animals such as *fish, horse, whale*, etc. *Peaceful* collocates with nouns referring to places such as *town, parkland, quarter, village, road;* activity such as *demonstration, coexistence, cohabitation, interaction, resistance*; events, times, means, etc.

43 In some cases, the adjective *likeable* is used with people, as in *He's seen as reasonable, easygoing and likeable*. In such cases, *likeable* refers to qualities such as pleasing, agreeable, and friendly which bring about a favourable regard.

44 In some cases, the adjective *lively* is used to describe events, as in *We had a lively discussion at the meeting*. In this case, *lively* means enthusiastic.

45 Another root, e.g. *love*, takes the suffixes *-able* and *-ly*. Both *loveable* and *lovely* are derived from *love*, but they differ in use. In *She's a very loveable person*, the adjective *loveable* means 'capable of being loved'. A loveable woman is one whose character is so attractive that it makes people love her. *Loveable* mainly collocates with nouns referring to people. In *Thank you for the lovely present*, the adjective *lovely* means 'having a striking appearance'. A lovely present is one that is so attractive on account of beauty. *Lovely* collocates mainly with nouns referring to objects.

46 Similar distinctions apply to the antonyms of these words. In *It was an appealing plan but quite impracticable*, the adjective *impracticable* means 'incapable of being practised'. An impracticable plan is one that could not be carried out. In *A 24-hour service would be impractical for a small organisation like this*, the adjective *impractical* means 'relating closely to practice'. An impractical service is one that is not sensible or realistic because it requires too much time or trouble.

47 Another interesting pair includes *personable* vs. *personal*. The two adjectives are derived from *person*, but they differ in use. In *The secretary is intelligent, hard-working and personable*, the adjective *personable* means 'showing personality'. A personable secretary is one who has an attractive appearance and a pleasant character. *Personable* collocates with nouns referring to people such as *companion, lecturer, reporter, secretary, spokesman*, etc. In *She has her own personal bodyguard*, the adjective *personal* means 'relating closely to a person'. A personal bodyguard is one that relates to an individual person, as opposed to other persons. *Personal* collocates with nouns referring to people such as *assist-*

ant, attendant, bodyguard, instructor, representative; things they own such as *car, computer, home page, records, weapon*, etc. The adjective *personal* can also mean making an offensive comment on someone's character or appearance, as in *Did you have to make such a personal remark about her new haircut*?

48 Similar pairs are *short-haired* vs. *hairy, light-headed* vs. *heady*, etc. In *He is short-haired*, the adjective *haired* means 'having hair of a specified kind'. Being short-haired means having short hair. In *She does not know my name. I was too hairy to tell her that*, the adjective *hairy* means 'having the trait of anger'. A hairy person is one who is excited. The adjective can also mean having a lot of hair on parts of the body other than the head, as in *He's very hairy, isn't he? Have you noticed his arms*? In *She became light-headed from the fever*, the adjective *headed* means 'having a head of a specified kind'. Being light-headed means feeling weak, for example through exhaustion or illness. In *She is known for her heady opinions*, the adjective *heady* means 'having the trait of rashness'. A heady opinion is one that is impulsive. The adjective can also mean excited and full of energy, as in *Working for such a newspaper was a heady experience for the journalist.*

References

Books and articles

Adams, Valerie. 1973. *An Introduction to Modern English Word-formation.* London: Longman.

Adams, Valerie. 2001. *Complex Words in English.* Essex: Longman.

Anshen, Frank & Mark Aronoff. 1984. 'Morphological productivity in historical perspective'. Paper read at the 4th International Conference on Historical Linguistics: Historical Semantics/Historical Word-Formation. Blazejewko, Poland.

Aronoff, Mark. 1976. *Word Formation in Generative Grammar*. Cambridge MA: MIT Press.

Aronoff, Mark. 1980. 'The relevance of productivity in a synchronic description of word formation'. In Jacek Fisiak. (ed.) *Historical Morphology*: 71–82.

Aronoff, Mark & Sungeun Cho. 2001. 'The semantics of *-ship* suffixation'. *Linguistic Inquiry* 32:167–173.

Aronoff, Mark & Kirsten Fudeman. 2005. *What is Morphology?* Oxford: Blackwell.

Baayan, Harald & Rochelle Lieber. 1991. 'Productivity and English derivation: A corpus-based study'. *Linguistics* 29: 801–843.

Bauer, Laurie. 1983. *English Word-formation.* Cambridge: Cambridge University Press.

Bauer, Laurie. 1988. *Introducing Linguistic Morphology*. Edinburgh: Edinburgh University Press.

Bauer, Laurie. 2001. *Morphological Productivity*. Cambridge: Cambridge University Press.

Beard, Robert. 1995. *Lexeme-Morpheme Base Morphology*. New York: State University of New York Press.

Beard, Robert, & Bogdan Szymanek. 1988. *Bibliography of Morphology, 1960–1985*. Amsterdam: Benjamins.

Biber, Douglas, Susan Conrad & Randi Reppen. 1998. *Corpus Linguistics: Investigating linguistic structure and use.* Cambridge: Cambridge University Press.

Bolinger, Dwight. 1977. *Meaning and Form*. London: Longman.

Booij, Geert. 2005. *The Grammar of Words*. Oxford: Oxford University Press.

Brugman, Claudia. 1988. *The Story of* over. *Polysemy, Semantics and the Structure of the Lexicon.* New York: Garland Press.

Bybee, Joan. 1985. *Morphology: An inquiry into the relation between meaning and form.* Amsterdam: Benjamins.

Carstairs-McCarthy, Andrew. 1992. *Current Morphology*. London: Routledge.

Casad, Eugene. 1995. 'Seeing it in more than one way'. In John Taylor & Robert Maclaury. (eds) *Trends in Linguistics, Language and the Cognitive Construal of the World*: 23–45.

Chomsky, Noam. 1957. *Syntactic Structures*. The Hague: Mouton.

Chomsky, Noam. 1965. *Aspects of the Theory of Syntax*. Mass: MIT Press.

Chomsky, Noam. 1995. *The Minimalist Program*. Cambridge: MIT Press.

Collins COBUILD. 1992. *English Grammar*. London: William Collins and Sons & Co.

Collins COBUILD. 1993. *Word Formation.* London: HarperCollins Publishers.

Collins, Peter. 1991. 'The modals of obligation and necessity in Australian English'. In Karin Aijmer & Bengt Altenberg. (eds) *English Corpus Linguistics*: *Studies in honour of Jan Svartvik*: 145–165.

Croft, William. 1995. 'Autonomy and functionalist linguistics'. *Language* 71: 490–532.

Croft, William. 1998. 'What (some) functionalists can learn from (some) formalists'. In Michael Darvell. *Functionalism and Formalism in Linguistics.* Vol. 1: 85–108.

Croft, William & D. Allen Cruse. 2004. *Cognitive Linguistics*. Cambridge: Cambridge University Press.

Crystal, David. 2002. *The English Language: A guided tour of the language.* London: Penguin Books.

Cutler, Anne. 1980. 'Productivity in word formation'. *Chicago Linguistic Society* 16: 45–51.

Deane, Paul. 1992. *Grammar in Mind and Brain: Explorations in cognitive syntax*. Berlin: Mouton de Gruyter.

Dewell, Robert. 1994. '*Over* again: Image-schema transformations in semantic analysis'. *Cognitive Linguistics* 5: 351–380.

Dirven, René. & Marjolijn Verspoor. (eds) 1998. *Cognitive Explorations of Language and Linguistics*. Amsterdam: Benjamins.

Dirven, René. & Günter Radden. (in press) *Cognitive English Grammar*. Amsterdam: Benjamins.

Dixon, Robert. 1991. *A New Approach to English Grammar on Semantic Principles*. Oxford: Clarendon.

Dressler, Wolfgang. 1985. *Morphology: The dynamics of derivation.* Ann Arbor: Kroma.

Evans, Vyvyan. 2003. *The Structure of Time: Language, meaning and temporal cognition.* Amsterdam: Benjamins.

Fabb, Nigel. 1988. 'English suffixation is constrained only by selectional restrictions'. *National Language and Linguistic Theory* 6: 527–539.

Fauconnier, Gills. 1985. *Mental Spaces: Aspects of meaning construction in natural language.* Cambridge: Cambridge University Press.

Fauconnier, Gills. 1997. *Mappings in Thought and Language.* Cambridge: Cambridge University Press.

Fillmore, Charles. 1977. 'Scenes-and-frames'. In Antonio Zampolli. (ed.) *Linguistic Structures Processing*: 55–81.

Fillmore, Charles. 1982. 'Towards a descriptive framework for spatial deixis'. In Robert J. Jarvella & Wolfgang Klein. (eds) *Speech, Place and Action*: 31–59.

Foley, William & Robert D. Van Valin. 1984. *Functional Syntax and Universal Grammar.* Cambridge Studies in Linguistics 38. Cambridge: Cambridge University Press.

Francis, W. Nelson. 1992. 'Language corpora B.C.' In Jan Svartvik. (ed.) *Directions in Corpus Linguistics: Proceedings of Nobel Symposium* 82: 17–32.

Geeraerts, Dirk. 1988. 'Cognitive grammar and the history of lexical semantics'. In Brygida Rudzka-Ostyn. (ed.) *Topics in Cognitive Linguistics*: 647–677.

Geeraerts, Dirk. 1989. 'Introduction: Prospects and problems of prototype theory'. *Linguistics* 27: 587–612.

Givón, Talmy. 1993. *English Grammar: A function-based introduction.* Vol. 1 & 2. Amsterdam: Benjamins.

Górska, Elzbieta. 1994. 'Moonless nights and smoke-free cities, or what can be without the other?' A cognitive study of privative adjectives in English. *Folia Linguistica* 28: 413–435.

Górska, Elzbieta. 2001. 'Recent derivatives with the suffix *-less*: A change in progress within the category of English privative adjectives'. *Studia Anglica Posnaniensia* 36: 189–202.

Haiman, John. 1985. *Iconicity in Syntax.* Amsterdam: Benjamins.

Halle, Morris. 1973. 'Prolegomena to a theory of word formation'. *Linguistics Inquiry* 4: 3–16.

Hamawand, Zeki. 2002. *Atemporal Complement Clauses in English. A Cognitive Grammar Analysis.* München: Lincom.

Hamawand, Zeki. 2003a. 'The construal of atemporalisation in complement clauses in English'. *Annual Review of Cognitive Linguistics* 1: 61–87.

Hamawand, Zeki. 2003b. 'For-to complement clauses in English: A cognitive Grammar Analysis'. *Studia Linguistica* 57: 171–192.

Hamawand, Zeki. 2005. 'The construal of salience in atemporal complement clauses in English'. *Language Sciences* 27: 193–213.

Haspelmath, Martin. 2002. *Understanding Morphology*. London: Arnold.
Heine, Bernd. 1997. *Cognitive Foundations of Grammar*. Oxford. Oxford University Press.
Hockett, Charles. 1954. 'Two models of grammatical description'. *Word* 10: 210–231.
Hopper, Paul. & Elizabeth Traugott. 1993. *Grammaticalisation*. Cambridge: Cambridge University Press.
Huddleston, Rodney & Geoffrey Pullum. 2002. *The Cambridge Grammar of the English Language*. Cambridge: Cambridge University Press.
Jackendoff, Ray. 1983. *Semantics and Cognition*. Cambridge: MIT Press.
Jackendoff, Ray. 1997. *The Architecture of the Language Faculty*. Cambridge: MIT Press.
Jensen, John. 1990. *Morphology. Word Structure in Generative Grammar*. Current issues in linguistic theory 70. Amsterdam: Benjamins.
Johnson, Mark. 1987. *The Body in the Mind: The bodily basis of meaning, imagination and reason*. Chicago: University of Chicago Press.
Katamba, Francis. 1993. *Morphology*. London: MacMillan Press Ltd.
Kaunisto, Mark. 1999. 'Electric/Electrical and Classic/Classical. Variation between the suffixes -ic and -ical'. *English Studies* 4: 343–370.
Kennedy, Graeme. 1991. 'Between and through: The company they keep and the functions they serve'. In Karin Aijmer & Bengt Altenberg. (eds) *English Corpus Linguistics*: *Studies in honour of Jan Svartvik*: 95–110.
Kreitzer, Anatol. 1997. 'Multiple levels of schematisation: A study in the conceptualisation of space'. *Cognitive Linguistics* 8: 291–325.
Lakoff, George. 1987. *Women, Fire and Dangerous Things: What categories reveal about the mind*. Chicago: University of Chicago Press.
Lakoff, George. 1990. 'The invariance hypothesis: is abstract reason based on image schemas?' *Cognitive Linguistics* 1: 39–74.
Lakoff, George & Mark Johnson. 1980. *Metaphors We Live By*. Chicago: University of Chicago Press.
Langacker, Ronald. 1987. *Foundations of Cognitive Grammar*. Vol. 1: *Theoretical Prerequisites*. Stanford: Stanford University Press.
Langacker, Ronald. 1988a. 'An overview of cognitive grammar'. In Brygida Rudzka-Ostyn. (ed.) *Topics in Cognitive Linguistics*: 3–48.
Langacker, Ronald. 1988b. 'A view of linguistic semantics'. In Brygida Rudzka-Ostyn. (ed.) *Topics in Cognitive Linguistics*: 49–90.
Langacker, Ronald. 1988c. 'The nature of grammatical valence'. In Brygida Rudzka-Ostyn. (ed.) *Topics in Cognitive Linguistics*: 91–125.
Langacker, Ronald. 1991a. *Foundations of Cognitive Grammar*. Vol. 2: *Descriptive Application*. Stanford: Stanford University Press.
Langacker, Ronald. 1991b. *Concept, Image and Symbol*. Berlin: Mouton de Gruyter.
Langacker, Ronald. 1994. 'Cognitive grammar'. In R. E. Asher. (ed.) *The Encyclopedia of Language and Linguistics* 2: 590–594.

Langacker, Ronald. 1997a. 'Consistency, dependency and conceptual grouping'. *Cognitive Linguistics* 8: 1–32.

Langacker, Ronald. 1997b. 'The contextual basis of cognitive semantics'. In Jan Nuyts & Eric Pederson. *Language and Conceptualisation*: 229–232.

Langacker, Ronald. 1999. *Grammar and Conceptualisation.* Berlin: Mouton de Gruyter.

Lee, David. 2001. *Cognitive Linguistics: An introduction.* Oxford: Oxford University Press.

Lees, Robert. 1960. *The Grammar of English Nominalisations.* The Hague: Mouton.

Lieber, Rochelle. 2004. *Morphology and Lexical Semantics*. Cambridge: Cambridge University Press.

Lieber, Rochelle. 2005. 'English word-formation processes'. In Pavol Stekauer & Rochelle Lieber. *Handbook of Word-Formation*: 375–427.

Lyons, John. 1968. *Introduction to Theoretical Linguistics*. Cambridge: Cambridge University Press.

Ljung, Magnus. 1974. *A Frequency Dictionary of English Morphemes*. Stockholm: AWE/Gebers.

Malkiel, Yakov. 1977. 'Why Ap-ish but Worm-y?' In Paul J. Hopper. (ed.) *Studies in Descriptive and Historical Linguistics*: 341–364.

Marchand, Hans. 1969. *The Categories and Types of Present-day English Word Formation. A Synchronic-diachronic Approach.* Munich: Beck.

Matthews, Peter. 1974. *Morphology*. Cambridge: Cambridge University Press.

McEnery, Tony & Andrew Wilson. 2001. *Corpus Linguistics*. Edinburgh: Edinburgh University Press.

Meyer, Charles. 2002. *English Corpus Linguistics*. Cambridge: Cambridge University Press.

Newmeyer, Frederick. 2000. *Language Form and Language Function.* Cambridge: MIT Press.

Nichols, Johanna. 1984. 'Functional theories of grammar'. *Annual Review of Anthropology* 13: 97–117.

Plag, Ingo. 1999. *Morphological Productivity. Structural Constraints in English Derivation.* Berlin: Mouton de Gruyter.

Plag, Ingo. 2003. *Word-Formation in English.* Cambridge: Cambridge University Press.

Prince, Ellen. 1991. 'Functional explanation in linguistics and the origins of language'. *Language and Communication* 11: 79–82.

Riddle, Elizabeth. 1985. 'A historical perspective on the productivity of the suffixes *-ness* and *-ity*'. In Jacek Fisiak. (ed.) *Historical Semantics Historical Word-Formation*: 435–461.

Rosch, Eleanor. 1975. 'Cognitive representation of semantic categories'. *Journal of Experimental Psychology* 104: 192–233.

Rosch, Eleanor. 1977. 'Human categorisation'. In Neil Warren. (ed.) *Studies in Cross-Cultural Psychology* 1: 3–49.

Rosch, Eleanor. 1978. 'Principles of categorisation'. In E. Rosch & B. B. Lloyd. (eds) *Cognition and Categorisation*: 27–48.

Rudzka-Ostyn, Brygida (ed) 1988. *Topics in Cognitive Linguistics*. Amsterdam: Benjamins.

Sandra, Dominiek & Sally Rice. 1995. 'Network analyses of prepositional meaning: Mirroring whose mind – The linguist's or the language user's?' *Cognitive Linguistics* 6: 89–130.

Saussure, Ferdinand. 1916. *Cours de Linguistique Générale*. Paris: Payot.

Selkirk, Elisabeth. 1982. *The Syntax of Words*. Cambridge MA: MIT Press.

Sinclair, John. 1991. *Corpus, Concordance and Collocation*. Oxford: Oxford University Press.

Spencer, Andrew. 1991. *Morphological Theory*. Oxford: Blackwell.

Spencer, Andrew. 2001. 'Morphology'. In Mark Aronoff & Rees-Miller. (eds) *The Handbook of Linguistics*: 213–237.

Stageberg, Norman. 1965. *An Introductory English Grammar*. New York: Holt, Rinehart and Winston Inc.

Stekauer, Pavol. 2000. *English Word-formation. A History of Research (1960–1995)*. Tübingen: Gunter Narr Verlag.

Stubbs, Michael. 2001. *Words and Phrases. Corpus Studies of Lexical Semantics*. Oxford: Blackwell.

Szymanek, Bogdan. 1998. *Introduction to Morphological Analysis*. Warszawa: Wydawinctwo Naukowe PWN.

Talmy, Leonard. 1983. 'How language structures space'. In Herbert Pick & Linda Arcedolo. (eds) *Spatial Orientation: Theory, research, and application*: 225-282.

Talmy, Leonard. 1985. 'Force dynamics in language and thought'. *Chicago Linguistic Society* 21:293–337.

Taylor, John. 1989. *Linguistic Categorisation. Prototypes in Linguistic Theory*. Oxford: Clarendon Press.

Taylor, John. 2002. *Cognitive Grammar*. Oxford: Oxford University Press.

Tognini-Bonelli, Elena. 2001. *Corpus Linguistics at Work*. Amsterdam: Benjamins.

Tyler, Andrea. & Vyvyan Evans. 2001. 'Reconsidering prepositional polysemy networks. The case of *over*'. *Language* 77: 724–765.

Ungerer, Friedrich & Hans-Jörg Schmid. 1996. *An Introduction to Cognitive Linguistics*. London: Longman.

Urdang, Laurence. 1982. *Suffixes and other Word-final Elements of English*. Detroit: Gale Research Company.

Vandeloise, Claude. 1994. 'Methodology and analyses of the preposition *in*'. *Cognitive Linguistics* 5: 157–184.

Vendler, Zeno. 1967. *Linguistics in Philosophy*. Ithaca, NJ: Cornell University Press.

Watters, John. 1985. 'The place of morphology in functional grammar: The case of the Ejagham verb system'. In A. M. Bolkstein, C. de Grool & J. L. Mackenzie. (eds) *Predicate and Terms in Functional Grammar*: 85–104.

Wierzbicka, Anna. 1988. *The Semantics of Grammar.* Amsterdam: Benjamins.

Zernik, Uri. 1991. *Lexical acquisition: Exploiting on-line resources to build a lexicon.* Hillsdale, NJ: Lawrence Erlbaum.

Usage manuals

Evans, Bergen & Cornelia Evans. 1957. *A Dictionary of Contemporary American Usage*. New York: Random House.

Fee, Margery & Janice McAlpine. 1997. *Guide to Canadian English Usage.* Oxford: Oxford University Press.

Fowler, Henry. 1996. *Modern English Usage.* Oxford: Oxford University Press.

Greenbaum, Sidney & Janet Whitcut. 1988. *Longman Guide to English Usage.* Essex: Longman.

Hughes, Barrie (ed). 1993. *The Penguin Working Words: An Australian guide to modern English usage*. Victoria: Viking.

Manser, Martin (ed.) 1991. *Bloomsbury Good Word Guide*. London: Bloomsbury.

MacKaskill, Stanley. 1981. *A Dictionary of Good English: A guide to current usage*. London: The MacMillan Press Ltd.

Partridge, Eric. 1961. *Usage and Abusage. A Guide in Good English.* London: Hamish Hamilton.

Peters, Pam. 1995. *The Cambridge Australian English Style Guide.* Cambridge: Cambridge University Press.

Peters, Pam. 2004. *The Cambridge Guide to English Usage*. Cambridge: Cambridge University Press.

Shipman, Robert. 1991. *A Pun My Word.* Maryland: Rowman & Littlefield Publishers, Inc.

Treble, H. A. & G. H. Vallins. 1961. *An ABC of English Usage*. Oxford: Clarendon Press.

Wood, Frederick. 1962. *Current English Usage: A concise dictionary.* London: MacMillan & Co. Ltd.

Dictionaries and thesauruses

Cambridge Advanced Learner's Dictionary Online. Available at: http://dictionary.cambridge.org

COBUILD English Dictionary. 1998. Glasgow: Harper Collins Publishers.

COBUILD English Dictionary and Thesaurus. 1993. Glasgow: Harper Collins Publishers.

COBUILD on CD-ROM. 1995. Glasgow: Harper Collins Publishers.

Hayakawa, Samuel. (no year). *Modern Guide to Synonyms and Related Words*. Darmstadt: Verlag Darmstädter Blätter.

Kirkpatrick, Betty. (ed.) 1998. *Roget's Thesaurus of English Words and Phrases*. London: Penguin Books.

Little et al. 1959. *The Oxford English Dictionary on Historical Principles*. London: Oxford University Press.

Longman Dictionary of Contemporary English. 1995. 3rd edition. London: Longman.

Longman Dictionary of English Language and Culture. 1992. 1st edition. London: Longman.

Longman Language Activator. 2002. Pearson Education Limited.

Merriam-Webster Dictionary Online. Available at: http://www.m-w.com.

Oxford Advanced Learner's Dictionary. 1995. 5th edition. Oxford: Oxford University Press.

Oxford Collocations Dictionary: for students of English. 2003. Oxford: Oxford University Press.

Oxford English Dictionary on CD-ROM. 1994. Oxford: Oxford University Press.

Oxford English Dictionary Online. Available at: http://www.oed.com

Urdang, Laurence. 1991. *The Oxford Thesaurus: An A-Z dictionary of synonyms*. Oxford: Clarendon Press.

Subject index

Suffix index

Adjective index

www.ingramcontent.com/pod-product-compliance
Lightning Source LLC
LaVergne TN
LVHW010444080826
844660LV00026B/1211

* 9 7 8 1 8 4 5 5 3 1 8 1 2 *